The Language of Evaluation

The Language of Evaluation
Appraisal in English

J. R. Martin
and
P. R. R. White

palgrave
macmillan

© J. R. Martin and P. R. R. White 2005

All rights reserved. No reproduction, copy or transmission of this publication may be made without written permission.

No paragraph of this publication may be reproduced, copied or transmitted save with written permission or in accordance with the provisions of the Copyright, Designs and Patents Act 1988, or under the terms of any licence permitting limited copying issued by the Copyright Licensing Agency, 90 Tottenham Court Road, London W1T 4LP.

Any person who does any unauthorised act in relation to this publication may be liable to criminal prosecution and civil claims for damages.

The authors have asserted their rights to be identified as the authors of this work in accordance with the Copyright, Designs and Patents Act 1988.

Hardback edition first published in 2005
This paperback edition first published in 2007 by
PALGRAVE MACMILLAN
Houndmills, Basingstoke, Hampshire RG21 6XS and
175 Fifth Avenue, New York, N.Y. 10010
Companies and representatives throughout the world.

PALGRAVE MACMILLAN is the global academic imprint of the Palgrave Macmillan division of St. Martin's Press, LLC and of Palgrave Macmillan Ltd. Macmillan® is a registered trademark in the United States, United Kingdom and other countries. Palgrave is a registered trademark in the European Union and other countries.

ISBN-13: 978–1–4039–0409–6 hardback
ISBN-10: 1–4039–0409–X hardback
ISBN-13: 978–1–4039–0410–2 paperback
ISBN-10: 1–4039–0410–3 paperback

This book is printed on paper suitable for recycling and made from fully managed and sustained forest sources. Logging, pulping and manufacturing processes are expected to conform to the environmental regulations of the country of origin.

A catalogue record for this book is available from the British Library.

Library of Congress Cataloging-in-Publication Data

Martin, J. R.
    The language of evaluation : appraisal in English / J.R. Martin and P.R.R. White.
    p. cm.
    Includes bibliographical references (p.) and index.
    ISBN 1–4039–0409–X (cloth)   1–4039–0410–3 (pbk)
    1. English language – Semantics. 2. English language – Usage. 3. Evaluation – Terminology. I. White, P.R.R. (Peter Robert Rupert), 1956– II. Title.

PE1585.M29 2005
420.1'43—dc22   2005043360

10 9 8 7 6 5 4 3 2 1
16 15 14 13 12 11 10 09 08 07

Printed and bound in Great Britain by
CPI Antony Rowe, Chippenham and Eastbourne

Contents

List of Figures	vii
List of Tables	ix
Acknowledgements	x
Preface	xi

1 Introduction   1
   1.1 Modelling appraisal resources   1
   1.2 Appraisal in a functional model of language   7
   1.3 Situating appraisal in SFL   33
   1.4 Appraisal – an overview   34
   1.5 Appraisal and other traditions of evaluative language analysis   38
   1.6 Outline of this book   40

2 Attitude: Ways of Feeling   42
   2.1 Kinds of feeling   42
   2.2 Affect   45
   2.3 Judgement   52
   2.4 Appreciation   56
   2.5 Borders   58
   2.6 Indirect realisations   61
   2.7 Beyond attitude   68
   2.8 Analysing attitude   69

3 Engagement and Graduation: Alignment, Solidarity and the Construed Reader   92
   3.1 Introduction: a dialogic perspective   92
   3.2 Value position, alignment and the putative reader   95
   3.3 The resources of intersubjective stance: an overview of engagement   97
   3.4 Engagement and the dialogistic status of bare assertions   98
   3.5 Heteroglossia: dialogic contraction and expansion   102
   3.6 Entertain: the dialogistic expansiveness of modality and evidentiality   104

3.7	Dialogistic expansion through the externalised proposition – attribution	111
3.8	The resources of dialogic contraction – overview: disclaim and proclaim	117
3.9	Disclaim: deny (negation)	118
3.10	Disclaim: counter	120
3.11	Proclaim: concur, pronounce and endorse	121
3.12	Proclaim: concur	122
3.13	Proclaim: endorsement	126
3.14	Proclaim: pronounce	127
3.15	Engagement, intertextuality and the grammar of reported speech	133
3.16	Graduation: an overview	135
3.17	Graduation: focus	137
3.18	Graduation: force – intensification and quantification	140
3.19	Force: intensification	141
3.20	Force: quantification	148
3.21	Force (intensification and quantification), attitude and writer–reader relationships	152
3.22	Analysing intersubjective positioning	153

4 Evaluative Key: Taking a Stance — 161
4.1	Introduction	161
4.2	Evaluative key in journalistic discourse – the 'voices' of news, analysis and commentary	164
4.3	Evaluative key and the discourses of secondary-school history	184
4.4	Stance	186
4.5	Signature	203
4.6	Evaluation and reaction	206
4.7	Coda …	207

5 Enacting Appraisal: Text Analysis — 210
5.1	Appraising discourse	210
5.2	War or Peace: a rhetoric of grief and hatred	212
5.3	Mourning: an unfortunate case of keystone cops	234
5.4	Envoi	260

References — 262

Index — 274

List of Figures

1.1	Ideational, interpersonal and textual metafunctions	8
1.2	Language strata	9
1.3	The intersection of strata and metafunctions	12
1.4	Network displaying dependent systems	14
1.5	Network displaying two simultaneous systems	15
1.6	Network displaying three simultaneous systems	15
1.7	Halliday's grammatical reading of modality	16
1.8	Representations of scaled systems (modality value)	16
1.9	A topological perspective on value and orientation	17
1.10	Kinds of meaning in relation to kinds of structure	18
1.11	Prosodic domain in Tagalog	23
1.12	Prosodic domain in English	23
1.13	Types of prosody	24
1.14	Cline of instantiation	25
1.15	Metafunctions in relation to field, mode and tenor	27
1.16	Register recontextualised by genre	32
1.17	Interpersonal semantic systems and tenor variables	34
1.18	An overview of appraisal resources	38
2.1	Judgement and appreciation as institutionalised affect	45
2.2	Modality and types of judgement (following Iedema *et al.* 1994)	54
2.3	Strategies for inscribing and invoking attitude	67
3.1	Engagement: contract and expand	104
3.2	Engagement – dialogic expansion	117
3.3	Engagement – contract: disclaim	122
3.4	The engagement system	133
3.5	A preliminary outline of graduation	138
3.6	Force: intensification – quality and process	141
3.7	Force: quantification	151
3.8	System network for graduation: force and focus	154
4.1	Reporter and writer voices: patterns of inscribed authorial judgement	169

4.2	Elaborated system of journalistic key	173
4.3	Journalistic keys – attitudinal profile	178
4.4	Journalistic voices and authorial sanction	182
4.5	The keys of history – network again	185
5.1	Bonding – the infusion of value in activity	212

List of Tables

1.1	Probability – value by orientation	13
1.2	Probability – subclassifying subjective realisations	14
1.3	Time frames for semiotic change	26
1.4	Interpersonal semantics in relation to lexicogrammar and phonology	35
1.5	Approaches to evaluation	39
2.1	Irrealis affect	48
2.2	Affect – un/happiness	49
2.3	Affect – in/security	50
2.4	Affect – dis/satisfaction	51
2.5	Affect – kinds of unhappiness	51
2.6	Judgement – social esteem	53
2.7	Judgement – social sanction	53
2.8	Types of appreciation	56
2.9	Sub-types of appreciation	57
2.10	Interactions between attitudinal invocation and attitudinal inscription	68
2.11	Example attitude analysis	71
2.12	Appraisal analysis conventions	73
2.13	Inscribed attitude in Proulx	74
2.14	Inscribed and invoked attitude in Proulx	75
2.15	Invoked attitude in Proulx	76
2.16	Inscribed attitude in 'Baby, please don't cry'	80
2.17	Inscribed attitude for Dad in 'Baby, please don't cry'	81
2.18	Inscribed attitude for Baby in 'Baby, please don't cry'	81
3.1	The monoglossic and the heteroglossic	100
3.2	Realisation options for pronouncement	131
3.3	A taxonomy of pronouncement realisations	132
3.4	The gradability of attitudinal meanings	136
3.5	The gradability of engagement values	136
3.6	Feature combinations for quality intensifications	149
3.7	Feature combinations for process intensifications	149
3.8	Feature combinations for quantification	152
3.9	Engagement analysis of Heffer text	158
4.1	Cline of instantiation – from system to reading	163
4.2	Cline of instantiation – evaluation	164
5.1	Overview of meta-relations	232

Acknowledgements

Copyright permissions and acknowledgements

'The Dad Department', by George Blair-West, from *Mother & Baby* magazine, June/July 1994, A. Bounty Publication, Sydney.

'What We Think of America', by Harold Pinter, Granta 77, March 14, 2002: 66–9.

'What We Think of America', by Doris Lessing, Granta 77, March 14, 2002: 52–4.

'Mourning', *HK Magazine*, September 21, 2001.

'Damn the Peaceniks for the faint hearts', by Carol Sarler, *Daily Express*, features pages, October 10, 2001.

'A few questions as we go to war', by William Raspberry. *Guardian Weekly*. Jan 2–8.

Other acknowledgements

Empire magazine, Emap Consumer Media, London for two extracts from the letters-to-the-editor page, November 2003 edition.

Extract from *The Shipping News*, Annie Proulx, London: Fourth Estate, 1993.

Extract from 'The Valley of Fear.' Part 1 'The Tragedy of Birlstone.' Chapter 1 'The Warning.', Arthur Conan Doyle, *The Penguin Complete Sherlock Holmes*. Harmondsworth: Penguin. 1981.

Extract from *On the Case with Lord Peter Wimsey* from, *Three complete novels: Strong Poison, Have his Carcase, Unnatural Death*, Dorothy L. Sayers, New York: Wings Books, 1991.

Preface

The impetus for this book grew out of work on narrative genres, principally undertaken by Guenter Plum and Joan Rothery at the University of Sydney through the 1980s. Their point was that interpersonal meaning was critical both to the point of these genres (as emphasised by Labov) and also to how we classified them. This encouraged us to extend the model of interpersonal meaning that we had available at the time (based largely on work by Cate Poynton on language and gender), especially in the direction of one that could handle affect alongside modality and mood.

The appraisal framework we're presenting here was developed in response to this need as part of the Disadvantaged Schools Program's Write it Right literacy project, which looked intensively at writing in the workplace and secondary school (from about 1990 to 1995). Jim was academic adviser to this project, in which Joan Rothery focussed on secondary school English and Creative Arts (working closely with Mary Macken-Horarik and Maree Stenglin). Peter joined the team, and drew on his background as a journalist to focus on media discourse (working closely with Rick Iedema and Susan Feez). Appraisal theory developed as we moved from one register to another, and shuttled among theory, description and applications to school-based literacy initiatives. Caroline Coffin focused on secondary school history in this project, and adapted appraisal analysis to this subject area. The main innovation in this period involved moving beyond affect to consider lexical resources for judging behaviour and appreciating the value of things, and the recognition of syndromes of appraisal associated with different voices in the media and discourses of history.

During the 1990s Jim was also supervising influential PhD work by Gillian Fuller, Mary Macken-Horarik and Henrike Körner. Fuller's heteroglossic perspective on evaluation in popular science, drawing on Bakhtin, was a major influence on the development of engagement as a resource for managing the play of voices in discourse. Körner specialised in legal discourse, and her work on graduation, especially the distinction between force and focus, was also foundational. Macken-Horarik's study of appraisal in secondary school narrative drew attention to the need for a more dynamic perspective on evaluation as it unfolded prosodically in discourse. More recently Sue Hood's application of appraisal theory to academic discourse led to further developments with respect to graduation, some of which we have incorporated here.

We are of course greatly indebted to these colleagues, and to all the functional linguists and educational linguists of the so called 'Sydney School' who gave value to our work. In 1998 Peter established his appraisal website and e-mail list, which has also proved a supportive context for the development of these ideas (www.grammatics.com/appraisal/). Our collective thanks to all of those, too numerous to mention, who have contributed to the ongoing discussions there. Thanks also to our SFL colleagues around the world who have engaged so helpfully with our ideas at meetings and over the net.

Of course none of this work would have been possible without the systemic functional linguistic theory that guides our endeavour. So a note of thanks as well to Michael Halliday, for his close attention to interpersonal meaning in language and for his design of the roomy theory that inspired this research.

Adelaide and Sydney, May 2005

1
Introduction

1.1 Modelling appraisal resources

This book is concerned with the interpersonal in language, with the subjective presence of writers/speakers in texts as they adopt stances towards both the material they present and those with whom they communicate. It is concerned with how writers/speakers approve and disapprove, enthuse and abhor, applaud and criticise, and with how they position their readers/listeners to do likewise. It is concerned with the construction by texts of communities of shared feelings and values, and with the linguistic mechanisms for the sharing of emotions, tastes and normative assessments. It is concerned with how writers/speakers construe for themselves particular authorial identities or personae, with how they align or disalign themselves with actual or potential respondents, and with how they construct for their texts an intended or ideal audience.

While such issues have been seen as beyond the purview of linguistic enquiry by some influential branches of twentieth-century linguistics, they have, of course, been of longstanding interest for functionally and semiotically oriented approaches and for those whose concern is with discourse, rhetoric and communicative effect. We offer here a new approach to these issues, developed over the last decade or so by researchers working within the Systemic Functional Linguistic (hereafter SFL) paradigm of M.A.K. Halliday and his colleagues. (See, for example, Halliday 2004/1994, Martin 1992b or Matthiessen 1995.) SFL identifies three modes of meaning which operate simultaneously in all utterances – the textual, the ideational and the interpersonal. Our purpose in the book is to develop and extend the SFL account of the interpersonal by attending to three axes along which the speaker's/writer's intersubjective stance may vary.

We attend to what has traditionally been dealt with under the heading of 'affect' – the means by which writers/speakers positively or negatively evaluate the entities, happenings and states-of-affairs with which their texts are concerned. Our approach takes us beyond many traditional accounts of 'affect' in that it addresses not only the means by which speakers/writers overtly encode what they present as their own attitudes but also those means by which they more indirectly activate evaluative stances and position readers/listeners to supply their own assessments. These attitudinal evaluations are of interest not only because they reveal the speaker's/writer's feelings and values but also because their expression can be related to the speaker's/writer's status or authority as construed by the text, and because they operate rhetorically to construct relations of alignment and rapport between the writer/speaker and actual or potential respondents.

Our concern is also with what has traditionally been dealt with under the heading of 'modality' and particularly under the headings of 'epistemic modality' and 'evidentiality'. We extend traditional accounts by attending not only to issues of speaker/writer certainty, commitment and knowledge but also to questions of how the textual voice positions itself with respect to other voices and other positions. In our account, these meanings are seen to provide speakers and writers with the means to present themselves as recognising, answering, ignoring, challenging, rejecting, fending off, anticipating or accommodating actual or potential interlocutors and the value positions they represent.

We also attend to what has been dealt with under headings such as 'intensification' and 'vague language', providing a framework for describing how speakers/writers increase and decrease the force of their assertions and how they sharpen or blur the semantic categorisations with which they operate.

By way of introduction to some of our principal analytical concerns and the approach we adopt, consider the following two text extracts. They are both taken from the letters-to-editor pages of the UK movie magazine, *Empire* (November 2003).

Letter 1

Mood-Altering Substance

I had to write and say what a brilliant magazine *Empire* is. I was sitting on my bed on the morning of September 1, the first day I had to go back to school, and I was naturally very depressed. I heard the letter box open and the latest edition of *Empire* was lying on the carpet. Even better was the discovery that once hastily torn open, I saw there was an article on the *Lord of the Rings: The Return of the King*. My bad mood immediately lifted and I was no longer dreading the return to school. Keep up the good work.

[name of letter-writer], via email

Letter 2

An Indefensible Position

Just a line to say how severely saddened I've been at all the negative reviews of *Tomb Raider 2*. I feel the whole venture has been a very affectionate homage to the action genre pre-1980, and tonally perfect, paying attention to pacing while also keeping ironic humour at bay. Why, it even ended in a genuinely affecting manner. Oh – and Angelina Jolie is one of the few real movie starts we have, in the old-fashioned sense of the word. You just couldn't take your eyes off her – totally charming.

[name of letter-writer], via email

For more crazy, way-out opinions, turn to page 112.

Letter 1 is an example of a text type which occurs with some regularity in leisure, life-style and special interest publications of this type – glowing endorsements of the magazine in question by an apparently extremely satisfied subscriber. While such a text may at first glance appear inconsequential, a closer analysis reveals points of significant interest for studies of evaluation and stance.

For a start, the writer's motivation for making such a public display of his approval and enthusiasm seems somewhat obscure. We can not help being slightly suspicious that such paeans of praise may have been concocted by the magazine's own staff (or their friends or family) and published in order to promote the magazine.[1] This very suspicion is of itself revealing. It points to a particular conception of what is normal or reasonable in the use of evaluative language in public communication, a conception which leads us to see such effusiveness as in some way aberrant or at least curious. The issue for us can not be simply a matter of the correspondent's positivity. We find unexceptional all manner of publicly-presented positive evaluations – for example, favourable arts reviews, positively-disposed journalistic commentaries, obituaries, and 'this-is-your-life' style television programmes. Rather, it would seem to be a matter of the manner and the targeting of the evaluation. We notice, for example, that the writer offers virtually nothing by way of actual assessment of the magazine's properties, no indication of where the magazine's supposed virtues lie, apart from the fact that it contained some material on *The Lord of the Rings*. Instead, the correspondent offers the mini narrative of his journey from despair to equanimity. His praise of the magazine is construed as a matter of the effect its arrival in his letter box has on his emotions and state of mind. Thus the text operates with an assumption that this individual, very personal response is in some way more broadly significant, that it carries evaluative significance for the magazine's readership generally.

As well, our attention is drawn to the social positionings and alignments which are in play here. By grounding his approval in this way in emotion rather than in assessment, the correspondent constructs himself as enthusiast or 'fan' rather than as expert. The construed relationship between correspondent and the addressed magazine staff is thus one of inequality. To praise another is, of course, to make a bid to bond with them in some way. In this case, the writer makes a public display of seeking to bond with the magazine's journalistic staff. In the absence, however, of any specific account of what it is the writer finds so worthy of merit in the magazine, other readers are largely excluded from this process of affiliation. Unless they also are 'fans' of the magazine, they lack the material necessary to decide whether they too would want to include themselves in this particular community of shared feeling and taste. We suspect that it is on the basis of this exclusion that we, as non-fans, find something gratuitous and inauthentic about this type of text.

This text, then, even though extremely short and perhaps 'inconsequential' in its subject matter, still demonstrates something of the subtlety and complexity of the intersubjective relationships and affiliations which are observable once we attend to the interpersonal and the evaluative in language. The extract is of even more obvious significance, perhaps, when we recognise that it exemplifies what would appear to be an increasingly conventionalised discursive persona – that of the popular cultural 'fan'. In *Working with Discourse*, Martin and Rose (2003) observe how devotees of Blues music (and in particular the Blues music of Stevie Ray Vaughan) have exploited the reader/buyer feedback and review pages of the online retailer Amazon.com to very publicly express their 'fandom' and thereby to construct a global community of shared feeling. Even though these web pages obviously serve the global capitalist purposes of Amazon.com (the fans' enthusiasm promotes the products on sale), as Jay Lemke has observed in personal communication, they also afford fans the possibility of some degree of resistance – the opportunity for some anti-global guerrilla tactics of a semiotic kind. The fans use the pages as a resource for articulating the particular terms of their community of shared feeling, for constructing a discursive framework of alignment and rapport by which enthusiasts from around the world can be brought together. In our letter we see clearly articulated the dialogistic terms by which such affiliations are constructed. Though, on the face of it, an entirely 'monologic' text, the letter obviously constructs a particular set of dialogic relationships. Most notably, it constructs an affiliation not only with the putative addressee (the magazine's journalistic staff) but also, through its highly personalised use of affect, with all those other readers who share the writer's enthusiasm (all the other 'fans'). The point of the letter, then, is one of assuming the existence of this particular community of shared feeling among the magazine's regular readership and of celebrating it.

The writer's identity as 'fan' is conveyed by several other objective lexico-grammatical markers of enthusiasm. Through the use of *I had to write and say* he construes his enthusiasm for the magazine as some form of external compulsion dictating his actions. Somewhat similar in effect are the text's use of exclamative fronting structures in which the Complement of a relational clause is moved into a textually marked position ahead of the Subject. This fronting occurs twice – in *what a brilliant magazine Empire is* (versus *Empire is a brilliant magazine*) and *Even better was the discovery that …* (versus *the discovery that … was even better*). Thus the fan's eagerness and enthusiasm find their expression in the choice of a marked grammatical structuring which fronts and hence foregrounds the evaluative terms *brilliant* and *even better*.

Note as well the use of *naturally* in,

> I was sitting on my bed on the morning of September 1, the first day I had to go back to school, and I was **naturally** very depressed.

Such terms are obviously interactive or dialogic in that the construed reader is thereby represented as sharing a particular set of values or attitudes with the writer – in this case a psychology in which it is the norm for school attendance to trigger distress and despair. The writer thus constructs a consensus with his intended readership based on 'commonsense'.

The letter, then, though only a few sentences long, demonstrates a range of issues relating to the often complex functionality of evaluative language. It has demonstrated the effects of the writer favouring one type of attitude (emotion) over other options – the choice gives rise to a particular discursive persona. And the fundamentally dialogic nature of evaluation has also been demonstrated, with this choice of attitudinal orientation, in conjunction with other intersubjective resources, construing relationships of alignment and rapport between the writer, the magazine and its regular readership.

Text 2 provides a contrast in that, rather than construing consensus, the writer set himself against what is apparently a very widely held view among film reviewers generally and the magazine's own writers more specifically, namely that *Tomb Raider 2* was a bad movie. We notice that this difference is reflected in the way the two writers frame their texts. As just noted, the first writer employs *I had to write and say* while the second writer begins with *Just a line to say …* . Tellingly the writer of the adversarial second text adopts a locution which, to some degree, diminishes or downplays the significance or weight of what he is about to contribute to the debate. He certainly does not present himself as under some external compulsion. As well, his contrary positive assessment of the film (that it was *a very affectionate homage …*) is explicitly cast as his opinion by means of the framer, *I feel*, thereby overtly allowing for the possibility that others may 'feel' differently.

Text 2, however, does share at least one significant feature with text 1. Its writer also grounds his attitudinal position in emotions – he begins by describing his sadness at the negativity of the *Tomb Raider* reviews. Reports of one's own emotional reactions are highly personalising. They invite the addressee to respond on a personal level, to empathise, sympathise or at least to see the emotion as warranted or understandable. In this, the two letter writers employ a similar intersubjective strategy. The similarity, however, is a relatively fleeting one. The second correspondent differs from the first in that, while starting with emotion, he then goes on to provide a number of specific, sometimes technical assessments in support of his viewpoint. Unlike the first writer, he constructs his role as being, not that of the fan, but that of the expert who would set himself up as the equal of the magazine's writers and other reviewers.

This discussion has served, then, as an introduction to the types of questions with which we will be concerned in the remainder of the book. We turn now to briefly describing the historical development of appraisal theory and to providing a brief sketch of its relationship to SFL, within which it has been developed and which it seeks to extend, and to other theories of the interpersonal and the evaluative.

1.2 Appraisal in a functional model of language

As indicated, our model of evaluation evolved within the general theoretical framework of SFL. Eggins 2004/1994 provides an accessible introduction to the 'Sydney' register of SFL which informed our work. For grammar, we relied on Halliday 2004/1994 and Matthiessen 1995 and for discourse analyses we used Martin 1992b (later recontextualised as Martin & Rose 2003). The most relevant reservoir of theoretical concepts is Halliday & Matthiessen 1999 (for thumbnail sketches of SFL theory see the introductory chapters in Halliday & Martin 1993 and Christie & Martin 1997). We'll now outline some of the basic parameters of SFL, by way of situating appraisal within a holistic model of language and social context.

1.2.1 Metafunction

At heart SFL is a multi-perspectival model, designed to provide analysts with complementary lenses for interpreting language in use. One of the most basic of these complementarities is the notion of kinds of meaning – the idea that language is a resource for mapping ideational, interpersonal and textual meaning onto one another in virtually every act of communication. Ideational resources are concerned with construing experience: what's going on, including who's doing what to whom, where, when, why and how and the logical relation of one going-on to another. Interpersonal resources are concerned with negotiating social relations: how people are interacting, including the feelings they try to share. Textual resources are concerned with information flow: the ways in which ideational and interpersonal meanings are distributed in waves of semiosis, including interconnections among waves and between language and attendant modalities (action, image, music etc.). These highly generalised kinds of meaning are referred to as metafunctions, as outlined in Figure 1.1.

In this book we are focussing on interpersonal meaning. Martin & Rose 2003 provide a sympathetic framework for dealing with interpersonal meaning in relation to meaning of other kinds. In addition, for ease of exposition, we are concentrating here on interpersonal meaning in written discourse. In this respect our presentation complements Eggins & Slade 1997, which deals with spoken language. Their participation in the development of appraisal analysis confirms our expectation that the tools developed here can be usefully applied to both spoken and written texts.

Up to about 1990, work on interpersonal meaning in SFL was more strongly oriented to interaction than feeling. This was the result of

8 The Language of Evaluation

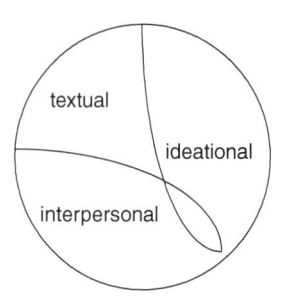

Figure 1.1 Ideational, interpersonal and textual metafunctions

Halliday's seminal work on the grammar of mood and modality (Halliday 1994) and its extension into the analysis of turn-taking in dialogue (speech function and exchange structure as introduced in Halliday 1984, Martin 1992b, Eggins & Slade 1997). Working with colleagues in the early 1990s we began to develop a more lexically-based perspective, triggered in the first instance by the need for a richer understanding of interpersonal meaning in monologic texts. Initially we were concerned with affect in narrative, and moved on to consider evaluation in literary criticism, the print media, art criticism, administrative discourse and history discourse as part of an action research project concerned with literacy in the workplace and secondary school (Iedema, Feez & White 1994, Iedema 1995, Martin 2000a, Martin 2001b). Since then the research has moved across many fields and the framework has stabilised somewhat around the categories outlined in Chapters 2 and 3 below. Readers interested in the ongoing development of appraisal are invited to join the discussions at www.grammatics.com/appraisal.

1.2.2 Realisation

The second lens we need to consider is realisation – the idea that language is a stratified semiotic system involving three cycles of coding at different levels of abstraction (see Figure 1.2). For spoken language the most concrete of these is phonology, which deals with organisation of phonemes into syllables, and their deployment in units of rhythm and intonation. For writing, of course, this level is concerned with graphology, and has to deal with the organization of letters into sentences (via intermediate units), alongside punctuation, layout and formatting. For the language of the deaf, this level is concerned with signing.

In SFL the next level of abstraction is referred to as lexicogrammar. It is concerned with the recoding of phonological and graphological patterns

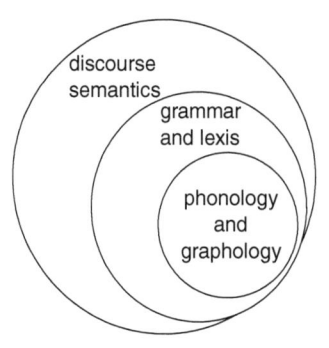

Figure 1.2 Language strata

as words and structures. The notion of recoding is critical here. Lexicogrammar is not made up of phonological or graphological patterns; rather it is realised through them. It is a more abstract level of organisation, not just a bigger one. One way to appreciate this is to note that both phonology[2] and grammar have their own compositional hierarchies. In English phonology we can recognise tone groups consisting of one or more feet, feet consisting of one or more syllables and syllables consisting of one or more phonemes; and for English grammar we have clauses consisting of one or more groups,[3] groups consisting of one or more words and words consisting of one or more morphemes. And the two hierarchies don't necessarily match up – we find clauses realised over two tone groups and one tone group realising two clauses, just as there are morphemes realised by one or more syllables (*dog, parrot, elephant*, etc.), and syllables realising one or two morphemes (*hat, hats; she, she's*). So it can't be the case that lexicogrammar consists of phonology. Lexicogrammar is a pattern of phonological patterns; that is to say, it is a more abstract level realised by a more concrete one.

The third level of abstraction will be referred to here as discourse semantics, to emphasise the fact that it is concerned with meaning beyond the clause (with texts in other words). This level is concerned with various aspects of discourse organisation, including the question of how people, places and things are introduced in text and kept track of once there (identification); how events and states of affairs are linked to one another in terms of time, cause, contrast and similarity (conjunction); how participants are related as part to whole and sub-class to class (ideation); how turns are organised into exchanges of goods, services and information (negotiation); and how evaluation is established, amplified, targeted and sourced (appraisal).

Appraisal is placed in discourse semantics for three reasons. First of all the realisation of an attitude tends to splash across a phase of discourse, irrespective of grammatical boundaries – especially where amplified. The following rave by a Stevie Ray Vaughan fan (from the Amazon website) accumulates a positive evaluation that is more than the sum of its clause-based parts:

> awesome! awesome! awesome! awesome! it's very worth buying. oh did i say that it's awesome! thank you. stevie ray!

Secondly, a given attitude can be realised across a range of grammatical categories, as in the following examples:

an <u>interesting</u> contrast in styles	adjective (Epithet)
the contrast in styles <u>interested</u> me	verb (Process)
<u>interestingly</u>, there's a contrast in styles	adverb (Comment Adjunct)

We need to move out of lexicogrammar to generalise the evaluative meaning common to this kind of scatter.

Finally, there is the question of grammatical metaphor (Halliday 1994, Halliday & Matthiessen 1999). This is the process whereby meaning is cooked twice as it were, introducing a degree of tension between wording and meaning. It's possible, for example, to nominalise the attitude just reviewed so that it comes out grammatically as a thing.

> the contrast in styles is of considerable <u>interest</u>

Phrased in this way a semantic process whereby something attracts our attention is rendered as a grammatical entity nominating a type of attraction. We could indeed have treated *an interesting contrast in styles* above along similar lines, since *contrast* is itself a nominalisation which was in fact unpacked (as *different*) in a review entitled 'An interesting contrast' as follows:

> His overall appearance, his stage presence, even his playing style are quite different in the two shows.

Grammatical metaphor also comes into play as far as attributing and grading opinions is concerned. Grammatically speaking this would involve modality, which we can realise through modal adverbs and/or modal verbs:

> Perhaps his playing style might be different.
> Probably his playing style would be different.
> Certainly his playing style must be different.

Alternatively we can draw on first person, present tense mental processes of cognition to establish degrees of certainty:

> I suspect his playing style is different.
> I believe his playing style is different.
> I know his playing style is different.

And where we do use this explicitly subjective form (Halliday 1994) the appropriate tag is to Stevie's playing style, not the speaker – because what we're negotiating is how he plays, not whether the speaker thinks:

> I suspect his playing style is different, isn't it?
> *I suspect his playing style is different, don't I?[4]

In these examples a semantic assessment of probability is reworked as a grammatical process of cognition. The tension between the levels gives rise to verbal play such as the following:

> 'I'm inclined to think—' said I. 'I should do so', Sherlock Holmes remarked impatiently. I believe that I am one of the most long-suffering of mortals; but I'll admit that I was annoyed at the sardonic interruption. 'Really, Holmes', said I severely, 'you are a little trying at times'. (Doyle 1981: 769)

In summary, our point here is that the degree of play between discourse semantics and lexicogrammar which Halliday's concept of grammatical metaphor affords is an important aspect of appraisal theory. And we can't draw on these insights unless we develop appraisal as a discourse semantic resource for meaning.

The complementarity of the metafunctional and realisational complementarities just reviewed is outlined in Figure 1.3.

Before turning to other relevant dimensions of SFL we should perhaps stress the Firthian perspective we take on realisation, namely that all levels make meaning. As far as interpersonal meaning is concerned

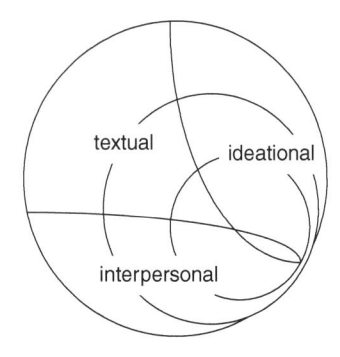

Figure 1.3 The intersection of strata and metafunctions

phonology contributes through intonation, phonaesthesia (eg sl-, gr-, -ump style series) and various features of voice quality which have tended to be marginalised as paralinguistic but appear far more central once appraisal systems are given their due. We do not accept, in other words, that a line of arbitrariness needs to be drawn between content and expression form as far as interpersonal meaning is concerned and would suggest that the commonplace mapping of Saussure's signifié-to-signifiant opposition onto content and expression is unhelpful when interpreting realisation in a functional model of language.

Similarly, we take lexicogrammar as a meaning making resource rather than a set of forms, following Halliday 1994 and Matthiessen 1995. It seems clear to us that Halliday's main contribution to grammatical theory has been to design a theory in which meaning can be modelled grammatically. We've relied on his 'meaning importing' perspective on the grammar of English in our work. In Hjelmslev's terms this means that we operate with a stratified content plane, in which both lexicogrammar and discourse semantics contribute layers of meaning to a text. The main complementarity between these strata has to do with the scope of our gaze – on meaning within the clause (lexicogrammar) as opposed to meaning beyond the clause (discourse semantics). Note in passing that interpreting grammatical metaphor as stratal tension with layers of meaning standing in a figure to ground relationship depends on a stratified content plane of just this kind.

1.2.3 Axis

Another critical dimension of analysis in SFL is axis – the yin/yang complementarity of system and structure. Although inherited directly from Firth, this opposition goes back to Saussure's consideration of paradigmatic and syntagmatic relations (the axes of choice and chain in language). For Firth, elements of structure in syntagmatic chains functioned as points of departure for systems. In phonology, for example, the CVC structure of a syllable would be explored paradigmatically in terms of the system of consonants that can operate initially as opposed to finally, and the system of vowels in between.

Halliday's main innovation of this work was to treat units of structure as a whole as points of departure for systems, and deriving their structure from choices made with respect to the unit as a whole. In phonology this would mean systems of syllables (Halliday 1992) and other higher units as required. In grammar it led to the development of elaborate paradigms of group and clause choices (Halliday 1976a) responsible for organising the structure of groups and clauses. This led in turn to the recognition of the metafunctional complementarities introduced above, and was critical to the development of grammars of meaning for English and Chinese (and many other languages over time; see Caffarel, Martin & Matthiessen 2004).

1.2.4 System

Traditionally paradigmatic relations are displayed in paradigms – tables plotting one dimension against another. In our discussion of grammatical metaphor above we looked at different kinds of probability (following Halliday 1994), including its value (high, median, low) and orientation (objective, subjective). These oppositions are presented as a matrix in Table 1.1.

As long as we are dealing with two dimensions this kind of display of paradigmatic relations works fairly well. Once we introduce subclassification however, for example the difference between explicitly subjective and implicitly subjective realisations, the picture becomes more complicated. We have to be more careful about labelling, and the formatting of borders (as in Table 1.2).

Table 1.1 Probability – value by orientation

	objective	subjective
low	perhaps	I suspect
median	probably	I believe
high	certainly	I know

14 *The Language of Evaluation*

If we try and introduce a third dimension (say usuality or obligation), things become more complicated still. Visually speaking we end up with a three dimensional cube, which can be drawn, but ends up hard to read and is not much used. In Chapter 2 below we present a number of appraisal systems as tables, limiting as far as possible the number of dimensions and the amount of subclassification involved.

Table 1.2 Probability – subclassifying subjective realisations

	objective	subjective: explicit	subjective: implicit
low	perhaps	I suspect	might
median	probably	I believe	would
high	certainly	I know	must

In order to cope with this additional complexity, Halliday designed images referred to as system networks to display paradigmatic relations. The names of rows and columns in paradigms are treated as features in systems of choice, and any feature can be an entry condition to another system. In Figure 1.4 the square bracket with the arrow leading into it represents a logical 'or'; the network says that subjective modality can be either explicit or implicit.

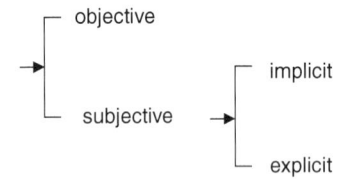

Figure 1.4 Network displaying dependent systems

Each of the two systems in Figure 1.4 is a binary system, but systems can contain any number of features. In general they contain two or three, since it is usually possible to find reasons for grouping features into smaller systems if a system with three or more features is proposed (see the discussion of Halliday's interpretation of value in relation to negativity, below).

Multidimensionality is handled by an angled bracket with the meaning of logical 'and'. This can be used to handle the cross-classification in Table 1.1 as outlined in Figure 1.5. This network says that modality can be either objective or subjective and either high, median or low. It maps value against orientation in other words.

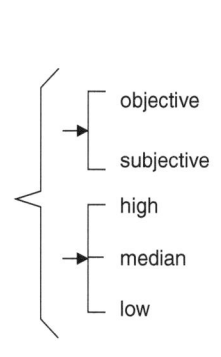

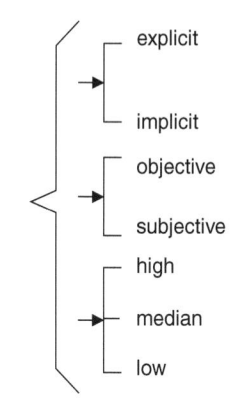

Figure 1.5 Network displaying two simultaneous systems

Figure 1.6 Network displaying three simultaneous systems

With this kind of imaging there is no limit to the number of dimensions that can be displayed. Since the implicit/explicit opposition holds for objective (*perhaps/it's possible*, etc.) as well as subjective modality we can in fact include this system as a third dimension, as in Figure 1.6. We'll use systems networks of this kind to display appraisal systems when we need to focus attention on subclassification of one system by another, or on multiple dimensions.

In grammar, system networks are used to represent categorical oppositions. Systems classify grammatical items as one kind of thing or another (not both and not something in between). So although the high/median/low value system presented above looks like a scale, the system network notation does not formalise it as such. In other words, the arrangement of features top-to-bottom in a system has no meaning. Halliday (1976a, 1994) in fact argues that grammatically speaking this system is not a scale, because median modalities interact differently with negation than high and low ones. With median probability, for example, we can freely transfer negativity between the modality and the proposition:

it's probable his playing styles aren't different
it's not probable his playing styles are different

Both of these are in some sense equivalent to *His playing styles won't be different*. With the high and low values however, if the negativity

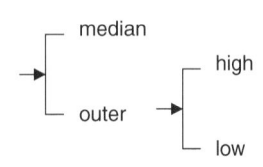

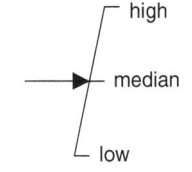

Figure 1.7 Halliday's grammatical reading of modality

Figure 1.8 Representation of scaled systems (modality value)

transfers, the value switches (from low to high or from high to low). Thus *it's possible that ... not* pairs with *It's not certain that ...*

it's possible his playing styles aren't different
it's not certain his playing styles are different

And *it's certain that ... not* pairs with *it's not possible that ...*

it's certain his playing styles aren't different
it's not possible his playing styles are different

Grammatically then, there is a motivated opposition between median modality and outer modality, which can then be divided into high and low. This interpretation is outlined in Figure 1.7.

As far as appraisal semantics is concerned, however, we have found it useful to interpret some systems as scaled and suspect that this may in fact be a distinctive feature of interpersonal semantic systems in general. For such meanings it is useful to employ the notion of values being located along a continuous scale extending from 'low' to 'high', with various intermediate points possible between these two extremes. Thus the sequence, *contented ^ happy ^ joyous ^ ecstatic*, can be analysed as representing a cline from the low intensity value of *contented* to the maximally high value of *ecstatic*. The modal values *possibly* [low] ^ *probably* [median] ^ *certainly* [high] can be similarly analysed. Sue Hood (personal communication) has suggested representing scalar systems as in Figure 1.8.

The introduction of scaled systems shifts our perspective from categorical to graded analysis. Technically speaking this is a shift from typology to topology. From a topological perspective we are interested in regions of meaning and the proximity of one meaning to another along a cline. For display purposes, we can plot one dimension against

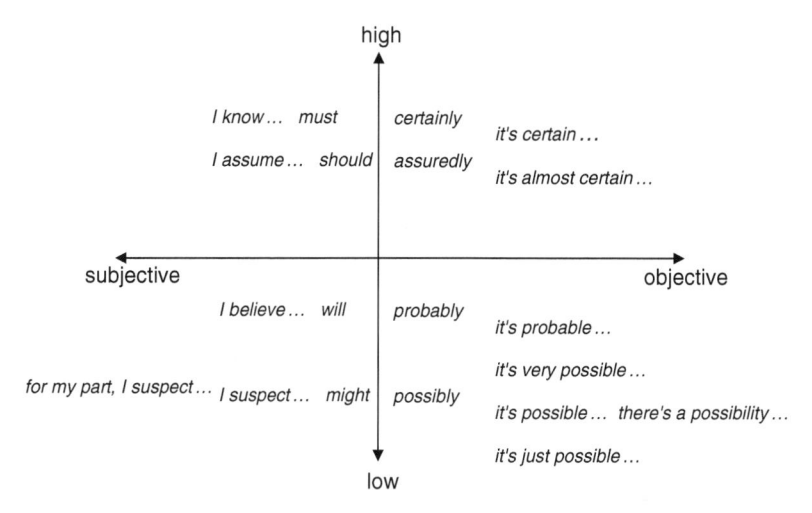

```
                        high
                         ▲
           I know...  must  │ certainly
                            │             it's certain...
           I assume... should│ assuredly
                            │             it's almost certain...
                            │
◄───────────────────────────┼──────────────────────────────►
subjective                  │                         objective
           I believe... will│ probably
                            │             it's probable...
                            │             it's very possible...
for my part, I suspect... I suspect... might│ possibly
                            │             it's possible... there's a possibility...
                            │             it's just possible...
                         ▼
                        low
```

Figure 1.9 A topological perspective on value and orientation

another[5] and arrange realisations in the image as closer to or farther away from one another. With modality, for example, we can treat both value and orientation as clines (from high to low and from subjective to objective) and consider degrees of subjectivity or objectivity, and a range of graded values. In Figure 1.9, we've included an extra-subjective and an extra-objective option (*for my part, I suspect* and *there's a possibility*), and values for hyper- and hypo-possibility (*very possible* and *just possible*). There are of course many other gradings to explore.

1.2.5 Structure

As noted above, in SFL system and structure are complementary faces of meaning potential. The system perspective foregrounds the notion of choice – language as a resource. The structure perspective foregrounds the inherent temporality of semiotic processes – they unfold through time, and phases of this process enter into interdependent relations with one another by way of signalling the meanings that are being made. Pike was the first linguist to acknowledge different kinds of incommensurable structuring principles, drawing on his reading in physics:

> Within tagmemic theory there is an assertion that at least three perspectives are utilized by Homo sapiens. On the one hand, he

often acts as if he were cutting up sequences into chunks – into segments or *particles* ... On the other hand, he often senses things as somehow flowing together as ripples on the tide, merging into one another in the form of a hierarchy of little *waves* of experiences on still bigger waves. These two perspectives, in turn, are supplemented by a third – the concept of *field* in which intersecting properties of experience cluster into bundles of simultaneous characteristics which together make up the patterns of his experience. [Pike 1982: 12–13]

Halliday (1979) takes the further step of associating kinds of structure with kinds of meaning. In Martin's terms (1995a, 1996), ideational meaning is associated with particulate structure, interpersonal meaning with prosodic structure and textual meaning with periodic structure (see Figure 1.10). Particulate structure is segmental, and we may find segments organised into mono-nuclear (orbital) or into multi-nuclear (serial) patterns. This kind of structure configures ideational meanings – for example the mono-nuclear nucleus/satellite relations of the Process and Medium to other participants and circumstances in a clause (with the Process/Medium as central, participants in orbit close to this centre, and circumstances in outer orbits); or of Classifier and Thing to pre- and post-modification in nominal groups (with the Classifier/Thing complex as central, and additional modification more and less gravitationally bound). The complementary serial patterns of realisation don't

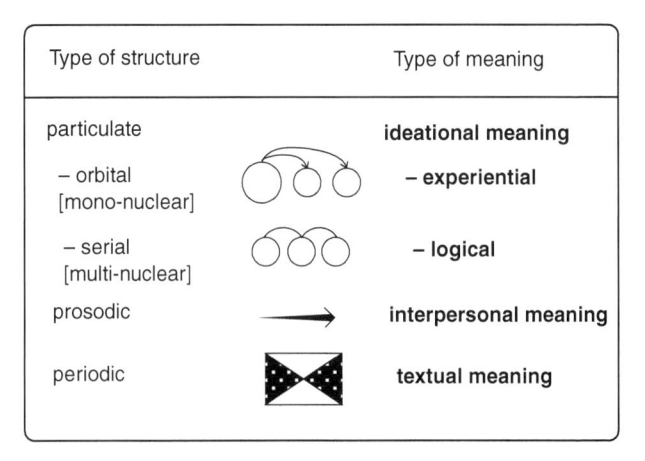

Type of structure		Type of meaning
particulate		**ideational meaning**
– orbital [mono-nuclear]		– experiential
– serial [multi-nuclear]		– logical
prosodic	→	**interpersonal meaning**
periodic		**textual meaning**

Figure 1.10 Kinds of meaning in relation to kinds of structure

have any one gravitational centre; rather the structure unfolds through segmental interdependencies such as those we find for projecting clauses (*I think he knows she feels* ...) or tense selections in the English verbal group (*had been feeling* – present in past in past). Periodic structure organises meaning into waves of information, with different wave lengths piled up one upon another. We are perhaps most familiar with this kind of pattern in phonology, where we can interpret a syllable as a wave of sonority, a foot as a wave of stressed and unstressed syllables, and a tone group as a wave of pre-tonic and tonic feet.[6] But information is organised into hierarchies of periodicity on all strata.

Halliday's comments on the prosodic nature of interpersonal structure are of particular relevance to appraisal analysis:

> The interpersonal component of meaning is the speaker's ongoing intrusion into the speech situation. It is his perspective on the exchange, his assigning and acting out of speech roles. Interpersonal meanings cannot easily be expressed as configurations of discrete elements ... The essence of the meaning potential of this part of the semantic system is that most of the options are associated with the act of meaning as a whole ... this interpersonal meaning ... is strung throughout the clause as a continuous motif or colouring ... the effect is cumulative ... we shall refer to this type of realisation as 'prosodic', since the meaning is distributed like a prosody throughout a continuous stretch of discourse. [Halliday 1979: 66–7]

Halliday of course is drawing here on Firth's phonological analysis, which emphasised non-segmental forms of realisation – including articulatory prosodies mapped across consonants clusters and syllables, vowel harmony, rhythm and intonation. Once we turn to lexicogrammar and discourse semantics, prosodic structure is arguably more difficult to model and understand, probably because it is the kind of structure that is most obscured by the evolution of alphabetic writing systems. We'll introduce three types of prosodic realisation here, which we have found useful for interpreting the ways in which appraisal operates as an ongoing cumulative motif.

saturation – this type of prosodic realisation is opportunistic; the prosody manifests where it can. A modality of possibility for example might be strung through the clause as a first person present tense mental process, a modal verb and a modal adjunct and picked up again in the tag. This kind of opportunistic realisation is similar to vowel harmony in phonology.

I suppose	he	might	possibly	have	mightn't	he
projecting mental process		modal verb	modal adjunct		modal verb (+neg)	

intensification – this type of realisation involves amplification; the volume is turned up so that the prosody makes a bigger splash which reverberates through the surrounding discourse. Intensification involves repetitions of various kinds, and is similar to the use of loudness and pitch movement for highlighting in phonology[7] (as noted by Poynton 1984, 1985, 1996):

> '**That**,' said her spouse, 'is a lie.' '**It's the truth**,' said she. 'It's a **dirty rotten stinking lousy bloody low filthy two-faced** lie,' he amplified. He's just a **lovely lovely lovely** guy; **Truly, TRULY** outstanding. **Gregsypookins** – five steps of 'diminutive' endearment (*Greg-s-y-poo-kin-s*).

A prosody can also increase in mass through submodification, exclamative structure or superlative morphology:

> You will find yourself laughing in awe of **how truly** great a SRV show could be.
>
> **What an** amazing album. 'Love Struck Baby' starts it off and is one of their **most** famous songs. 'Testify' is one of the great**est** songs Stevie ever did.

domination – in this kind of realisation the prosody associates itself with meanings that have other meanings under their scope. In English grammar, Halliday's Mood function works in this way by construing the arguability of a clause – the 'nub' of the argument. This function has been foregrounded in popular culture through the idiolect of Yoda in the Star Wars epics. Where standard English places the Mood function first in the clause, Yoda places it last.

> [standard: Mood ^ Residue sequencing]
> I can – sense a disturbance in the force.
> He was – full of anger.

[Yoda: Residue ^ Mood sequencing]
Sense a disturbance in the force – I can.
Full of anger – he was.

For an earlier generation, Monty Python attracted attention to the arguability function of this interpersonal nub:

It's just contradiction!
– No it isn't.
– It is!
– It is not.
Well an argument isn't just contradiction.
– It can be.
– No it can't. [from Monty Python's Flying Circus]

As illustrated, the Mood function sets up the mood of the clause (declarative, interrogative, imperative, etc.), alongside its modality and polarity. The rest of the clause, called Residue by Halliday, functions as the domain of these meanings. This is reflected in standard and non-standard English through the interaction of negative polarity in Mood and indefinite deixis in Residue. In the words of Australian boxing champion Jeff Fenech:

'If you don't get **no** publicity, you don't get **no** people at the fight,' ... 'If you don't get **no** bums on seats you don't get paid ... Anyway I enjoy it.'

(cf. standard: If you don't get **any** publicity for **any** fights in **any** papers from **any**one ...)

With this kind of prosodic realisation then, although the relevant interpersonal meanings may be realised locally (in the Mood function) they colour a longer stretch of discourse by dominating meanings in their domain (cf. McGregor 1997 on scopal meaning).

A comparable effect is achieved by associating interpersonal meaning with the crest of an informational wave. Interpersonal Themes in English (Halliday 2004/1994) construe an attitude towards the meanings of the clause which follow in the Rheme. Exclamatives, clause initial comment adjuncts (including swearing) and intensified wh interrogatives all function in this way. We might interpret this as a co-option of periodic structure by a prosody.

> All of the hits are here from the albums 'Couldn't Stand the Weather' and 'Texas Flood,' plus so much more. Along with the band that night (Thursday, Oct. 4 1984) was The Roomful of Blues, a group of musicians who play the brass section. **What a** great job they did!
>
> **Unfortunately for us** SRV appeared in the production-poor 80's; **fortunately for us**, we have excellent live recordings to if not replace then bring into perspective his real greatness.
>
> Our leaders are too holy and innocent. And faceless. I can understand if Mr (F.W.) de Klerk says he didn't know, but **dammit**, there must be a clique, there must have been someone out there who is still alive and who can give a face to 'the orders from above' for all the operations.
>
> **Why, oh why**, did he have to leave us so young?

Similarly languages might choose to associate interpersonal meaning with the head of a unit, on which the rest of the unit is hypotactically dependent. Tagalog uses its hypotaxis linker *na/ng* in this way to establish the prosodic domain of modality (and other interpersonal functions).

> sigurado **-ng** u-uwi ka ng bahay ngayon hapon
> certain LK go home you-sg house today afternoon
> 'You'll certainly go home to your house this afternoon.'

Using Halliday's α β notation for hypotaxis, we can show the prosodic effect of this association in Figure 1.11.

The explicitly subjective modality metaphors introduced above for English work in the same way by setting up modality as the head clause on which the propositions which is being modalised depends (see Figure 1.12).

> α   I cannot believe
> β   that his death and the murder of so many others in the last terrible weeks has not prompted an immediate response from the government!

```
certainty  ──────────────────────────────→
   sigurado ──── –ng
      α          ↓
              uuwi ka ng bahay ngayon hapon
                           β
```

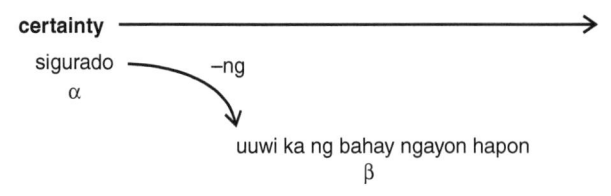

Figure 1.11 Prosodic domain in Tagalog

```
obligation  ──────────────────────────────→
  I cannot believe ──── that
       α                  ↓
                     his death and the murder of so many others
                     in the past terrible weeks has not prompted
                     an immediate response from the government
                                          β
```

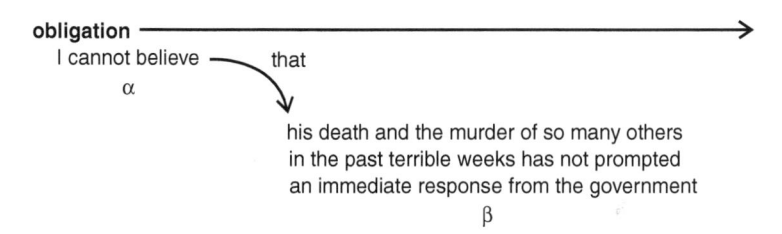

Figure 1.12 Prosodic domain in English

We've used examples from grammar to illustrate saturation, intensification and domination as prosodic realisation principles here. By way of summary these strategies are outlined diagrammatically in Figure 1.13. The same strategies work at the level of discourse semantics, and will be explored at that level as required later in the book.

1.2.6 Instantiation

A further complementarity we need to consider is that of instantiation in relation to realisation. Whereas realisation is a scale of abstraction, involving the recoding of one pattern of meanings as another (as introduced above), instantiation is a scale of generalisation, involving our perspective on inertia and change – are we trying to stand back and get an overall picture of what is going on or are we standing right up close, microscopically subsumed in the deconstruction of an instance, or are we somewhere in between? Halliday's analogy here is weather and climate (Halliday & Matthiessen 1999), weather being the capricious flux we experience day to day, and climate the relatively comforting inertia we try to use to plan. Critically, weather and climate are the same thing, looked at in different ways; climate is a generalisation of weather patterns, and weather is an instance of climatic trends. In SFL the concept of instantiation is used to explore the metastablity of systems – how they change globally in ways that matter (eg global warming) and how

24 *The Language of Evaluation*

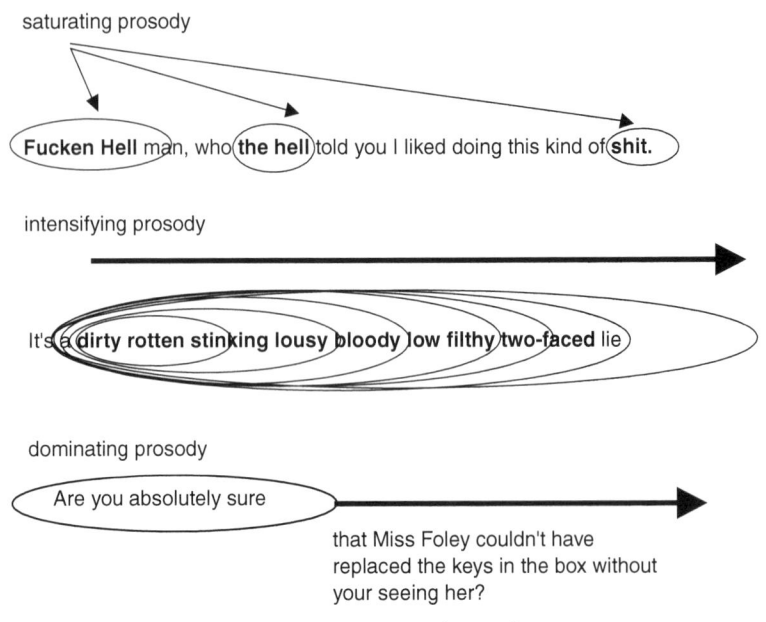

saturating prosody

Fucken Hell man, who the hell told you I liked doing this kind of shit.

intensifying prosody

It's a dirty rotten stinking lousy bloody low filthy two-faced lie

dominating prosody

Are you absolutely sure that Miss Foley couldn't have replaced the keys in the box without your seeing her?

Figure 1.13 Types of prosody

they vary locally in ways that apparently don't (eg daily temperature variations). Theoretically speaking local variation is always nudging the system as a whole in one direction or another, just as every shot a batsman plays changes his strike rate (and every run her average). But for the most part, the changes are too small to take notice of. And we don't hear a contradiction when the weatherwoman says that today's temperature is 26°, 2° above average (when today's temperature has in fact changed that average).

Although instantiation is a cline, linguists have tended to fix their gaze, implicitly or explicitly, at certain levels of generalisation. At one end of the scale we have the notion of system – in SFL the meaning potential that functions as a general resource for the community of speakers under consideration. Towards the other end we have the notion of text – the spoken or written instance of the system under investigation. Register and genre theory deals with sub-systems (with functional variation according to language use). Between this level of generality and instances, Halliday & Matthiessen propose the notion of text type for collections of instances which are too small to generalise as registerial or generic sub-systems. To this scale we can usefully add the

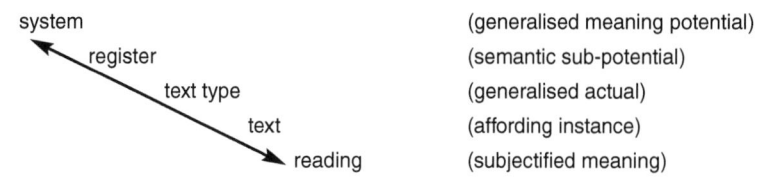

```
system                    (generalised meaning potential)
  ↖ register              (semantic sub-potential)
      ╲ text type         (generalised actual)
         ╲ text           (affording instance)
            ↘ reading     (subjectified meaning)
```

Figure 1.14 Cline of instantiation

notion of reading, since texts themselves have more than enough meaning potential to be read in different ways, depending on the social subjectivity of readers (see Figure 1.14). The ultimate instance is thus the reading which a text affords, not the text itself; and as discourse analysts we need to continually remind ourselves that our analyses are always socially positioned readings and that we need to declare our 'interests' as best we can.

By way of declaration here, in this book we are proposing appraisal as a discourse semantic system. In Chapter 4 we will consider sub-systems of appraisal which we refer to as keys and signatures. More so than other semantic systems we have explored, appraisal analyses focuses attention on the meanings a text affords and the reading positions which focus on this potential in different ways. We explore some of the reasons for this in Chapter 2. Throughout the book we have tried as far as possible to draw attention to the reading which is 'naturalised' by the overall trajectory of the meanings in a text.

Instantiation makes room for both modernist and post-modernist perspectives as far as metastability is concerned. In modernity, linguistics was very much concerned with uncovering the system underlying the use of language, with some theorists[8] going so far as to suggest that instances of language use were not suitable data for an investigation of this kind. Radical post-structuralism has mounted a serious challenge to this idealism, rejecting the notion of grand systems and championing subjectified readings as the meaning of a text. Polarisation of this kind is not conducive to an explanation of language change, which has to address the relation of systems to instances since it's through instances that systems negotiate both stability and change.

1.2.7 Genesis

Where instantiation focuses on the synergy of specific instances in relation to general systems, genesis is concerned with how far we look

Table 1.3 Time frames for semiotic change

logogenesis	'instantiation of the text'	**unfolding**
ontogenesis	'development of the individual'	**growth**
phylogenesis	'expansion of the culture'	**evolution**

through time when we consider semiotic change. Halliday & Matthiessen 1999 develop an outline of time-frames involving the terms logogenesis, ontogenesis and phylogenesis, as outlined in Table 1.3. Logogenesis is concerned with the relatively short time-frame associated with the unfolding of a text; ontogenesis considers the development of semiotic repertoires in the individual; and phylogenesis deals with the evolution of the reservoir of meanings which give identity to a culture.

In a model of this kind, phylogenesis provides the environment for ontogenesis which in turn provides the environment for logogenesis. In other words, where a culture has arrived in its evolution provides the social context for the linguistic development of the individual, and the point an individual is at in their development provides resources for the instantiation of unfolding texts. Conversely, logogenesis provides the material (ie semiotic goods) for ontogenesis, which in turn provides the material for phylogenesis; in other words, texts provide the means through which individuals interact to learn the system. And it is through the heteroglossic aggregation of individual systems (that are always already social systems), through the changing voices of us all in other words, that the semiotic trajectory of a culture evolves. Language change in this model is read in terms of an expanding meaning potential, a key feature of semiotic systems as they adapt to new discursive and material environments.

In this book we focus on the shortest of these time frames, considering appraisal as it unfolds in texts – through prosodies, shifts in key and the phases and staging of various genres. For work on the ontogenesis of appraisal see Painter 2003. There is almost no work on phylogenesis using this framework as far as we are aware; Martin 2002a includes some fanciful speculations in relation to the evolution of evaluation in discourses of reconciliation.

1.2.8 Context

Unlike other functional theories, SFL has developed as both an intrinsic and extrinsic theory of language function. SFL's internal model of language function was introduced in 1.2.1 above which dealt with metafunctions. By the 1970s this trinocular functionality had been projected onto social context as a resonating external model of language use, involving the categories field, mode and tenor. During the 1980s in Sydney this model was further developed in relation to the concept of genre (Martin 1999a). We'll assume this stratified register and genre model of context here and explore it in general terms in relation to appraisal analysis.

1.2.9 Register

Martin 1992b refers to the level of analysis comprised of the social context categories field, mode and tenor as register. Register is a more abstract level of analysis than discourses semantics, since it is concerned with patterns of discourse patterns. Hjelmslev makes a useful distinction between connotative and denotative semiotics, defining connotative semiotics as semiotic systems which have another semiotic system as their expression plane. In his framework, denotative semiotics have their own expression plane (for example language is realised through its own expression form – phonology, graphology or signing). In these terms, register is a connotative semiotic realised through language. The SFL model of register categories correlating with metafunctions (in the proportions ideational is to field as textual is to mode as interpersonal is to tenor) is outlined in Figure 1.15.

Field is concerned with the discourse patterns that realise the domestic or institutionalised activity that is going on. Technically speaking a field is a set of activity sequences that are oriented to some global institutional purpose. These activity sequences of course involve participants,

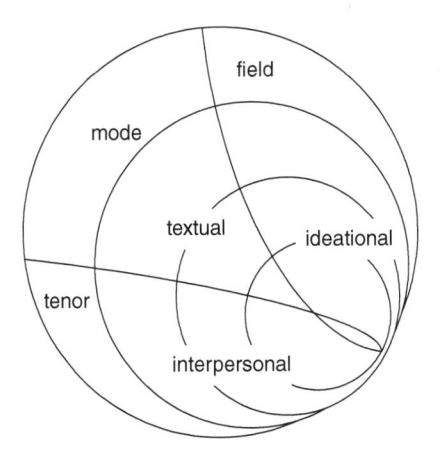

Figure 1.15 Metafunctions in relation to field, mode and tenor

process and circumstances that are themselves organised into taxonomies which in turn distinguish one field from another. In this book we are mainly concerned with interpersonal meaning and so field analysis will not play a central role. That said, we must stress that feelings are always feelings about something – about the activity sequences and taxonomies enacting one field or another. And communities are formed not simply around shared values but around shared values about communal activity. So we will have to address the interface of appraisal resources and field at various points in our discussion. Our discussion of key in Chapter 3 will look in particular at the bonding of appraisal with ideational meaning in the fields of history and the print media.

For relevant work on field, exploring everyday language, technicality and abstraction, on technology and bureaucracy, and on the discourses of humanities, social science and science see Halliday & Martin 1993, Hasan & Williams 1996, Martin & Veel 1998, Christie 1999, Unsworth 2000, Hyland 2000, Martin & Wodak 2003.

Mode deals with the channelling of communication, and thus with the texturing of information flow from one modality of communication to another (speech, writing, phone, SMS messages, e-mail, web pages, letters, radio, CD, television, film, video, DVD, etc.). One important variable is the amount of work language is doing in relation to what is going on. In some contexts language may have a small role to play since attendant modalities are heavily mediating what is going on (eg image, music, action). In other contexts language may by and large be what is going on, sometimes to the point where abstract terms are considerably removed from sensuous experience we might expect to touch, taste, feel, hear or see. This range of variation is sometimes characterised as a cline from language in action to language as reflection.

Another key variable is the complementary monologue through dialogue cline. This scale is sensitive to the effects of various technologies of communication on the kind of interactivity that is facilitated. The key material factors here have to do with whether interlocutors can hear and see one another (aural and visual feedback) and the imminence of a response (immediate or delayed).

We have no doubt that appraisal resources are sensitive to mode in a number of ways. Our work on written monologic modes here can be usefully compared with Eggins & Slade's 1997 studies of evaluation in casual conversation. But at this stage the interaction of appraisal and mode variation is by and large a research frontier. Mode is further explored in Halliday & Martin 1993, Martin & Veel 1998 and Martin & Wodak 2003. For SFL perspectives on the modalities accompanying language see

O'Toole 1994, Kress & van Leeuwen 1996 on images (Goodman 1996, Jewitt & Oyama 2001, Stenglin & Iedema 2001 provide useful introductions), van Leeuwen 1999 on music and sound and Martinec 1998, 2000a, b, c, 2001 on action. As a result of these studies multimodal discourse analysis has become a very exciting area of work in functional linguistics (Kress & van Leeuwen 1996), inspired in part by the new electronic modalities of communication enabled by personal computing technologies (Baldry 1999). It's relation to appraisal analysis is flagged in Martin 2001a, Martin 2004.

Because of our focus on interpersonal meaning, tenor is the register variable which is most relevant to our discussion. Halliday 1985b characterises tenor as follows:

> **Tenor** refers to who is taking part, to the nature of the [communicative] participants, their statuses and roles: what kinds of role relationship obtain, including permanent and temporary relationships of one kind or another, both the types of speech roles they are taking on in the dialogue and the whole cluster of socially significant relationships in which they are involved. [Halliday 1985b/9:12]

His ideas were developed through the 1980s in Sydney, mainly by Poynton, whose pioneering work on gender, affect, naming practices and amplification in the nominal group laid the foundation for the development of appraisal theory through the 1990s (Poynton 1984, 1985, 1990a, b, 1993, 1996). Drawing on this work, we can identify power and solidarity as two key tenor variables – the vertical and horizontal dimensions of interpersonal relations as it were (referred to as status and contact by Poynton 1985 and Martin 1992b).

In post-colonial societies the five most general factors which position us in relation to tenor are generation, gender, ethnicity, capacity and class. By generation we refer to inequalities associated with maturation; gender covers sex and sexuality based difference; ethnicity is concerned with racial, religious and other 'cultural' divisions; capacity refers to abilities and disabilities of various kinds; class is based on the distribution of material resources and is arguably the most fundamental dimension since it is the division on which our post-colonial economic order ultimately depends. Our positioning begins at birth in the home, and all five factors condition access to the various hierarchies we encounter beyond domestic life – in education, religion, recreation and the workplace. At the same time, all factors function as a basis for affiliation – as relatives, friends, lovers, team-mates, colleagues, comrades and so on.

Poynton 1985 outlines important realisation principles for both power and solidarity, principles which unfortunately to date have not been properly explored. For power, she considers 'reciprocity' of choice to be the critical variable. Thus social subjects of equal status construe equality by having access to and taking up the same kinds of choices, whereas subjects of unequal status take up choices of different kinds. Terms of address are one obvious exemplar in this area. It is easy to imagine an English-speaking academic addressing an Asian student by their first name, and they in turn addressing the academic as Professor, just as it is easy to image colleagues addressing one another by their first names (as Peter and Jim). But for an Asian student to address their Professor as Jim would come as a surprise, whatever the expressed naming preferences of the academic in question. Ethnicity, generation and the student–teacher relationship all facilitate non-reciprocal address. From this example we can see that it is not just a question of reciprocity, but also of the different kinds of choices that might be available for interlocutors in dominant and deferential positions. As far as appraisal is concerned, this principle affects who can express feelings and who can't, what kinds of feelings are expressed, how strongly they are expressed, and how directly they are sourced.

For solidarity Poynton suggests the realisation principles of 'proliferation' and 'contraction'. Proliferation refers to the idea that the closer you are to someone the more meanings you have available to exchange. One way of thinking about this is to imagine the process of getting to know someone and what you can talk about when you don't know them (very few things) and what you can talk about when you know them very well (almost anything). In appraisal terms this might involve appreciation of the weather to begin, judgements of politicians, sporting heroes and media personalities as the relationship develops, moving on to emotional reactions to family, friends and lovers as intimacy develops. Social subjects differ about how much proliferation is appropriate when. Sitting with a group of British and Australian colleagues at a seafood restaurant in Seattle, Peter and Jim were once surprised to have their waiter sit down and describe his reactions to various items on the menu without being asked for his opinion about a specific item. His attempt to construe good friendly service was read as intrusive by the 'outsiders', and allowances had to be made on the part of the visiting social semioticians for cultural differences (happily furnished as they were with yet another travel story from America which they would use to bond with family, friends and colleagues back home).

Contraction refers to the amount of work it takes to exchange meanings, and the idea that the better you know someone the less explicitness it takes. Poynton exemplifies this in part through naming, pointing out that knowing someone very well involves short names, whereas knowing them less well favours longer ones. For outsiders, Stevie Ray Vaughan might be introduced as *Texas bluesman Stevie Ray Vaughan* for example, whereas for hardcore fans just his initials will do:

Texas bluesman Stevie Ray Vaughan
Stevie Ray Vaughan
Stevie Ray
Stevie
SRV

With appraisal, contraction affects the amount of work required to exchange a feeling. Imagine a dinner party featuring a colleague renowned for big-noting himself – who embarks, yet again, on a self-promotional excursion. Friends familiar with this behaviour need only to catch one another's eye to comment; an embarrassed friend might simply address the colleague by name, using intonation to express exasperation. For those less familiar with the 'unspoken' evaluation, a query later in the evening might be required, eliciting perhaps some gossip or a judgemental story genre involving explicitly pejorative terms (Eggins & Slade 1997).

The general point here is that as far as solidarity is concerned, the better you know someone the more feelings you will share and the less you need to say to share them. And proliferation and contraction are best read as semiotic resources for negotiating intimacy and distance, since relationships are dynamic processes unfolding over time.

As can be seen from the exemplification of power and solidarity realisation principles, appraisal is being treated here as a resource for construing tenor. Technically speaking then it operates in discourse semantics as one of the realisations of tenor. This treatment contrasts with Poynton's model of tenor which placed affect alongside power and solidarity[9] in register. This goes back in part to a reference in Halliday 1978: 33 to John Pearce who included the 'degree of emotional charge' in a relationship as part of tenor (in Doughty *et al*. 1972: 185–6). We suspect in retrospect that one reason affect was pushed back to this level was the strong interactional focus in work on interpersonal meaning at the level of discourse semantics during the 1980s, when the emphasis was on the semantics of mood and modality in relation to turn-taking (speech function and exchange structure analysis as outlined in

Martin 1992b). In the 1990s, when the focus shifted to the semantics of feeling, it seemed more natural to locate this work in discourse semantics as a pattern of lexicogrammatical patterns construing evaluation. In Poynton's model affect was in any case acknowledged as a tenor variable unlike the others in that its operation was optional, whereas power and solidarity are ever present. As noted, we will treat appraisal as a discourse semantic resource here, which is deployed to construe power and solidarity. Our expectation is that these two variables, taken together with Poynton's realisation principles, will be sufficient to generalise appraisal patterns across texts without having to propose an additional affect oriented variable at the level of register.

1.2.10 Genre

During the 1980s, in Sydney, the analysis of functional variation in language was pushed beyond the field, mode and tenor framework just introduced to include a more abstract level of patterning called genre (Martin 1999a). This stratified model of social context is outlined in Figure 1.16. In this model genre is a system comprising configurations of field, mode and tenor selections which unfold in recurring stages of discourse – a pattern of register patterns in other words. In our applied work we adopted a working definition of genre as a staged, goal oriented social process (Martin 1997b, 2000c, 2001c). Social because we participate

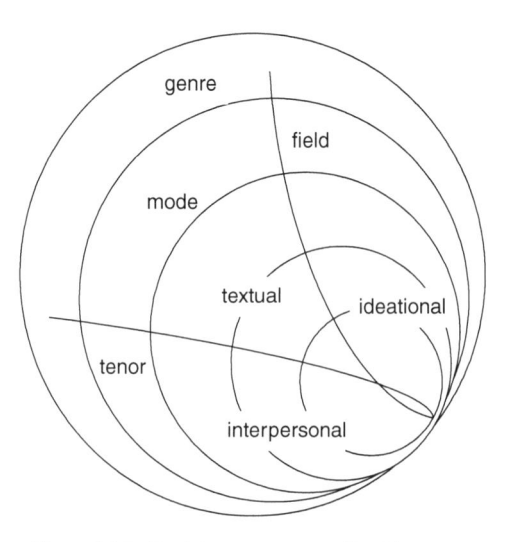

Figure 1.16 Register recontextualised by genre

in genres with other people; goal oriented because we use genres to get things done and feel a sense of frustration when we don't resolve our telos; staged because it usually takes us a few steps to reach our goals.

The number of recognisably distinct genres in any culture may be quite large, but not unmanageably so. In contemporary western culture we can informally name many spoken genres whose patterns of meaning are more or less predictable, such as *greetings, service encounters, casual conversations, arguments, telephone enquiries, instructions, lectures, debates, plays, jokes, games* and so on; and within each of these general types, we could name many more specific genres. From the perspective of appraisal we are interested in the range of evaluations the genre draws on to achieve its goals and how it plays out these evaluations from one stage of the genre to another. Eggins & Slade 1997 consider appraisal in a number of spoken genres from this point of view, including narratives of various kinds and gossip. In this book we'll examine a number of mainly written texts, dealing with their generic structure as we go.

As far as generic structure is concerned, from the perspective of interpersonal meaning we are more interested in the rhetorical organisation of a text than its logic. We're asking questions about how the genre negotiates power and solidarity with readers, and how unfolding prosodies of appraisal contribute to that negotiation. In functional linguistics this style of analysis has tended to focus on narrative (eg Martin & Plum 1997); we'll broaden this here to include a range of genres from the print media and from the discourse of history (drawing on earlier work by Coffin 1997, Iedema 1997 and White 1997).

1.3 Situating appraisal in SFL

On the basis of the complementarities introduced above we can locate appraisal as an interpersonal system at the level of discourse semantics. At this level it co-articulates interpersonal meaning with two other systems – negotiation and involvement. Negotiation complements appraisal by focussing on the interactive aspects of discourse, speech function and exchange structure (as presented in Martin 1992b). Eggins & Slade 1997 present a detailed SFL framework for analysing interactive moves in casual conversation.

Involvement complements appraisal by focussing on non-gradable resources for negotiating tenor relations, especially solidarity. The terms of address introduced above in relation to Poynton's work fall into this area, along with expletives (and related euphemisms) and interjections (these will be related to attitude in Chapter 2 below). Lexical resources

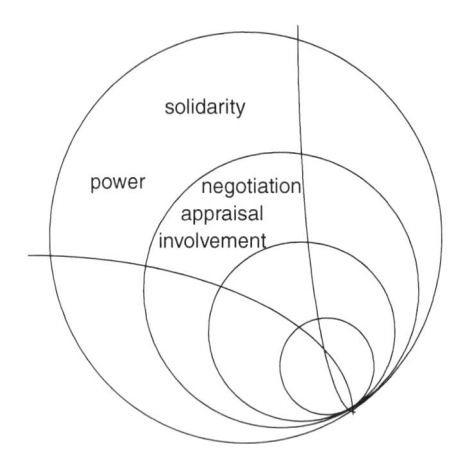

Figure 1.17 Interpersonal semantic systems and tenor variables

which function as signals of group affiliation can also be considered here, including slang (cf. Halliday 1976b on the criminal argot he refers to as anti-language), and technical and specialised lexis (and attendant acronyms). To this collection we could add secret scripts and pig-latins, and various markers of social dialect (accent, non-standard morphology, semantic style, etc.). We have not worked much in this area and do not intend our canvas of resources to be exhaustive here. Our intention is simply to flag the existence of a wide array of resources that are used to negotiate group identity and so co-operate with appraisal and negotiation in the realisation of tenor relations.

An outline of tenor in relation to these interpersonal semantic systems is presented in Figure 1.17.

A guide to the range of phonological and lexicogrammatical patterns realizing negotiation, appraisal and involvement is presented in Table 1.4. The table is intended as an orientation to the meanings involved, without claiming to be exhaustive. At the level of tenor, power and solidarity need to be considered in relation to all three discourse semantic systems, although as noted above involvement is especially tuned to the negotiation of group membership (thus solidarity). That said, social groups have status, and so the implications of affiliation for power relations cannot be ignored.

1.4 Appraisal – an overview

As we can see from Figure 1.17 and Table 1.4, appraisal is one of three major discourse semantic resources construing interpersonal meaning

Table 1.4 Interpersonal semantics in relation to lexicogrammar and phonology

Register	Discourse semantics	Lexicogrammar	Phonology
Tenor	**Negotiation** – speech function – exchange	– mood – tagging	– tone (& 'key')
power (status)	**Appraisal** – engagement – affect – judgement – appreciation – graduation	– 'evaluative' lexis – modal verbs – modal adjuncts – polarity – pre/numeration – intensification – repetition – manner; extent	– loudness – pitch movement – voice quality – phonaesthesia – [formatting]
solidarity (contact)		– logico-semantics – vocation	
	Involvement – naming – technicality – abstraction – anti-language – swearing	– proper names – technical lexis – specialised lexis – slang – taboo lexis – grammatical metaphor	– 'accent' ... – whisper ... – actronyms – 'pig latins' – secret scripts

(alongside involvement and negotiation). Appraisal itself is regionalised as three interacting domains – 'attitude', 'engagement' and 'graduation'. **Attitude** is concerned with our feelings, including emotional reactions, judgements of behaviour and evaluation of things. **Engagement** deals with sourcing attitudes and the play of voices around opinions in discourse. **Graduation** attends to grading phenomena whereby feelings are amplified and categories blurred.

Attitude is itself divided into three regions of feeling, 'affect', 'judgement' and 'appreciation'. **Affect** deals with resources for construing emotional reactions, for example feeling of shock in relation to the events of 9/11:

> The terrible events of the past week have left us with feelings – in order of occurrence – of **horror, worry, anger,** and now, just a **general gloom.** (Mourning 2001)

Judgement is concerned with resources for assessing behaviour according to various normative principles, for example criticism of the Australian Prime Minister, John Howard's neo-conservative government:

> Worse, this is a **mean** administration, a **miserly, mingy, minatory** bunch if ever there was one. [Carlton 2000: 38]

Appreciation looks at resources for construing the value of things, including natural phenomena and semiosis (as either product or process), for examples a fan's rave review of a Stevie Ray Vaughn CD:

> ... and, as a bonus, a **very psychedelic, destructive** (literally!), **cathartic** and **liberatory** version of Jimi Hendrix's 'Third stone from the sun'. [Amazon.com online reviews]

As can be seen our approach to feelings is a fairly encompassing one, moving well beyond linguistic construal of emotion into domains where attitude is deployed to control behaviour and manage taste. Our framework for analysing attitude is presented in Chapter 2 below.

Broadly speaking **engagement** is concerned with the ways in which resources such as projection, modality, polarity, concession and various comment adverbials position the speaker/writer with respect to the value position being advanced and with respect to potential responses to that value position – by quoting or reporting, acknowledging a possibility, denying, countering, affirming and so on. In the following example, the writer begins by affirming baldly that what he says is true (*not making this up*), uses a long chain of projection and quotation marks to carefully attribute the charge of terrorism (a passenger **said** he **heard** a man **call** himself a 'Bosnian terrorist'), and then counters the expectations he's set up by letting us in parenthetically on what *in fact* was said:

> Meanwhile (and we're not making this up), two Indian nationals on a flight from Singapore to Hong Kong were detained at Changi Airport after an American passenger said he heard one of the men calling himself a 'Bosnian terrorist.' (The man in fact said he was a 'bass guitarist.') [Mourning 2001]

In Chapter 3 we develop a social dialogic perspective on these resources which looks at whether or not and how speakers acknowledge alternative positions to their own – monoglossic or heteroglossic discourse (after Bakhtin, eg 1981).

Graduation is concerned with gradability. For attitude, since the resources are inherently gradable, graduation has to do with adjusting the degree of an evaluation – how strong or weak the feeling is. This kind of **graduation** is called 'force'; realisations include intensification, comparative and superlative morphology, repetition, and various graphological and phonological features (alongside the use of intensified lexis – *loathe* for *really dislike*, and so on). In general there seem to be more resources for turning the volume up than for turning it down:

raise <u>so</u> touchy, <u>infinitely more</u> naked, <u>quite</u> clinical, <u>most</u> dangerous

lower <u>a little</u> upset, <u>somewhat</u> upset, the <u>least bit</u> more information

In the context of non-gradable resources graduation has the effect of adjusting the strength of boundaries between categories,[10] constructing core and peripheral types of things; this system is called 'focus' and is exemplified below:

sharpen a fully-fledged, award-winning, gold-plated monster; all alone

soften a word ... spelled somewhat like terrorists; about 60 years old

Note the complementarity of **force** and **focus** in the following responses to a Nigerian scamster by one of his exasperated 'victims' [Column 8 2002 – *Sydney Morning Herald*]:

force singularly, extraordinarily, incredibly, bewilderingly stupid ....

focus Some <u>pure essence of</u> stupid so uncontaminated by anything else as to be beyond the laws of stupidity that we know.

Graduation systems are further developed in Chapter 3. An overview of these appraisal systems is presented as Figure 1.18. For synoptic introductions to the system see Martin 2000a, Martin & Rose 2003; the appraisal website and discussion group provide internet access to these tools: www/grammatics.com/appraisal/; Macken-Horarik & Martin 2003 includes a number of recent papers drawing on this model.

38 *The Language of Evaluation*

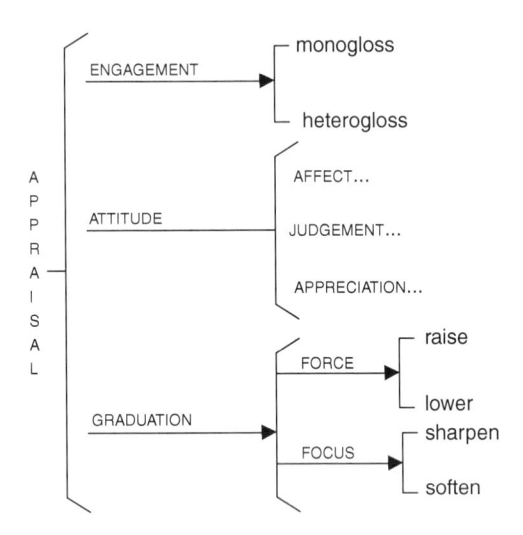

Figure 1.18 An overview of appraisal resources

1.5 Appraisal and other traditions of evaluative language analysis

Appraisal is related to work on evaluation in other models in various ways; we will not attempt a comprehensive summary here (Ochs 1989 and Macken-Horarik & Martin 2003 offer helpful orientations to the literature). Hunston & Thompson 2000a provide the most relevant overview, and make a useful distinction between opinions about entities and opinions about propositions. Opinions about entities are canonically attitudinal and involve positive and negative feelings; opinions about propositions on the other hand are canonically epistemic and involve degrees of certainty. Hunston & Thompson note that the former tend to be realised lexically and the latter grammatically. Idealising along these lines we might oppose affect on the one hand to modality on the other. Comparable oppositions are found in Ochs & Schiefflen 1989, Biber & Finnegan 1989, Bybee & Fleischman 1995 and Conrad & Biber 2000 among others. A somewhat similar opposition operates in Hunston's own distinction between 'value' which operates on what she terms the 'interactive plane' (assessments of propositions in a text by propositions which follow in the text), and 'value' which operates on what she terms the 'autonomous plane' (assessments of experiential world phenomena, typically in terms of whether they are 'good' or 'bad', but not confined to this dichotomy). Hunston, however, teases out a

Table 1.5 Approaches to evaluation

Approaches to evaluation	'entity focussed'	'proposition focussed'
Chafe & Nichols 1986		evidentiality
Ochs & Schiefflen 1989	affect specifiers	affect intensifiers
Biber & Finnegan 1989	affect	evidentiality
Wierzbicka 1990b	emotion	
Bybee & Fleischman 1995	evaluation	modality
Niemeier & Dirven 1997	emotion	
Conrad & Biber 2000	attitudinal stance	epistemic stance
Hunston & Thompson 2000	opinions about entities	opinions about propositions
Hunston 2000	'status' and 'value' on the 'autonomous plane'	'status' and 'value' on the 'interactive plane'

further axis of variation in evaluative orientation by distinguishing between 'value' (as just outlined) and 'status'. On the interactive plane evaluations of 'status' act to determine the proposition's type – for example, whether it is a 'fact', an assessment, an assumption, a recommendation, and so on. Additionally, there is work which focuses more on one side than the other – eg Chafe & Nichols' 1986 epistemically-oriented work on evidentiality, or Niemeier & Dirven's 1997 and Wierzbicka's 1990b attitudinally-oriented work on emotion (a selective overview of terminology is offered in Table 1.5).

Of course, as Hunston & Thompson point out, it's not always easy to maintain this opposition, whether we are looking at realisations in a given language or their function in discourse. As with Labov's developing work on evaluation and intensity in narrative (Labov 1972, 1982, 1984, 1997), categories tend to broaden out to cover a wide range of meanings brought together under some kind of disposition-oriented umbrella.

Further complicating this picture is the literature on hedging, beginning with Lakoff 1972 on fuzzy boundaries (invoking proto-type theory) and taken up and extended by Brown & Levinson 1987 as one tool for negotiating face. By Hyland 1998 the term hedging refers to linguistic resources which indicate either 'a lack of commitment to the truth value of an accompanying proposition' or 'a desire not to express that commitment categorically' (Hyland 1998: 1). In a definition of this kind Lakoff's original focus on vagueness (further developed in Channel 1984) seems to have been extended well into the realm of evidentiality through the notion of 'degree of commitment'.

Our own position, as outlined above, takes **attitude** as in some sense focal and distinguishes **engagement** and **graduation** as distinct resources (for adopting a position with respect to propositions and for scaling intensity or degree of investment respectively). Compared with some work on affect, our concept of **attitude** moves beyond emotion to deal more comprehensively with feelings, including **affect**, **judgement** and **appreciation**. **Engagement** is comparable in many respects to evidentiality, but our social perspective, inspired by Bakhtin's dialogism, contrasts with the truth functional orientation of more philosophically influenced approaches. As far as **graduation** is concerned, we establish resources for intensification (**force**) and for adjusting boundaries (**focus**) as distinct systems, both concerned with modulating meaning by degree. We thus adopt more of a separating approach to hedging, setting degree of commitment apart from 'fuzzification'; and in general terms we adopt more of a separating approach to evaluation, keeping **attitude** distinct from its sourcing and intensification. This in part reflects our history – as noted above we began worrying about affect in various types of narrative and moved on from there to a range of other educationally significant genres (Christie & Martin 1997) and casual conversation (Eggins & Slade 1997). More importantly it reflects the fact that we developed our approach within the general theoretical framework of SFL, in the context of its rich developing descriptions of phonology/graphology and signing, lexicogrammar, discourse semantics, register and genre and multimodality. As far as concurrent work is concerned, appraisal is probably most closely related to the concept of stance, as developed by Biber and his colleagues in their corpus based quantitative studies (eg Conrad & Biber 2000, Precht 2003).

Compared with work on evidentiality (eg Chafe & Nichols 1986, Ochs 1989), to date appraisal research has concentrated on English. Our theoretical affiliation is clearly social constructionist (Harré 1987) rather than universalist (Wierzbicka 1986), and so cross-cultural perspectives on evaluation such as those undertaken by Lutz appear to us to provide the most appropriate orientation to work on appraisal across languages and cultures (Lutz 1982, 1986, 1988, Lutz & Abu-Lughod 1990, Lutz & White 1986).

1.6 Outline of this book

As noted above, Chapter 2 below deals with **attitude**, while **engagement** and **graduation** are the concern of Chapter 3. Then in Chapter 4 we look at appraisal from the perspective of register, looking at the way in which syndromes of appraisal selection organise themselves into distinctive sub-registers (technically keys). Finally in Chapter 5 we illustrate our analytical approach by considering two texts in some detail. In this chapter we are particularly concerned to relate patterns of appraisal to context, concentrating on how evaluation is used to negotiate social relations.

Obviously in a rapidly developed and intractable area of this kind, there can be no final word. So we'll simply end this chapter by quoting from ourselves, for the benefit of fellow Trekkies (fans of the television Science Fiction series, *Star Trek*) who missed out on our aspirations last time round:

> In the course of the Star Trek Next Generation episodes Unification I and II, Spock and Data are at work together on an encrypted Romulan communication. Engaging Spock in conversation, Data takes an interest in the fact that whereas he, an android with no feelings, has spent his lifetime trying to acquire some so as to become more human, Spock, a Vulcan/human born with emotions, has spent his lifetime suppressing them. It is salutary to note that of all the Enterprise crew, it is only the lexicogrammars of Spock and Data that contemporary linguistics has begun to describe. Perhaps, as this volume heralds for evaluative language, it is time to explore strange new worlds, seeking out new life, where few linguists have gone before. [Martin 2000a: 175]

A little harsh on what has been achieved perhaps; but not far wrong in terms of all the work on evaluation we have yet to do.

Notes

1. We don't, of course, have any compelling reason to believe that this actually was the case. Our suspicions, in this sense, are without substantive foundation and we imply no actual wrong-doing on the part of the magazine's staff.
2. To simplify the exposition, we'll stop dealing separately with graphology at this point in the discussion.
3. Actually groups or phrases, after Halliday 1994.
4. The tag is only acceptable here as a double-take, following a pause.
5. Theoretically of course these regions are multidimensional, involving any number of relevant intersecting dimensions of meaning; as with paradigms, however, it is hard to read the intersection of more than two dimensions at a time.
6. Longer wavelengths have been proposed for media discourse in work by van Leeuwen 1982 and Martinec 2000.
7. Comparable to the use of formatting for highlighting in graphology.
8. Chomsky of course is the best known of these, for various reasons the apotheosis of modernity one would have to say (cf. de Beaugrande 1997, Martin 1997a).
9. Poynton 1985 in fact uses the term status for power and contact for solidarity; her tripartite model of tenor and terminology was adopted in Martin 1992b.
10. Readers who enjoyed the recent Indian movie *Monsoon Wedding* will have been amused by the event manager's recurrent use of 'exactly and approximately' in his undertakings; from the perspective of **graduation**, he appears to be using contradictory focus in a misguided effort to increase force.

2
Attitude: Ways of Feeling

2.1 Kinds of feeling

In this chapter we outline a framework for mapping feelings as they are construed in English texts, referring to this system of meanings as **attitude**. This system involves three semantic regions covering what is traditionally referred to as emotion, ethics and aesthetics. Emotion is arguably at the heart of these regions since it is the expressive resource we are born with and embody physiologically from almost the moment of birth (Painter 2003). We will refer to this emotive dimension of meaning as **affect**.

Affect is concerned with registering positive and negative feelings: do we feel happy or sad, confident or anxious, interested or bored? In the following example the feelings construed are unhappy ones as a member of Australia's Stolen Generation recounts her experience of being separated from her siblings.

> [2.1] So this meant the **grieving** took place again. The **grief** came for my younger sister and two brothers whom I thought I would never see again. The day I left the Orphanage – that was a **very sad** day for me. I was **very unhappy**, and the memories came back. There was nowhere to turn. You was on your own. I was again in a different environment ... I had no choice but to stick it out. With the hardships going and thinking of my sister and brothers which I left at the Orphanage. **My heart full of sorrows** for them. [*Bringing Them Home* 1997: 12]

Judgement deals with attitudes towards behaviour, which we admire or criticise, praise or condemn. Australia's treatment of Indigenous people, responsible for the negative **affect** in 2.1 is strongly challenged in the following comment from late last century.

[2.2] You have almost exterminated our people, but there are enough of us remaining to expose the **humbug** of your claim, as white Australians, to be a **civilised, progressive, kindly and humane** nation. By your **cruelty** and **callousness** towards the Aborigines you stand **condemned** ... If you would openly admit that the purpose of your Aborigines Legislation has been, and now is, to exterminate the Aborigines completely so that not a trace of them or of their descendants remains, we could describe you as **brutal**, but **honest**. But you dare not admit openly that what you hope and wish is for our death! You **hypocritically** claim that you are trying to 'protect' us; but your modern policy of 'protection' (so-called) is killing us off just as surely as the pioneer policy of giving us poisoned damper and shooting us down like dingoes!
[*Bringing Them Home* 1997: 46]

Appreciation involves evaluations of semiotic and natural phenomena, according to the ways in which they are valued or not in a given field. Michael Ondaatje's novel *Anil's Ghost*, about post-colonial struggle and human rights abuses in Sri Lanka, is commended to prospective readers in positively glowing terms:

[2.3] **Virtually flawless**, with **impeccable** regional details, **startlingly original** characters, and a **compelling** literary plot that borders on the thriller, Ondaatje's **stunning** achievement is to produce an **indelible** novel of **dangerous beauty**. *USA Today* [Previews M Ondaatje *Anil's Ghost* Toronto: Vintage. 2000: i]

As partially reflected in the examples just considered, attitudinal meanings tend to spread out and colour a phase of discourse as speakers and writers take up a stance oriented to **affect**, **judgement** or **appreciation**. We offer three longer examples here to illustrate this predilection for prosodic realisation, which according to Halliday (1979) is characteristic of interpersonal meaning in general across levels of language.

Affect (emotions; reacting to behaviour, text/process, phenomena)

[2.4] ... It might have been said that Jack Aubrey's **heart had been sealed off**, so that he could accept his misfortune **without it breaking**; and **that sealing-off** had turned him into a **eunuch as far as emotion was concerned**. ... whereas in former times Captain Aubrey, like his hero Nelson and so many of his contemporaries, had been **somewhat given to tears** – he had **wept with joy** at the masthead of his first command; **tears** sometimes wetted the lower part of his fiddle when he played particularly moving passages; and **cruel sobs** had racked him at many a shipmate's funeral by land or sea – he was now **as hard and dry-eyed as** any man could well be. He had parted from Sophie and the children at Ashgrove Cottage with no more than a **constriction in his throat** which made his farewells sound painfully harsh and **unfeeling** ... [O'Brian 1997a: 10]

Judgement (ethics; evaluating behaviour)

[2.5] 'The temptation is the same whatever the country: it is often to the lawyer's interest to make **wrong** seem **right**, and **the more skilful** he is the more he succeeds. Judges are even more exposed to temptation, since they sit every day; though indeed it is a temptation of a different sort: the have **enormous powers**, and if they choose they may be **cruel, oppressive, froward** and **perverse** virtually without control – they may interrupt and **bully**, further their political views, and **pervert the course of justice**. I remember in India we met a Mr Law at the dinner the Company gave us, and the gentleman who made the introductions whispered to me in a reverential tone that he was known as "the **just** judge". What an **indictment** of the bench, that one, one alone, among so many, should be **so** distinguished.' [O'Brian 1997b: 226–8]

Appreciation (aesthetics; evaluating text/process, natural phenomena)

[2.6] 'To tell you the truth, Maturin, on a **perfect** vernal day like this, I find nothing **so pleasant** as sitting on a **comfortable** chair in the sun, with green, green grass stretching away, the sound of bat and ball, and the sight of cricketers. Particularly such cricketers as these: did you see how Maitland glanced that ball away to leg? A **very pretty** stroke. Do not you find watching **good** cricket **restful, absorbing**, a **balm** to the anxious, harassed mind?' 'I do not. It seems to me, saving your presence, **unspeakably tedious**.' 'Perhaps some of the **finer** shades may escape you. Well played, sir! Oh very well played indeed. That was **as pretty** a late cut as I have ever seen – how they run, ha ha ...' [O'Brian 1997b: 189–90]

Alongside this prosodic disposition, **attitude** involves gradable meanings, which have the potential to be intensified and compared – as with several items in 2.1–2.6 above. Feelings have depth, in other words, a feature we can perhaps interpret as affording their tendency to spill out and sprawl over a phase of discourse. This aspect of attitudinal meaning will be dealt with in the discussion of **graduation** in Chapter 3.

very sad, very unhappy, full of sorrows, the more skilful, virtually flawless, startlingly original, so pleasant, very pretty, finer, as pretty

One way to think about **judgement** and **appreciation** is to see them as institutionalised feelings, which take us out of our everyday common sense world into the uncommon sense worlds of shared community values. In these terms, **judgement** reworks feelings in the realm of proposals about behaviour – how we should behave or not; some of these proposals get formalised as rules and regulations administered by church and state. **Appreciation** on the other hand reworks feelings as propositions about the value of things – what they are worth or not; some of these valuations get formalised in systems of awards (prices, grades, grants, prizes, etc.). Of course, as Painter 2003 demonstrates, learning about **judgement** and **appreciation** begins in the home in the very first stages of linguistic development as caregivers struggle to tame the wild will and voracious tastes of the emotional volcanoes they have brought into their lives. An outline of this orientation to **affect** at the heart of institutionalised feelings is offered as Figure 2.1.

ethics/morality (rules and regulations)
feeling institutionalised as proposals

JUDGEMENT

AFFECT

APPRECIATION

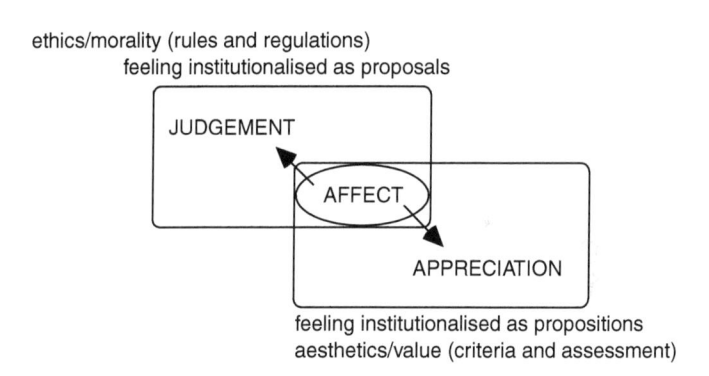

feeling institutionalised as propositions
aesthetics/value (criteria and assessment)

Figure 2.1 Judgement and appreciation as institutionalised affect

2.2 Affect

Because we are developing **attitude** as a discourse semantic system, we can expect its realisations to diversify across a range of grammatical structures. And this is certainly true of **affect**. In terms of Halliday 1994, these realisations comprise modification of participants and processes, affective mental and behavioural processes, and modal Adjuncts:

- affect as 'quality'
  - describing participants   a **sad** captain   Epithet
  - attributed to participants the captain was **sad**   Attribute
  - manner of processes   the captain left **sadly**   Circumstance

- affect as 'process'[1]
  - affective mental   his departure **upset** him   Process (effective)
                                he **missed** them   Process (middle)
  - affective behavioural   the captain **wept**   Process

- affect as 'comment'
  - desiderative   **sadly**, he had to go   Modal Adjunct

Beyond this of course we find the usual range of grammatical metaphors (Halliday 1994), including nominalised realisations of qualities (*joy, sadness, sorrow*) and processes (*grief, sobs, constriction in his throat*).

In order to classify emotions we adopted the strategy of mapping out the terrain as systems of oppositions. It is not clear to us, having been trained as grammarians, how to motivate a lexis-oriented classification of this kind; nor have we been able to find relevant strategies of argumentation in the field of lexicography or corpus linguistics. Thus our maps of feeling (for **affect**, **judgement** and **appreciation**) have to be treated at this stage as hypotheses about the organisation of the relevant meanings – offered as a challenge to those concerned with developing appropriate reasoning, as a reference point for those with alternative classifications and as a tool for those who need something to manage the analysis of evaluation in discourse.

By way of classifying **affect**, we in fact drew on the following six factors, several of which are foregrounded in the grammar of English (after Halliday 1994) and so we assumed of highly generalised relevance to the question of types of emotion. For purposes of this discussion we'll call the conscious participant experiencing the emotion an Emoter, and the phenomenon responsible for that emotion a Trigger.

i. Are the feelings popularly construed by the culture as positive (good vibes that are enjoyable to experience) or negative ones (bad vibes that are better avoided)? We are not concerned here with the value that a particular uncommon sense psychological framework might place on one or another emotion (cf. 'It's probably productive that you're feeling sad because it's a sign that …').

Attitude: Ways of Feeling 47

- positive affect   the captain was **happy**
- negative affect   the captain was **sad**

ii. Are the feelings realised as a surge of emotion involving some kind of embodied paralinguistic or extralinguistic manifestation, or more internally experienced as a kind of emotive state or ongoing mental process? Grammatically this distinction is constructed as the opposition between behavioural (eg *She smiled at him*) versus mental (eg *She liked him*) or relational (eg *She felt happy with him*) processes.

- behavioural surge   the captain **wept**
- mental process/state   the captain **disliked** leaving/the captain felt **sad**

iii. Are the feelings construed as directed at or reacting to some specific emotional Trigger or as a general ongoing mood for which one might pose the question 'Why are you feeling that way?' and get the answer 'I'm not sure.' Grammatically this distinction is constructed as the opposition between mental processes (<u>*She*</u> *likes* <u>*him*</u>/<u>*he*</u> *pleases* <u>*her*</u>) and relational states (<u>*she's*</u> <u>*happy*</u>). With the mental processes both the Emoter and the Trigger of the emotion are participants (Senser and Phenomenon) and thus directly implicated in the process; with relational states the Emoter and the emotion are the participants (Carrier and Attribute), pushing the Trigger to an optional circumstantial position (*she's happy* <u>*with him/about that*</u>).

- reaction to other   the captain **disliked** leaving/leaving **displeased** the captain
- undirected mood   the captain was **sad**

Passive mental processes of the 'please' type fall between these poles (*she's pleased by him*), especially where the Phenomenon is left implicit (*she's pleased*) – in which case instances are typically hard to categorise as mental or relational. We can think of this region of meaning as a scale graded along the following lines:

mental
↑ she likes him
| he pleases her
| she's pleased by him

48 *The Language of Evaluation*

⎰ she's pleased
⎪ she's pleased with him
⎪ she's very pleased
⎰ she's happy
relational

iv. How are the feelings graded – towards the lower valued end of a scale of intensity or towards the higher valued end; or somewhere in between? We don't wish at this stage to imply that low, median and high are discrete values (as with **modality** – cf. Halliday 1994: 358–9), but expect that most emotions offer lexicalisations that grade along a evenly clined scale (cf. the discussion of sadness below).

- low   the captain **disliked** leaving
- median   the captain **hated** leaving
- high   the captain **detested** leaving

v. Do the feelings involve intention (rather than reaction), with respect to a stimulus that is irrealis (rather than realis). Grammatically this distinction is constructed as the opposition between desiderative and emotive mental processes (*I'd like to* vs *I like it*); for further discussion of the grammar at issue here see Davidse 1991, Halliday 1994, Lock 1996, Matthiessen 1995.

- realis   the captain **disliked** leaving
- irrealis   the captain **feared** leaving

Irrealis **affect** always seems to implicate a Trigger, and so can be outlined as in Table 2.1 (setting aside parameter iii).

Table 2.1 Irrealis affect

DIS/INCLINATION	Surge (of behaviour)	Disposition
fear	tremble shudder cower	wary fearful terrorised
desire	suggest request demand	miss long for yearn for

Attitude: Ways of Feeling 49

vi. The final variable in our typology of **affect** groups emotions into three major sets having to do with un/happiness, in/security and dis/satisfaction. The un/happiness variable covers emotions concerned with 'affairs of the heart' – sadness, hate, happiness and love; the in/security variable covers emotions concerned with ecosocial well-being – anxiety, fear, confidence and trust; the dis/satisfaction variable covers emotions concerned with telos (the pursuit of goals) – ennui, displeasure, curiosity, respect.

- un/happiness   the captain felt **sad/happy**
- in/security   the captain felt **anxious/confident**
- dis/satisfaction the captain felt **fed up/absorbed**

The un/happiness set of meanings is probably the first to come to mind when we think about emotions, and is included in all of the inventories we have encountered. It involves the moods of feeling happy or sad, and the possibility of directing these feelings at a Trigger by liking or disliking it (see Table 2.2).

In/security covers our feelings of peace and anxiety in relation to our environs, including of course the people sharing them with us. In stereotypically gendered communities the feelings here are associated with 'mothering' in the home – tuned to protection from the world outside (or not) (see Table 2.3).

Table 2.2 Affect – un/happiness

UN/HAPPINESS	Surge (of behaviour)	Disposition
unhappiness		
misery	whimper	down [low]
[mood: 'in me']	cry	sad [median]
	wail	miserable [high]
antipathy	rubbish	dislike
[directed feeling: 'at you']	abuse	hate
	revile	abhor
happiness		
cheer	chuckle	cheerful
	laugh[2]	buoyant
	rejoice	jubilant
affection	shake hands	be fond of
	hug	love
	embrace	adore

50 *The Language of Evaluation*

Table 2.3 Affect – in/security

IN/SECURITY	Surge (of behaviour)	Disposition
insecurity		
disquiet	restless	uneasy
	twitching	anxious
	shaking	freaked out
surprise	start	startled
	cry out	jolted
	faint	staggered
security		
confidence	declare	together
	assert	confident
	proclaim	assured
trust	delegate	comfortable with
	commit	confident in/about
	entrust	trusting

Dis/satisfaction deals with our feelings of achievement and frustration in relation to the activities in which we are engaged, including our roles as both participants and spectators. In stereotypically gendered communities the feelings here are associated with 'fathering' (and mentoring in general) – tuned to learning and accomplishment. These oppositions take us to the borders of **affect** as it is popularly perceived, as reflected in Star Trek characters like Spock (a human/Vulcan hybrid who suppresses emotion) and Data (an android who feels none) – who occasionally express their fascination with things (typically triggered by what they regard as human eccentricity). Directed emotions in this region are sensitive to how active a role we are playing in the activity we're reacting to. We get angry as frustrated participants in an activity, but fed up as spectators; we're pleased with our own achievements, but charmed by others' (see Table 2.4).

The examples we've provided in these tables are by no means exhaustive, but included simply to give the gist of the range of meanings involved and emphasise the fact that the choice of one lexical item or another always involves grading the depth of feeling. To reinforce this point we've taken just one cell, for the mood 'unhappy', and blown it up in Table 2.5 by including a broader spectrum of meanings from Roget's Thesaurus – and in doing so we've included only a few of the meanings elaborated in Roget. In order to do justice to this kind of lexical elaboration we would need to develop semantic topologies for

Table 2.4 Affect – dis/satisfaction

DIS/SATISFACTION	Surge (of behaviour)	Disposition
dissatisfaction		
ennui	fidget yawn tune out	flat stale jaded
displeasure	caution scold castigate	cross, bored with angry, sick of furious, fed up with
satisfaction		
interest	attentive busy industrious	involved absorbed engrossed
pleasure	pat on the back compliment reward	satisfied, impressed pleased, charmed chuffed, thrilled

Table 2.5 Affect – kinds of unhappiness

Affect	Positive	Negative
dis/inclination	miss, long for, yearn for	wary, fearful, terrorised
un/happiness	cheerful buoyant, jubilant; like, love, adore	sad, melancholy, despondent; cut-up, heart-broken … broken-hearted, heavy-hearted, sick at heart; sorrowful … grief-stricken, woebegone … dejected …; dejected, joyless, dreary, cheerless, unhappy, sad; gloomy, despondent, … downcast, low, down, down in the mouth, depressed …; weepy, wet-eyed, tearful, in tears …
in/security	together, confident, assured; comfortable, confident, trusting	uneasy, anxious, freaked out; startled, surprised, astonished
dis/satisfaction	involved, absorbed, engrossed; satisfied, pleased, chuffed/ impressed, charmed, thrilled	flat, stale, jaded; cross, angry, furious; bored with, sick of, fed up with

each cell, designed around various intersecting parameters – a project well beyond the scope of this book.

2.3 Judgement

With **judgement** we move into the region of meaning construing our attitudes to people and the way they behave – their character (how they measure up). In general terms **judgements** can be divided into those dealing with 'social esteem' and those oriented to 'social sanction'. **Judgements of esteem** have to do with 'normality' (how unusual someone is), 'capacity' (how capable they are) and 'tenacity' (how resolute they are); **judgements** of **sanction** have to do with 'veracity' (how truthful someone is) and 'propriety' (how ethical someone is). **Social esteem** tends to be policed in the oral culture, through chat, gossip, jokes and stories of various kinds – with humour often having a critical role to play (Eggins & Slade 1997). Sharing values in this area is critical to the formation of social networks (family, friends, colleagues, etc.). **Social sanction** on the other hand is more often codified in writing, as edicts, decrees, rules, regulations and laws about how to behave as surveilled by church and state – with penalties and punishments as levers against those not complying with the code. Sharing values in this area underpins civic duty and religious observances.

Illustrative realisations for **social esteem** are presented in Table 2.6 for **normality**, **capacity** and **tenacity**. The range of meanings listed is not exhaustive, and the examples have not been graded along a high through median to low scale. As with **affect**, we can recognise positive and negative evaluations – traits we admire alongside those we criticise. It must also be stressed that we provide such a list of terms only as a general guide to the meanings which are at stake here. When it comes to language use in context, it is often the case that a given lexical item will vary its attitudinal meaning according to that context. Thus, though in the table below we list *slow* as encoding a value of negative **capacity** (**social esteem**), in other contexts it can convey an entirely different and positive evaluative meaning – as in 'the slow food movement' (referring to an approach to food preparation and dining which sets itself against what are seen as the failings of 'fast food'). The list, therefore, should not be treated as a dictionary of the value of **judgement** which can be mechanically applied in a text analysis.

Illustrative realisations for **social sanction** are presented in Table 2.7 for **veracity** and **propriety**, including positive and negative evaluations – behaviour we praise alongside that we condemn. Practising Catholics

Attitude: Ways of Feeling 53

Table 2.6 Judgement – social esteem

SOCIAL ESTEEM	Positive [admire]	Negative [criticise]
normality 'how special?'	lucky, fortunate, charmed ...; normal, natural, familiar ...; cool, stable, predictable ...; in, fashionable, avant garde ...; celebrated, unsung ...	unlucky, hapless, star-crossed ...; odd, peculiar, eccentric ...; erratic, unpredictable ...; dated, daggy, retrograde ...; obscure, also-ran ...
capacity 'how capable?'	powerful, vigorous, robust ...; sound, healthy, fit ...; adult, mature, experienced ...; witty, humorous, droll ...; insightful, clever, gifted ...; balanced, together, sane ...; sensible, expert, shrewd ...; literate, educated, learned ...; competent, accomplished ...; successful, productive ...	mild, weak, whimpy ...; unsound, sick, crippled ...; immature, childish, helpless ...; dull, dreary, grave ...; slow, stupid, thick ...; flaky, neurotic, insane ...; naive, inexpert, foolish ...; illiterate, uneducated, ignorant ...; incompetent; unaccomplished ...; unsuccessful, unproductive ...
tenacity 'how dependable?'	plucky, brave, heroic ...; cautious, wary, patient ...; careful, thorough, meticulous tireless, persevering, resolute ...; reliable, dependable ...; faithful, loyal, constant ...; flexible, adaptable, accommodating ...	timid, cowardly, gutless ...; rash, impatient, impetuous ...; hasty, capricious, reckless ...; weak, distracted, despondent ...; unreliable, undependable ...; unfaithful, disloyal, inconstant ...; stubborn, obstinate, wilful ...

Table 2.7 Judgement – social sanction

SOCIAL SANCTION 'mortal'	Positive [praise]	Negative [condemn]
veracity [truth] 'how honest?'	truthful, honest, credible ...; frank, candid, direct ...; discrete, tactful ...	dishonest, deceitful, lying ...; deceptive, manipulative, devious ...; blunt, blabbermouth ...
propriety [ethics] 'how far beyond reproach?'	good, moral, ethical ...; law abiding, fair, just ...; sensitive, kind, caring ...; unassuming, modest, humble ...; polite, respectful, reverent ...; altruistic, generous, charitable ...	bad, immoral, evil ...; corrupt, unfair, unjust ...; insensitive, mean, cruel ...; vain, snobby, arrogant ...; rude, discourteous, irreverent ...; selfish, greedy, avaricious ...

among our readership may recognise a shift from **social esteem** to **social sanction** comparable to that from venial to mortal sins. For the rest of us, it's perhaps more a question of who we turn to for help – too much negative **esteem**, and we may need to visit a therapist; too much negative **sanction**, and a lawyer may need to be called in.

54 *The Language of Evaluation*

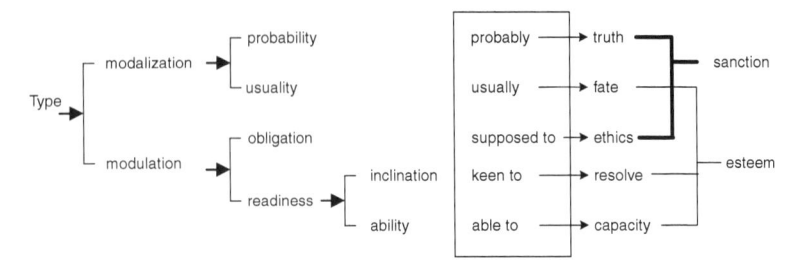

```
                    ┌─ probability          probably ──→ truth ─┐
       ┌ modalization ─┤                                         ├── sanction
       │            └─ usuality             usually ──→ fate ──┤
Type ──┤
       │            ┌─ obligation           supposed to ──→ ethics ─┐
       └ modulation ─┤                                               ├── esteem
                    │          ┌─ inclination   keen to ──→ resolve ─┤
                    └ readiness ─┤                                   │
                               └─ ability      able to ──→ capacity ─┘
```

Figure 2.2   Modality and types of judgement (following Iedema *et al*. 1994)

The parameters for organising **judgement** reflect grammatical distinctions in the system of modalisation (Halliday 1994), in the following proportions – normality is to usuality, as capacity is to ability, as tenacity is to inclination, as veracity is to probability, as propriety is to obligation. In early work our terms for the major types of **judgement** were closer to these modal oppositions, as reflected in Figure 2.2 (fate for normality, resolve for tenacity, truth for veracity, ethics for propriety).

Halliday's work on mood, modality and interpersonal metaphor provides the bridge between interpersonal grammar and appraisal which underpins these connections (Halliday 1994, Martin 1992b, 1995b; see also Lemke 1998). Beginning with propositions, we can construct a series of realisations for both probability, usuality and capacity which begins with congruent realisations and pushes through metaphorical ones towards lexis which is clearly appraising in nature. In this way modalisations of probability in Mood can be related to lexicalised **judgements** of **veracity**:

He's naughty.
He's **certainly** naughty.
It's **certain** he's naughty.
It's **true** he's naughty.
   It's **true, honest, credible, authentic, bogus**, etc.   [judgement: veracity]

Similarly, modalities of usuality can be related to **judgements** of normality:

He's naughty.
He's **often** naughty.

It's **usual** for him to be naughty.
It's **normal** for him to be naughty.
It's **normal, average, fashionable, peculiar, odd,** etc.
[judgement: normality]

Likewise for ability and capacity:

He **can** go.
He's **able** to go.
He's **capable** of going.
He's **strong** enough to go.
He's **healthy enough, mature enough, clever enough,** etc.
[judgement: capacity]

For proposals, modulations of inclination can be related to lexicalised tenacity:

I'**ll** go.
I'm **determined** to go.
I'm **intent** on going.
I'm **resolved**.
I'm **resolute, steadfast, unyielding, unflinching,** etc.
[judgement: tenacity]

And modulations of obligation can be related to lexicalised **judgements** of propriety:

Go.
You **should** go.
You're **supposed** to go.
It's **expected** you'll go.
It'd be **unfair** for you to go.
It'd be **corrupt, insensitive, arrogant, selfish, rude,** etc.
[judgement: propriety]

Reasoning along these lines, we can position interpersonal grammar (mood and modality) and appraisal on a cline, with grammaticalised realisations at one end and lexicalised realisations at the other – and with Halliday's modality metaphors construing meaning in between (Martin 2000b).

2.4 Appreciation

With **appreciation** we turn to meanings construing our evaluations of 'things', especially things we make and performances we give, but also including natural phenomena – what such things are worth (how we value them). In general terms **appreciations** can be divided into our 'reactions' to things (do they catch our attention; do they please us?), their 'composition' (balance and complexity), and their 'value' (how innovative, authentic, timely, etc.).

Illustrative realisations for **appreciation** are presented in Table 2.8 for **reaction, composition** and **valuation**. The range of meanings listed is not exhaustive, and the examples have not been graded along a high through median to low scale. As with **affect** and **judgement**, we can recognise positive and negative evaluations – properties we value alongside those we do not.

Table 2.8 Types of appreciation

	Positive	Negative
Reaction: impact 'did it grab me?'	arresting, captivating, engaging ...; fascinating, exciting, moving ...; lively, dramatic, intense ...; remarkable, notable, sensational ...	dull, boring, tedious ...; dry, ascetic, uninviting ...; flat, predictable, monotonous ...; unremarkable, pedestrian ...
Reaction: quality 'did I like it?'	okay, fine, good ... lovely, beautiful, splendid ...; appealing, enchanting, welcome ...	bad, yuk, nasty ...; plain, ugly, grotesque ...; repulsive, revolting, off-putting ...
Composition: balance 'did it hang together?'	balanced, harmonious, unified, symmetrical, proportioned ...; consistent, considered, logical ...; shapely, curvaceous, willowly ...	unbalanced, discordant, irregular, uneven, flawed ...; contradictory, disorganised ...; shapeless, amorphous, distorted ...
Composition: Complexity 'was it hard to follow?'	simple, pure, elegant ...; lucid, clear, precise ...; intricate, rich, detailed, precise ...	ornate, extravagant, byzantine ...; arcane, unclear, woolly ...; plain, monolithic, simplistic ...
Valuation 'was it worthwhile?'	penetrating, profound, deep ...; innovative, original, creative ...; timely, long awaited, landmark ...; inimitable, exceptional, unique ...; authentic, real, genuine ...; valuable, priceless, worthwhile ...; appropriate, helpful, effective ...	shallow, reductive, insignificant ...; derivative, conventional, prosaic ...; dated, overdue, untimely ...; dime-a-dozen, everyday, common; fake, bogus, glitzy ...; worthless, shoddy, pricey ...; ineffective, useless, write-off ...

Of these variables valuation is especially sensitive to field since the value of things depends so much on our institutional focus. Stevie Ray Vaughan's blues, for example, is much appreciated by his fans for its authenticity:

> real, definitive, true, pure, authentic, raw, hardcore, vintage, classic, this-is-what-the-blues-are-all-about, essence ...

As one fan remarks on the Amazon website, 'If you can't appreciate the music on this cd, then you aren't a fan of true, god-blessed American music. Stevie Ray Vaughan absolutely RIPS on this cd!' In an academic field like linguistics, on the other hand, contributions are more likely to be valued for thoughtful innovation (or its apparent lack):

> penetrating, illuminating, challenging, significant, deep, profound, satisfying, fruitful, ground-breaking ...
>
> shallow, ad hoc, reductive, unconvincing, unsupported, fanciful, tendentious, bizarre, counterintuitive, perplexing, arcane ...

Grammatically, as Suzanne Eggins has suggested to us, we might think of **reaction**, **composition** and **valuation** in relation to mental processes – the way we look at things (our gaze). **Reaction** is related to affection (emotive – 'it grabs me', desiderative – 'I want it'); **composition** is related to perception (our view of order); and **valuation** is related to cognition (our considered opinions). Alternatively, the **appreciation** framework might be interpreted metafunctionally – with **reaction** oriented to interpersonal significance, **composition** to textual organisation and **valuation** to ideational worth (as summarised in Table 2.9 below).

Clearly there are strong links between the **appreciation** variable **reaction** and **affect** (as outlined above), including derivationally related lexis. Nevertheless we think it is important to distinguish between construing the emotions someone feels (**affect**) and ascribing the power

Table 2.9 Sub-types of appreciation

appreciation	mental process type	metafunction
reaction	affection	interpersonal
composition	perception	textual
valuation	cognition	ideational

to trigger such feelings to things:

affect   appreciation: reaction
I'm sad/weeping   *a weepy rendition of the song*

Similarly, positive and negative valuations of something imply positive and negative **judgements** of the capacity of someone to create or perform. But we consider it useful to distinguish between **judgements** of behaviour and evaluations of things.

judgement: capacity   appreciation: valuation
a brilliant scholar   *a penetrating analysis*

We'll return to these links in our discussion of borders (section 2.5) and of inscriptions and tokens (section 2.6) below.

Although our general framework for analysing **attitude** has stabilised over the years as we move from one register to another, we believe (as noted above) that there is a need to develop social semiotic principles for classifying lexis which are not available to us at this time. We are not sure whether these will emerge from corpus studies or from the development of reasoned argumentation (or some combination of the two). In the meantime we are stuck with the fine tuning enabled by thesauri, dictionaries and manual text analysis as **attitude** is further explored.

2.5 Borders

As inherently gradable meanings, the canonical grammatical realisation for **attitude** is adjectival; so it makes sense to try and establish grammatical frames for distinguishing kinds of **attitude** with respect to this kind of realisation. For **affect**, a useful distinguishing frame is a relational attributive process with a conscious participant involving the verb *feel*:

Affect

{person feels **affect** about something}
{it makes person feel **affect** that [proposition]}
I feel **happy** (about that/that they've come).
It makes me feel **happy** that they've come.

For **judgement**, a relational attributive process ascribing an **attitude** to some person's behaviour proves useful (cf. Lemke 1998):

Judgement
{it was **judgement** for person/of person to do that}
{(for person) to do that was **judgement**}
It was **silly** of/for them to do that.
(For them) to do that was **silly**.

For **appreciation**, a mental process ascribing an **attitude** to a thing can be used as a diagnostic:

Appreciation
{Person consider something **appreciation**}
{Person see something as **appreciation**}
I consider it **beautiful**.
They see it as **beautiful**.

Additional framing is explored in Niemeier and Dirven 1997; it may be that a more delicate exploration of frames will help interrogate the subcategorisation of **affect**, **judgement** and **appreciation** suggested above.

As we have already indicated, the source and target of evaluation are also criterial. The source of **affect** is of course conscious participants, including persons, human collectives and institutions (Halliday & Matthiessen 1999):

woman, boy, mother, striker, streaker, lawyer, client, teacher, student ...
family, team, platoon, class, professoriate, clergy, congregation, judiciary ...
government, commission, court, council, board, company, senate, tribunal ...

And the behaviour of these conscious participants is the target of **judgement**. Appreciation on the other hand targets things, whether concrete or abstract, material or semiotic. Thus the different codings for 'skill' in the examples below.

he <u>played</u> **skilfully**	judgement
he's a **skilful** <u>player</u>	judgement
it was a **skilful** <u>innings</u>	appreciation

Where nominal groups construe a conscious participant in an institutional role or name a complex process as a thing then virtually the same attitudinal lexis can be used either to **judge** or **appreciate**, as exemplified below (although not always with exactly the same meaning).

judgement	appreciation
he proved a fascinating player	it was fascinating innings (impact)
he proved a splendid player	it was a splendid innings (quality)
he proved a balanced player	it was a balanced innings (balance)
he proved an economical player	it was an economical innings (complexity)
he proved an invaluable player	it was an invaluable innings (valuation)
he was an average player	it was an average innings (normality)
he was a strong player (capacity)	it was a strong innings
he was a brave player (tenacity)	it was a brave innings
he was an honest player (veracity)	it was an honest innings
he was a responsible (propriety)	it was a responsible innings

Clause frames for comparable meanings can be much less flexible:

It was balanced of them to come.	[judging behaviour??]
I consider it honest.	[appreciating a concrete thing??]

Alongside these complementarities, there is a small set of attitudinal lexis which arguably construes both **affect** and **judgement** at the same time:

guilty, embarrassed, proud, jealous, envious, ashamed, resentful, contemptuous ...

These items construe an emotional reaction to behaviour we approve or disapprove of:

I felt guilty about cancelling.
I felt proud that they'd won.

The terms *disgust/revolt* arguably combine **affect** with **judgement** or **appreciation** along similar lines (cf. *they/it revolted me*):

I felt disgusted with them for provoking him. [affect/judgement]
I felt disgusted with/by the smell. [affect/appreciation]

We'll suggest a way of analysing these apparent hybrid realisations at the end of section 2.6 below.

With attitudinal lexis in general, however, the clause frames introduced above and the nature of the source and target of evaluation can be used to distinguish among **affect**, **judgement** and **appreciation**.

2.6 Indirect realisations

To this point we have considered evaluation that has been directly inscribed in discourse through the use of attitudinal lexis. In a text like the following this would mean that we focus on the phrases *fighting mad* and *tears were falling down* as far as **affect** is concerned, by way of considering evaluation in this part of Indigenous singer Archie Roach's anthem for the Stolen Generations (as published in Rose 1996):

> One dark day on Framingham
> Came and didn't give a damn
> My mother cried go get their dad
> He came running **fighting mad**
> Mother's **tears were falling down**
> Dad shaped up he stood his ground
> He said you touch my kids and you fight me
> And they took us from our family
> Took us away
> They took us away
> Snatched from our mother's breast
> Said this was for the best
> Took us away [Rose 1996: 81]

But a restrictive focus of this kind would clearly not do justice to the affectual response Roach's story evokes for most listeners. His account of being stolen from his family by white authorities is more moving than this. Even with the direct inscription of **affect** removed, we can still infer the anger Archie's father felt:

> My mother cried go get their dad ...
> Dad shaped up he stood his ground
> He said you touch my kids and you fight me [Rose 1996: 81]

Similarly we can hardly resist empathising with the agony we presume Archie must have felt at being taken from his home. Although he says nothing explicit about his own feelings, they are plain to see:

> As Archie Roach got up to sing the words of the song Uncle Ernie had played on his gum leaf, he also indicated his **anguish** at being taken from his parents, and how he had gone on, not to the better life promised at the time by the white authorities, but to face discrimination and destitution. 'I've often lived on the streets and gone without a feed for days and no-one ever said sorry to me.' [Sitka 1998]

The general point here is that the selection of ideational meanings is enough to invoke evaluation, even in the absence of attitudinal lexis that tells us directly how to feel. At first blush it might seem that analysing the evaluation invoked by ideational selections introduces an undesirable element of subjectivity into the analysis. On the other hand, avoiding invoked evaluation of this kind amounts to a suggestion that ideational meaning is selected without regard to the attitudes it engenders – a position we find untenable. In this context it is important to distinguish between individual and social subjectivity – between readers as idiosyncratic respondents and communities of readers positioned by specific configurations of gender, generation, class, ethnicity and in/capacity. When analysing invoked evaluation it is certainly critical to specify one's reading position as far as possible with respect to the latter variables; and also to declare whether one is reading a text compliantly,[3] resistantly or tactically.

By a tactical reading we refer to a typically partial and interested reading, which aims to deploy a text for social purposes other than those it has naturalised; resistant readings oppose the reading position naturalised by the co-selection of meanings in a text, while compliant readings subscribe to it. For example, our use of Roach's verse to illustrate inscribed and invoked **attitude** is a tactical one, serving our purposes as linguists, not his as a social activist and spokesman for Australia's Indigenous peoples. Reading compliantly would have positioned us as Australians sympathetic to, and shamed by, Roach's experiences; reading resistantly we might have sided with Australian Prime Minister John Howard in refusing to apologise publicly for this genocidal behaviour by generations of white Australians.

Beyond this, when we suggest that a text naturalises a reading position we mean as far as evaluation is concerned that it will be fairly directive in the kinds of **attitude** it wants readers to share. In part these will be co-articulated by any attendant modalities of communication – potentially including paralanguage (voice quality, facial expression, gesture, bodily stance), dress, musical accompaniment, images, dance and so on (Roach's anguish, for example, is clearly inscribed in his soulful singing and moving melody). Beyond this the prosodic nature of the realisation of interpersonal meanings such as **attitude** means that inscriptions tend to colour more of a text than their local grammatical environment circumscribes. The inscriptions act as sign-posts, in other words, telling us how to read the ideational selections that surround them. Restoring Roach's lyrics, the inscription *fighting mad* certainly colours his father's futile attempt to defend his children:

> My mother cried go get their dad
> He came running **fighting mad**
> Mother's tears were falling down
> Dad shaped up he stood his ground
> He said you touch my kids and you fight me
> And they took us from our family [Rose 1996: 81]

This is arguably sign-posting that is not required for sympathetic readers; but it is important in this regard to imagine a society in which taking children from Indigenous families (up to 50,000 of them on some early estimates; cf. Manne 1998, 2001) was common practice, and publicly defended as humane treatment in the best interests of the children themselves. A society of this kind has surely regarded its Indigenous peoples as less than human, perhaps incapable of the emotions Roach inscribes here. And for us, a society which refuses to apologise publicly for behaviour of this kind continues to subscribe to a comparable racist stance.

For another example of prosodic realisation and the interaction of inscription and invocation, consider the following text, from Indigenous art critic Eric Michaels. Michaels is evaluating the phenomenal desert art paintings covering the doors of Yuendumu school (and by now the doors on houses throughout the community as a whole), which he appreciates as a *spectacular, remarkable* and *major* response to

64   *The Language of Evaluation*

the 1983 headmaster's *modest* suggestion – thereby establishing a prosody of positive evaluation, further reinforced by the positive inscriptions of **affect** (*excitement, interest, pleasure, pride, enthusiastic*).

> In 1983, the new school headmaster (Mr Terry Lewis) brought considerable excitement to the Yuendumu community by his interest in and support of traditional Warlpiri culture and language. One of his more **modest** suggestions was to make the school look less 'European' by commissioning senior men to paint the school doors with traditional designs. The results were **more spectacular** than anyone envisaged.
>
> Both European and Aboriginal residents of Yuendumu took considerable pleasure and pride in the <u>achievement</u>. Visitors to the community were equally enthusiastic, and word about these **remarkable** paintings began to spread. My own response was to see this <u>accomplishment</u> as a **major** one for contemporary international art as well as an <u>achievement</u> in indigenous culture. For me, these doors seemed to strike a chord with issues and images that were being negotiated in the art galleries of Sydney, Paris and New York. [Michaels 1987: 135]

Out of context, Michaels' terms *achievement, accomplishment* and *achievement* again to describe these doors might be taken as non-attitudinal – as simple nominalisations of a completed activity; and this is perhaps a plausible reading of *achievement* the first time it is used. As the text unfolds, and the prosody of positive **appreciation** is developed, however, one is drawn to an attitudinal reading; second time round *achievement* means 'the accomplishment, after a lot of effort, of something good'. By the time Michaels compares the doors with issues and images being negotiated in the art capitals of the world, there is no doubt about the positive **appreciation** his ideational selections are designed to invoke. Inscribed **attitude**, in other words, launches and subsequently reinforces a prosody which directs readers in their evaluation of non-attitudinal ideational material under its scope.

Complementing this, ideational meaning can be used not just to invite but to provoke an attitudinal response in readers. This is one function of lexical metaphor. Earlier in the song we introduced above, Roach draws on this resource to compare the treatment of Indigenous people with that of animals:

> This story's right, this story's true
> I would not tell lies to you
> Like the promises they did not keep

> And how they fenced us in like sheep
> Said to us come take our hand
> Sent us off to mission land
> Taught us to read, to write and pray
> Then they took the children away ...[Rose 1996]

Comparable metaphors are used in *Bringing Them Home*, a 1997 government report on the Stolen Generations:

> We was bought **like a market**. We was all lined up in white dresses, and they'd come round and pick you out **like you was for sale**. [BTH 90]
> I remember all we children being **herded up, like a mob of cattle**, and feeling the humiliation of being graded by the colour of our skins for the government records. [BTH 186]

In none of these examples does the Indigenous voice explicitly judge white authorities as inhumane, but the treatment of people as commercial goods arguably does more than evoke a **judgement** – it provokes one. Here's an extended example from journalist Bob Ellis, criticising John Howard's 1990s economic rationalism:

> John Howard says he knows how vulnerable people are feeling in these times of economic change. He does not. For they are feeling **as vulnerable as a man who has already had his arm torn off by a lion, and sits in the corner holding his stump and waiting for the lion to finish eating and come for him again**. This is something more than vulnerability. It is injury and shock and fear and rage. And he does not know the carnage that is waiting for him if he calls an election. And he will be surprised. [Ellis 1998]

The **affect** (felt by ordinary Australians) and **judgement** (of Howard) provoked by the metaphor are more than clear.

Somewhat less provocative, but still indicating that an evaluation is being invoked, is the use of non-core vocabulary that has in some sense lexicalised a circumstance of manner by infusing it into the core meaning of a word. Comparative manner is infused in this way in *herd* (in the metaphor cited above), which means 'gather together the way livestock are'; similarly *gallop* means 'run like a horse', and implicates a **judgement** of a person running in this way.

Simple intensification is also indicative, presumably because it grades a process and grading is an inherent feature of attitudinal vocabulary. A core lexical item like *break* for example can be intensified in various ways and by various degrees:

> demolish, damage, dismantle, break down, undermine, break up, smash, shatter, smash to smithereens, tear to bits, tear to shreds, pull to pieces ...

Former Labor Prime Minister Paul Keating uses *smash* in his famous Redfern Park speech to characterise the treatment of Indigenous culture by invading Europeans, implicating negative **judgement** as he does so (a **judgement** confirmed by following inscriptions to be sure):

> ... It begins, I think, with that act of recognition
> Recognition that it was we who did the dispossessing.
> We took the traditional lands and **smashed** the traditional way of life.
> We brought the diseases. The alcohol.
> We committed the murders.
> We took the children from their mothers.
> We practised discrimination and exclusion.
> It was our ignorance and our prejudice.
> And our failure to imagine these things being done to us.
> With some noble exceptions, we failed to make the most basic human response and enter into their hearts and minds.
> We failed to ask – how would I feel if this were done to me?
> [Keating 1992]

In traditional terms we might say that these non-core vocabulary items infused with manner connote **attitude** rather than denote it; as such they lie somewhere between affording an **attitude** and provoking it, and so are more sensitive to co-text and reading position for interpretation than lexical metaphor and direct inscriptions. There is a range of other mechanisms by which can similarly 'connote' or 'flag' attitude, and which likewise fall between affording an **attitude** and provoking it. Construing some action or event as contrary to expectation is one such mechanism. Consider by way of example the following,

> This is another book by an American who writes about the pleasures and pains of owning a house in France. Barry, <u>however</u>, is something of an exception because, unlike other authors in this genre, she does not <u>actually</u> live in her house in France. Her profiles of Gallic rusticity and meditation on the French way of life are derived from visits of <u>only</u> two or three weeks each year and her experience of village life seems confined to finding a neighbor to keep her keys for her and

someone to garage her car while she's away. [online book review – Amazon.com]

There are several indicators of counter-expectancy here (for example *however, actually* and *only two or three weeks*) which act to alert the reader that attitudinal values (positive/negative) are at stake. The ideational content of itself might, of course, have led the reader to this same negative viewpoint. But the point is that the reviewer has here intruded into the text to explicitly evaluate Barry's behaviour as contrary to expectation and by this flags a negative orientation to the author and her book.

The various strategies for inscribing and invoking **attitude** introduced above are outlined in Figure 2.3. Options can be usefully read top-down as a cline from 'inscribe' to 'afford' according to the degree of freedom allowed readers in aligning with the values naturalised by the text. Both lexical metaphor and non-core vocabulary have the effect of intensifying feeling, and so can be usefully compared with the intensification resources reviewed as 'force' in the graduation section of Chapter 3 below.

Recognition of inscribed and invoked **attitude** means that we might allow for double codings of the borderline categories introduced in Figure 2.3. Where players are explicitly judged in a role, an invoked **appreciation** of their accomplishments might be recognised; similarly, where an activity is explicitly appreciated as a thing, a **judgement** of whoever accomplished it might be invoked (see Table 2.10).

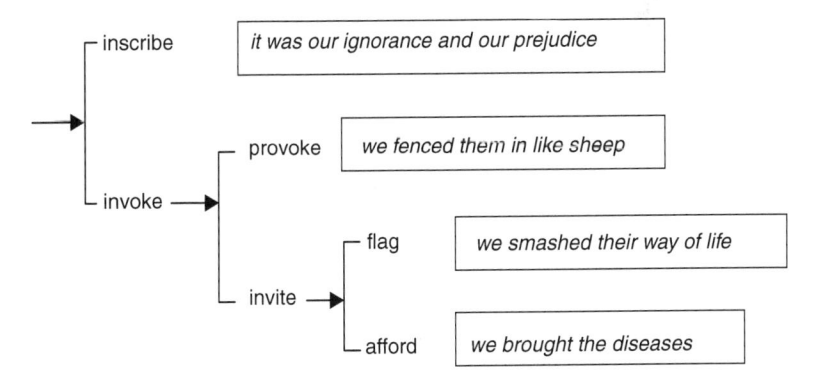

```
┌─ inscribe ──── it was our ignorance and our prejudice
│
│              ┌─ provoke ──── we fenced them in like sheep
└─ invoke ─────┤
               │              ┌─ flag ──── we smashed their way of life
               └─ invite ─────┤
                              └─ afford ── we brought the diseases
```

Figure 2.3 Strategies for inscribing and invoking attitude

68 *The Language of Evaluation*

Table 2.10 Interactions between attitudinal invocation and attitudinal inscription

Inscribed judgement & invoked appreciation	Inscribed appreciation & invoked judgement
he proved a fascinating player	it was fascinating innings (impact)
he proved a splendid player	it was a splendid innings (quality)
he proved a balanced player	it was a balanced innings (balance)
he proved an economical player	it was an economical innings (complexity)
he proved an invaluable player	it was an invaluable innings (valuation)
he played average (normality)	it was an average innings
he played strongly (capacity)	it was a strong innings
he played bravely (tenacity)	it was a brave innings
he played honestly (veracity)	it was an honest innings
he played responsibly (propriety)	it was a responsible innings

Reasoning along the same lines, the hybrids introduced in section 2.5 above that construe an **attitude** to something we approve or disapprove of can be treated as **affectual** inscriptions invoking (ie implying) **judgement** or **appreciation** (*guilty, embarrassed, proud, jealous, envious, ashamed, resentful, contemptuous; disgust/revolt*).

2.7 Beyond attitude

In order to scale our presentation of attitudinal resources down to something manageable we have focussed on gradable lexical items construing evaluation. This places swearing beyond the scope of our study, since it involves non-gradable lexis. Swearing is clearly used however to construe strong feelings, as in the narrative evaluation below:

> You know, and I'd think that was some sort of record. And that was real absolute lunacy, doing that. We wouldn't do it again, but **my God** we had a ball doing it though, didn't we? (addressed to partner) We really had a good time. You know, but there was so much work. [Plum 1988: 222]

Emotional outbursts of this kind are hard to classify as **affect**, **judgement** or **appreciation** on their own. In some texts they can be read as amplifying attendant inscriptions; so we could in principle treat *my God* as intensifying *had a ball* above if we want to include it in our analysis.

In other texts it is harder to say precisely which kind of **attitude** is being construed:

> Fucken Hell man, who the hell told you I liked doing this kind of shit. On Saturday I saw Brian and Brendon and his Girlfriend at Waterloo, I was waiting to catch the **bloody** bus, anyway they started talking to me so that killed alot of time. Anyway I had to go to the Laundromat Yesterday and I saw my ex-boyfriend man he looks **fucken** ugly **god** knows what I went out with him, he looks like a **fucken dickhead** ... [Martin 1997c: 312–23]

Perhaps in general we should simply treat expletives, related euphemisms (*gosh, darn*, etc.) and interjections (*ugh, phew, gr-r-r-r, ow, whew, tut-tut*, etc.) as outbursts of evaluation which are underspecified as far as type of **attitude** is concerned. Jordens 2002 however makes the point that in a specific register, particular types of swearing and other exclamations may be associated with particular types of **attitude** – for example *oh, man, ohhhh, whoa, oh heavens, oh god, oh crikey* and *oh shit* with insecurity in his interviews with patients under treatment for colonic cancer.

Interjections bring us to the borders of what is normally considered language, comprised as they are of apparently residual protolanguage material (as Halliday 1975 and Painter 1984, 1998 would describe it). As work on interpersonal meaning evolves, the traditional distinction between language and paralanguage certainly needs to be reconsidered – a step we will not be pursuing here. But work on paralanguage (gesture, facial expression, laughter, voice quality, loudness, etc.) and attendant modalities of communication (image, music, movement, etc.) are central arenas for further research on the realisation of **attitude** as we move from a functional linguistic to a more encompassing social semiotic perspective. The realisation of **attitude** in images and their interaction with verbal text is explored in Martin 2001a.

2.8 Analysing attitude

Section 2.7 concludes our introduction to the system of **attitude** up to the point in delicacy we decided to develop here. For the remainder of the chapter we'll consider the realisation of **attitude** as it unfolds in discourse, focussing on three example texts. The first of these is a phase of Annie Proulx's *The Shipping News*, concerned with Quoyle's frustrated apprenticeship as a small town newspaper reporter.

70   *The Language of Evaluation*

> Quoyle brought over his copy. 'Al isn't in yet,' he said, squaring up the pages, 'so I thought I'd give it to you.'
>
> His friend did not smile. Was on the job. Read for a few seconds, lifted his face to the fluorescent light. 'Edna was in she'd shred this. Al saw it he'd tell Punch to get rid of you. You got to rewrite this. Here, sit down. Show you what's wrong. They say reporters can be made out of anything. You'll be a test case.'
>
> It was what Quoyle had expected.
>
> 'Your lead,' said Partridge. 'Christ!' He read aloud in a high-pitched singsong.
>
>> Last night the Pine Eye Planning Commission voted by a large margin to revise earlier recommendations for amendments to the municipal zoning code that would increase the minimum plot size of residential properties in all but downtown areas to seven acres.
>
> 'It's like reading cement. Too long. Way, way, way too long. Confused. No human interest. No quotes. Stale.' His pencil roved among Quoyle's sentences, stirring and shifting. 'Short words. Short sentences. Break it up. Look at this, look at this. Here's your angle down here. That's news. Move it up.'
>
> He wrenched the words around. Quoyle leaned close, stared, fidgeted, understood nothing.
>
> 'O.K., try this
>
>> Pine Eye Planning Commission member Janice Foxley resigned during an angry late-night Tuesday meeting. 'I'm not going to sit here and watch the poor[4] people of this town get sold down the river,' Foxley said.
>>
>> A few minutes before Foxley's resignation the commission approved a new zoning law by a vote of 9 to 1. The new law limits minimum residential property sizes to seven acres.
>
> 'Not very snappy, no style, and still too long,' said Partridge, 'but going in the right direction. Get the idea? Get the sense of what's news? What you want in the lead? Here, see what you do. Put some spin on it.'
>
> Partridge's fire never brought him to a boil. After six months of copy desk fixes Quoyle didn't recognise news, had no aptitude for detail. He was afraid of all but twelve or fifteen verbs. Had a fatal flair for the passive. 'Governor Murchie was handed a bouquet by first grader Kimberley Plud,' he wrote and Edna, the crusty rewrite woman, stood up and bellowed at Quoyle. 'You lobotomized moron. How the hell can you hand a governor?' Quoyle another sample of the semi-illiterates who practiced journalism nowadays. Line them up against the wall! [Proulx 1993: 7–8]

As is customary in discourse analysis we can begin with either a 'top-down' or a 'bottom-up' perspective. For **attitude** this means starting with prosodies and working down to their realisations or starting with realisations and working back to the 'mood' of a text. One useful technique for exploring prosodies is to use colour coding, involving just a few fairly general categories (such as **affect, judgement** and **appreciation**) and mapping unfolding motifs. This is however too expensive for publication in an academic monograph, so for this text we'll start bottom-up, beginning with inscriptions – and use a table to display results. The abbreviations we're using are as follows:

+	'positive attitude'
–	'negative attitude'
des	'affect: desire'
hap	'affect: un/happiness'
sec	'affect: in/security'
sat	'affect: dis/satisfaction'
norm	'judgement: normality'
cap	'judgement: capacity'
ten	'judgement: tenacity'
ver	'judgement: veracity'
prop	'judgement: propriety'
reac	'appreciation: reaction'
comp	'appreciation: composition'
val	'appreciation: valuation'

By setting up separate columns for **affect, judgement** and **appreciation** (see Table 2.11) these evaluations can be notated alongside the lexicogrammatical items construing them. For **judgement** and **appreciation**, it is also useful to note the source of the **attitude** (who is judging or appreciating) and what is being appraised (who is being judged and what is being appreciated). Normally we interpret speakers and writers as the source of evaluations, unless **attitude** is projected as the speech or thoughts of an additional appraiser.[5] So whereas the narrator judges

Table 2.11 Example attitude analysis

Appraising items	Appraiser	Affect	Judgement	Apprec'tion	Appraised
wrong	Partridge			–val	Q's copy
no aptitude			–cap		Quoyle
lobotomised moron	Edna		–cap		Quoyle

Quoyle as having no aptitude for detail, it's Partridge who values his original copy as wrong, and Edna who adjudges him a moron; we'll just leave a blank for the default position (ie writer/speaker sourced appraisal) in order to avoid having to write 'narrator' over and over again for Proulx's text.

We acknowledge of course that a narrator's voice may align with that of one or another character in a story, and that analysis of the source of appraisal may have to be adjusted to take this into account. We won't pursue this issue of 'point of view' here, but would stress in passing that evaluation is one of the main narrative resources used to indicate whose voice a writer is narrating from. As narrator, for example, Proulx is relatively sympathetic to Quoyle, aligning readers to empathise with him, for all his failings; and this contrasts sharply with the views of Quoyle's colleagues during his apprenticeship, especially with Edna's criticisms. Because of this play of sympathy and antipathy that we grow habituated to as the novel unfolds, we hear Edna, not Proulx, slamming Quoyle and his like as semi-literates who should be shot – in spite of the fact that these evaluations are not explicitly projected by Proulx directly or indirectly as speech or thought:

> Partridge's fire never brought him to a boil. After six months of copy desk fixes Quoyle didn't recognise news, had no aptitude for detail. He was afraid of all but twelve or fifteen verbs. Had a fatal flair for the passive. 'Governor Murchie was handed a bouquet by first grader Kimberley Plud,' he wrote and Edna, the crusty rewrite woman, stood up and bellowed at Quoyle. 'You lobotomized moron. How the hell can you hand a governor?' **Quoyle another sample of the semi-illiterates who practiced journalism nowadays. Line them up against the wall!**

Affect can be coded in a framework of this kind by treating the emoter as appraiser, and the trigger of the emotion, if recoverable, as appraised. This makes sense if we interpret the appraiser as the person who is feeling something (whether emoting, judging or appreciating), and the appraised as the person, thing or activity that is being reacted to. This of course is stretching the everyday meaning of the terms appraiser and appraised, something we have learned to live with to standardise coding and which we feel a technical redefinition of the terms affords; analysts who find this unhelpful may prefer to code **affect** separately from **judgement** and **appreciation** using the terms emoter and trigger as introduced above.

Attitude: Ways of Feeling 73

We also find it useful to distinguish negative feelings from positive feelings that are grammatically negated, thus drawing a distinction between *sad* and *not happy*; by notating grammatical negation as 'neg', we can code *not happy* as 'neg +hap', opposed to *sad* as '-hap'. Morphological negation (eg *unhappy, insecure*) on the other hand is not arguable, since it is realised lexically, outside Halliday's Mood function;[6] so we will code it as negative rather than negated **attitude** (ie -hap for *unhappy*, neg +hap for *not happy*) (see Table 2.12).

Our reading of the attitudinal inscriptions in Proulx's text are outlined in Table 2.13. Most of the explicit **attitude** is projected, mainly as Partridge's comments (and as Edna's comments and thoughts); we have annotated this in the appraiser column, using double quotes (") for speech and single quotes (') for thought (following Halliday 1994). Most of the evaluation is **appreciation**, directed at Quoyle's copy, handing over to negative **judgement** of his aptitude as a reporter later on; inscribed **affect**, mainly Quoyle's, is a further motif.

As we can see, evaluation in this phase of discourse focuses on what news is in terms of getting it right or wrong as far as the field of journalism is concerned:

wrong, too long, confused, stale, not very snappy, no style

right, short, spin

For this field we have taken the term *news* as positive appreciation, since it is used to refer to newsworthy information that is valuable enough to print.

And at this stage of his apprenticeship Quoyle is a bad reporter:

no aptitude for detail, fatal flair for the passive, lobotomized moron, semi-illiterates

One of these negative **judgements** involves name-calling (Edna's *you lobotomised moron*).The *Collins Cobuild Dictionary* explains this term by saying that 'if you refer to someone as a moron, you are showing that

Table 2.12 Appraisal analysis conventions

Appraising items	Appraiser	Affect	Judgement	Apprec'tion	Appraised
not smile	Partridge	neg +hap			Q's arrival
afraid	Quoyle	−sec			most verbs

74 *The Language of Evaluation*

Table 2.13 Inscribed attitude in Proulx

Appraising items	Appraiser	Affect	Judgement	Apprec'tion	Appraised
not smile	Partridge	neg +hap			Q's arrival
wrong	Partridge"			−val	Q's copy
too long	Partridge"			−comp	Q's lead
way (x3) too long	Partridge"			−comp	Q's lead
confused	Partridge"			−comp	Q's lead
stale	Partridge"			−reac	Q's lead
short	Partridge"			+comp	∞Q's lead[7]
Short	Partridge"			+comp	∞Q's lead
news[8]	Partridge"			+val	angle
fidgeted	Quoyle	−sat			P's editing
not very snappy	Partridge"			neg +reac	revised copy
no style	Partridge"			neg +val	revised copy
too long	Partridge"			−comp	revised copy
right direction	Partridge"			+val	revised copy
news	Partridge"			+val	revised copy
want	P" Quoyle	+des			news
spin	Partridge"			+val	revised copy
news				+val	Q's copy
no aptitude			neg + cap		Quoyle
afraid	Quoyle	−sec			most verbs
fatal flair			−cap		Quoyle
crusty			−ten		Edna
bellowed[9]	Edna	−hap			Quoyle
lobotomised moron	Edna"		−cap		Quoyle
semi-illiterates	Edna'		−cap		Quoyle (& kind)

you think they are **very stupid'**, and terms such as these can be graded (*you complete moron, you total idiot, you absolute imbecile*, etc.). On these grounds it seems appropriate to include pejorative names as inscriptions of attitude. Some further examples from the 'moron' set are listed below:

> moron, imbecile, idiot, half-wit, numbskull, blockhead, simpleton, boofhead, dimwit, slowcoach, thickhead, peabrain ...

Proulx's effort to endear readers to Quoyle, in spite of his failings, is most clearly exemplified here in her description of his *fatal flair for the passive* which we have coded as negative **judgement** (incapacity). The term *flair* normally collocates with positive **judgements** (a natural ability to do something well), and in this context positions readers to sympathise with Quoyle not simply as stupid but as an unfortunate victim of his own consuming predispositions.

Attitude: Ways of Feeling 75

Table 2.14 Inscribed and invoked attitude in Proulx

Appraising items	Appraiser	Affect	Judgement	Apprec'tion	Appraised
squaring up				t, +comp	Q's copy
not smile	Partridge	neg +hap			Q's arrival
on the job	Partridge	t, +sat			P's work
shred	P" Edna'			t, −val	Q's copy
get rid of	P" Al"		t, −cap		Quoyle
wrong	Partridge"			−val	Q's copy
test case	Partridge"		t, −cap		Quoyle
[Christ!]	Partridge"			−val	Q's copy
high-pitched singsong				t, −react	Q's copy
like reading cement	Partridge"			t, −react	Q's copy
too long	Partridge"			−comp	Q's lead
way (x3) too long	Partridge"			−comp	Q's lead
confused	Partridge"			−comp	Q's lead
no human interest	Partridge"			t, −react	Q's lead
no quotes	Partridge"			t, −react	Q's lead
stale	Partridge"			−reac	Q's lead
short	Partridge"			+comp	∞Q's lead
short	Partridge"			+comp	∞Q's lead
news	Partridge"			+val	Q's angle
wrenched				t, −comp	Q's copy
fidgeted	Quoyle	-sat			P's editing
understood nothing			t, −cap		Quoyle
not very snappy	Partridge"			neg +reac	revised copy
no style	Partridge"			neg +val	revised copy
too long	Partridge"			−comp	revised copy
right direction	Partridge"			+val	revised copy
news	Partridge"			+val	revised copy
want	P" Quoyle	+des			news
spin	Partridge"			+val	revised copy
fire	Patridge	t, +des			Q's copy
never ... boil			t, −cap		Quoyle
news				+val	Q's copy
didn't recognise			t, −cap		Quoyle
no aptitude			neg +cap		Quoyle
afraid	Quoyle	−sec			most verbs
fatal flair				−cap	Quoyle
crusty				−ten	Edna
bellowed	Edna	−hap			Quoyle
lobotomized moron	Edna"			−cap	Quoyle
[how the hell ...]	Edna"			−comp	Q's passive
semi-illiterates	Edna'			−cap	Quoyle & kind
line them up ...	Edna'		t, −cap		Quoyle & kind

Invoked **attitude** is added to the analysis in Table 2.14, using the notation 't,' for ideational tokens/invocations (eg 't, +comp' for *squaring up*). Swearing has also been included in the table, as explosions of **attitude** registering Partridge's and Edna's exasperation with the poor quality Quoyle's work (*Christ* and *the hell*). Since projection is a recursive system

76 *The Language of Evaluation*

Table 2.15 Invoked attitude in Proulx

Appraising items	Appraiser	Affect	Judgement	Apprec'tion	Appraised
squaring up				t, +comp	Q's copy
shred	P" Edna'			t, −val	Q's copy
high-pitched singsong				t, −react	Q's copy
like reading cement	Partridge"			t, −react	Q's copy
no human interest	Partridge"			t, −react	Q's lead
no quotes	Partridge"			t, −react	Q's lead
wrenched				t, −comp	Q's copy
[Christ!]	Partridge"			−val	Q's copy
[how the hell …]	Edna"			−comp	Q's passive
get rid of	P" Al"		t, −cap		Quoyle
test case	Partridge"		t, −cap		Quoyle
understood nothing			t, −cap		Quoyle
never..boil			t, −cap		Quoyle
didn't recognise			t, −cap		Quoyle
line them up …	Edna'		t, −cap		Quoyle & kind

the appraiser column includes some examples of one character projecting another's evaluation (eg Partridge saying Al would tell Punch to fire Quoyle).

The main function of the tokens is to extend the negative prosodies of **appreciation** (bad copy) and **judgement** (incompetent reporter) inscribed by the explicitly evaluative items, as outlined in Table 2.15. Some of the tokens provoke evaluation via lexical metaphor (*test case, like reading cement, Partridge's fire never brought him to a boil*); and both *shred* and *wrench* arguably imply evaluation because of the intensified manner in their meaning ('cut or tear **into very small pieces**', 'pull or twist **violently**').

We'll draw our discussion of this text to a close here, without pretending to have exhausted its evaluative meaning. Humour, broadly speaking, clearly has a role to play. Partridge, for example, mocks Quoyle by reading his lead aloud in a high-pitched singsong. For his part, Quoyle is scared of verbs, fatally attracted to the passive and sentenced to face the firing squad for his troubles – a life-threatening scenario we read as amusing (as too far over the top to be taken literally). And Quoyle is commodified as a *sample* semi-literate, not an *example* of one, a sarcastic collocation adding bite to Edna's blast. Unfortunately, pleading ignorance, we'll have to place humour beyond the scope of our discussion here; for ground-breaking work on humour in relation to appraisal in casual conversation see Eggins & Slade 1997.

Since Proulx's text foregrounds **judgement** and **appreciation**, we'll turn now to a text from an Australian parenting magazine which concentrates on affect. This text constitutes the 'Dad Department' for the June/July 1994 edition of *Mother & Baby* (A Bounty Publication):

Baby, please don't cry

> Becoming a parent unleashes a torrent of new emotions in dads too – never more so than when your child is inconsolable. Ask George Blair-West.

At last, you are in dreamland. My Goddess of Laughter, the Princess-of-all-that-is-Good. Your skin so smooth and soft. The squeals of sheer and utter joy that you unleashed only a few hours ago echo in my mind. I had to come and look at you. It is all I can do not to reach out and kiss you. But my feelings can't afford for you to wake again.

You cried so hard after we put you down. My heart hurt. It was all I could do not to rush to your side. And then you screamed your cry. I had to come to your door. You had no idea, but I was only feet away. Wanting. Wanting to hold you in my arms. You would have settled within seconds – but it would have been for my benefit, not yours.

It must have been scary, imprisoned by those hard white bars. You felt all alone. It was black with darkness. You probably thought we had left you forever. Abandoned. What a scary word. But of course you don't know the word – you only know the feeling.

Do you remember? Last night I came to you. You had been crying for us, calling 'Mummy' and then, when that didn't work, 'Daddy, Daddy'. After 20 minutes I couldn't take it any longer. Mummy said 'no'. She knew. I didn't mean to make it worse for you – I'm sorry. You gave me that big hug. You were so relieved to see me. I felt like a white knight on a shining charger. But, probably like every man who thinks he is Sir Lancelot, I soon realised I could not save you. I had to go, you see. And you cried for 30 minutes more because I had taught you that this would make me come to you.

Tonight you settled after 35 minutes. I'm getting better, aren't I? If it were not for me you might have only taken 15 minutes tonight. Don't worry. As Mummy says, we know you are okay because you were laughing when you went to bed. Remember? You wanted two kisses from each of us and you couldn't stop giggling when I blew on your tummy.

It was only when we shut the door and left you that the fear must have closed in. But if you wake during the night we'll be in here like a flash – you just wait and see. Mind you, that was how this problem started. You'd been doing fine till you got sick a week ago. I guess having us sit up with you and rocking you to sleep for four nights in a row threw you off your game, huh?

Now you have finally settled. You sleep the sleep of the cotton-soft breath. I'm glad one of us is over this, for even as I watch I know you went to sleep in exhausted desperation. After a while you will realise that we can leave you and come back again. At 18 months you're too young to understand 'later' or 'tomorrow'. Such complicated words. You probably do not even know you are 18 months! I wish I could explain. I especially wish I could explain to you that you're safe when we leave you and turn out the light.

You know, there are times when you can feel pretty helpless as a big person. I guess this is part of the training for getting through life. It scares me when I think of how far we have to go and what could go wrong – but I wouldn't want it any other way. So you, and I, have to suffer for a little longer. Together, if we really, really try, with Mummy's help, I think – no, I'm sure – we can beat this. Dream sweetly. [*Mother & Baby* 1994]

Since there is so much **affect** in the text it is useful taking the analysis a step further in delicacy than we attempted for Proulx, subcategorising realis **affect** as follows:

unhappiness
    misery   whimper, cry, wail; down, sad, miserable
    antipathy   rubbish, abuse, revile; dislike, hate, abhor

happiness
    cheer   chuckle, laugh, rejoice; cheerful, buoyant, jubilant
    affection   shake hands, hug, embrace; fond, loving, adoring

insecurity
    disquiet   restless, twitching, shaking; uneasy, anxious, freaked out
    surprise   start, cry out, faint; taken aback, surprised, astonished

security
    confidence   declare, assert, proclaim; together, confident, assured
    trust   delegate, commit, entrust; comfortable with, confident in, trusting

dissatisfaction
    ennui   fidget, yawn, tune out; flat, stale, jaded
    displeasure   caution, scold, castigate; cross, angry, furious

satisfaction
    interest   attentive, busy, flat out; involved, absorbed, engrossed
    pleasure   pat on the back, compliment, reward; satisfied, pleased, chuffed

Our reading of inscribed **attitude** in 'Baby, please don't cry' is presented as Table 2.16. The article contains some **appreciation**, but very little **judgement**; overwhelmingly it focusses on the emotions of father and child. This is an interesting play of **attitude** for part of a magazine dedicated to constructing norms for good and bad parenting. Perhaps the message being constructed here is that while good parenting involves sensitive new age guys ('snaggy' dads) learning to get in touch with their emotions, they also have to learn to manage them, in tune with the needs of mother and child (about which, of course, mother knows best).

The 'torrent of new emotions' unleashed in Dad is outlined in Table 2.17. Dad is constructed as wrestling with desire – giving in and feeling guilty, but trying to be strong and follow the prescriptions of the 'controlled crying' regime being implemented.

Baby, for her part, is presented as inconsolable when abandoned and happy only when her parents are around; she has to suffer with her Dad until she learns to 'settle' – see Table 2.18.

Compared with Proulx, there is very little invoked **attitude** since so much is explicitly inscribed. Some of the parents' behaviour could be read as tokens of **affect**:

to hold you in my arms

(you probably thought) we had left you forever

I blew on your tummy

And there is some lexical metaphor, enhancing **judgements** of baby and Dad. Note in passing the re-reading of *laughter* (**affect**) and *good* (**appreciation**) in the context of the metaphor, now taken as **judgements** of baby's good-natured **capacity** and **propriety**.

My Goddess of Laughter [+capacity]

the Princess-of-all-that-is-Good [+propriety]

I felt like a white knight on a shining charger [+capacity]

… man who thinks he is Sir Lancelot, I soon realised I could not save you [−capacity]

we'll be in here like a flash [+propriety]

Table 2.16 Inscribed attitude in 'Baby, please don't cry'

Appraising items	Appraiser	Affect	Judgement	Apprec'tion	Appraised
Laughter	Bub	cheer			(various)
good				+val	(various)
so smooth and soft				+val	B's skin
squeals of ... utter joy	Bub	cheer			Dad
∞ ... not to ... kiss	Dad	neg aff.			Bub
my feelings can't ...	Dad	(various)			Bub
cried so hard	Bub	misery			parents leave
settled	Bub	∞conf.			∞Dad return
my heart hurt	Dad	misery			Bub crying
screamed your cry	Bub	displ.			parents gone
wanting	Dad	desire			come in
wanting	Dad	desire			hold Bub
benefit				+val	hold Bub
scary	Bub	disquiet			imprisoned
felt all alone	Bub	disquiet			parents gone
abandoned	Bub	disquiet			parents gone
scary				−reac	'abandoned'
the feeling	Bub	disquiet			abandoned
crying for us	Bub	displ.			parents gone
I couldn't take it	Dad	displ.			Bub crying
I'm sorry	Dad	misery	−prop		visiting
worse				−val	being alone
that big hug	Bub	affection			Dad
so relieved	Bub	confident			see Dad
cried for 30 minutes	Bub	misery			Dad gone
better			+cap		Dad
don't worry	Bub	∞ dis.q			parents gone
okay				+val	Bub
were laughing	Bub	cheer			
kisses	parents	∞affect			
couldn't stop giggling	Bub	cheer			... on tummy
fear	Bub	disquiet			parents gone
this problem				−val	Bub crying
sick			−cap		Bub
settled	Bub	confident			exhausted
glad	Dad	cheer			Bub settled
exhausted desperation	Bub	ennui			parents gone
complicated				−comp	words
wish	Dad	desire			explain
especially wish	Dad	desire			explain ...
safe				+val	Bub
feel pretty helpless			−cap		big person
scares	Dad	disquiet			how far to go
wrong				−val	how far to go
wouldn't want	Dad	neg des.			life
have to suffer	Dad & Bub	disquiet			settling
sweetly				+val	∞dream

Attitude: Ways of Feeling 81

Table 2.17 Inscribed attitude for Dad in 'Baby, please don't cry'

Appraising items	Appraiser	Affect	Judgement	Apprec'tion	Appraised
∞ ... *not to ... kiss*	Dad	neg aff.			Bub
my feelings can't ...	Dad	(various)			Bub
my heart hurt	Dad	misery			Bub crying
wanting	Dad	desire			come in
wanting	Dad	desire			hold Bub
I couldn't take it	Dad	displ.			Bub crying
I'm sorry	Dad	misery	−prop		visiting
kisses	parents	∞affect			
glad	Dad	cheer			Bub settled
wish	Dad	desire			explain
especially wish	Dad	desire			explain ...
scares	Dad	disquiet			how far to go
wouldn't want	Dad	neg des.			life
have to suffer	Dad and Bub	disquiet			settling

Table 2.18 Inscribed attitude for Baby in 'Baby, please don't cry'

Appraising items	Appraiser	Affect	Judgement	Apprec'tion	Appraised
squeals of ... utter joy	Bub	cheer			Dad
cried so hard	Bub	misery			parents leave
settled	Bub	∞conf.			∞Dad return
screamed your cry	Bub	displ.			parents gone
scary	Bub	disquiet			imprisoned
felt all alone	Bub	disquiet			parents gone
abandoned	Bub	disquiet			parents gone
the feeling	Bub	disquiet			abandoned
crying for us	Bub	displ.			parents gone
that big hug	Bub	affection			Dad
so relieved	Bub	confident			see Dad
cried for 30 minutes	Bub	misery			Dad gone
don't worry	Bub	∞disq			parents gone
were laughing	Bub	cheer			
couldn't stop giggling	Bub	cheer			... on tummy
fear	Bub	disquiet			parents gone
settled	Bub	confident			exhausted
exhausted desperation	Bub	ennui			parents gone
have to suffer	Dad and Bub	disquiet			settling

Additional metaphor is used to intensify Baby's affectual disposition.

you are in dreamland
imprisoned by those hard white bars
threw you off your game
You sleep the sleep of the cotton-soft breath

The text is a useful one for considering the reading position naturalised by the **attitude** and who it might accommodate. Jim's reaction is basically to reach for the nearest bucket, longing for the not so distant time when men didn't have emotions, or if they did, didn't say anything about them. Undercutting this is his suspicion that this text has been written by a woman, for women – with this particular torrent of emotions a thoroughly feminine concoction.[10] Complete alienation in other words. Whether a community of snaggy dads exists that would actually bond with this portrayal of fatherhood is an interesting question. The dad in question is perhaps even less helpful than the more traditional kind who let women deal with children through the night; he wants to be involved but makes a mess of things, and has to have his emotions managed by mum – who now has two 'babies' to take care of instead of one. What's certain is that there's nothing post-patriarchal about the child-rearing presented here; men are constructed as self-indulgent incompetent oafs and totally dependent on the wisdom of their mothering partners. Perhaps what we have here is simply a passion play for the enjoyment of women with traditional values – a man-mocking celebration of motherhood, legitimising the article's position in a magazine which is after all called *Mother & Baby*.[11]

The third text we'll consider is a letter addressed to Peter Whimsey, from his assistant Katherine Climpson in Dorothy Sayers' murder mystery *Strong Poison*. Sayers uses graphology (italics and small caps) to foreground the evaluation in Climpson's letter, drawing our attention to the special nature of the relationship between Climpson (a working woman) and Whimsey (an artistocrat and amateur detective) as it is played out in this part of the book.

My dear Lord Peter,

I feel sure you will be anxious to hear, at the *earliest possible* moment *how* things are *going*, and though I have only been here *one* day, I really think I have *not* done so *badly*, all things considered!

My train got in quite late on Monday night, after a *most dreary* journey, with a *lugubrious* wait at *Preston*, though thanks to your kindness in insisting that I should travel *First-class*, I was not really at all tired! Nobody can realise what a *great* difference these extra comforts make, especially when one is getting on in years, and after the *uncomfortable* travelling which I had to endure in my days of poverty, I feel that I am living in almost *sinful* luxury! The carriage was *well* heated – indeed, *too much so* and I should have liked the window down, but that there was a *very fat* business man, *muffled* to the eyes in *coats* and *woolly waistcoats* who *strongly* objected to fresh air! Men are such HOT-HOUSE

PLANTS nowadays, are they not, quite unlike my dear father, who would never permit a *fire* in the house *before* November the 1st, or after March 31st even though the thermometer was at *freezing-point*!

I had no difficulty in getting a comfortable room at the Station Hotel, *late* as it was. In the *old* days, an *unmarried woman arriving alone at midnight with a suitcase* would hardly have been considered *respectable* – what a wonderful difference one finds today! I am *grateful* to have lived to see such changes, because whatever old-fashioned people may say about the greater *decorum* and *modesty* of women on Queen Victoria's time, those who can remember the old conditions know how *difficult* and *humiliating* they were!

Yesterday morning, of course, my *first* object was to find a *suitable boarding-house*, in accordance with your instructions, and I was *fortunate* enough to hit upon this house at the *second* attempt. It is very well run and *refined*, and there are three *elderly ladies* who are *permanent* boarders here, and are *well up* in all the GOSSIP of the town, so that nothing could be more *advantageous* for our purpose! ...

That gave me quite a *good* opportunity to ask about the *house*!! Such a *beautiful* old place, I said, and did anybody live there? (*Of course* I did not blurt this out *all at once* – I waited till they had told me of the many *quaint spots* in the district that would interest an artist!) Mrs. Pegler, a very *stout*, FUSSY old lady, with a LONG TONGUE (!) was able to tell me *all* about it. My dear Lord Peter, what I do *not* know now about the *abandoned wickedness* of Mrs. Wrayburn's early life is really NOT WORTH KNOWING!! But what was *more to the point* is that she told me the *name* of Mrs. Wrayburn's *nurse-companion*. She is a MISS BOOTH, a retired nurse, about *sixty* years old, and she lives *all alone* in the house with Mrs. Wrayburn, except for the *servants*, and a *housekeeper*. When I heard that Mrs. Wrayburn was so *old*, and *paralysed* and *frail*, I said was it not very *dangerous* that Miss Booth should be the only attendant, but Mrs. Pegler said the housekeeper was a *most trustworthy* woman who had been with Mrs. Wrayburn for many years, and was *quite* capable of looking after her any time when Miss Booth was out. So it appears that Miss Booth does go out sometimes! Nobody in this house seems to *know* her *personally*, but they say she is often to be seen in the town in *nurse's uniform*. I managed to extract quite a good description of her, so if I should happen to meet her, I daresay I shall be *smart* enough to *recognise* her! ...

I will let you know as *soon* as I get the *least bit* more information.

Most sincerely yours,
Katherine Alexandra Climpson [Sayers 1991: 98–100]

Sayers' formatting gives prominence to both inscribed and invoked attitude. The inscriptions are as follows:

> *not* done so *badly*; a *most dreary* journey; a *lugubrious* wait; travel *First-class*; the *uncomfortable* travelling; almost *sinful* luxury; *well* heated; indeed, *too*

much so [heated]; would hardly have been considered *respectable*; I am *grateful*; the greater *decorum* and *modesty* of women on Queen Victoria's time; how *difficult* and *humiliating* [the old conditions]; a *suitable boarding-house*; I was *fortunate* enough; very well run and *refined*; nothing could be more *advantageous*; a *good* opportunity; a *beautiful* old place; the many *quaint spots*; *not* know now about the *abandoned wickedness* of Mrs. Wrayburn's early life; what was *more to the point*; so *old*, and *paralysed* and *frail*; not very *dangerous*; a *most trustworthy* woman; quite capable; I shall be *smart* enough to *recognise her*

There are a few more invocations than inscriptions, most of which involve grading of some kind and so are in this respect inviting evaluation. We've highlighted intensification in bold face below (pending a more detailed discussion in Chapter 3):

the *earliest possible* moment; **how** things are *going*; only been here **one** day; *Preston*; a **great** difference [travelling first class]; a **very** *fat* business man; **muffled to the eyes** in *coats* and *woolly waistcoats*; **strongly** objected; **never** permit a *fire* in the house *before* November the 1st; even though the thermometer was at **freezing-point**; *late* **as** it was; the *old* days; an *unmarried woman arriving alone at midnight with a suitcase*; my **first** object; the **second** attempt; three *elderly ladies*; **permanent** boarders; **well up** in **all** the GOSSIP of the town; the *house*; *Of course* I did not **blurt** this out **all at once;** a **very** *stout*, FUSSY old lady, with a LONG TONGUE; **all** about it; the *name* of Mrs. Wrayburn's *nurse-companion;* about *sixty* years old; and she lives **all** *alone* in the house with Mrs. Wrayburn, except for the *servants*, and *a housekeeper*; Nobody in this house seems to *know* her *personally*; in *nurse's uniform*; to *recognise* her; I will let you know **as soon as** I get the **least bit more** information

Small caps are used to give prominence to five evaluations, which don't appear to be functioning differently from the italicised inscriptions and invocations:

Men are such HOT-HOUSE PLANTS nowadays

all the GOSSIP of the town

a very *stout*, FUSSY old lady, with a LONG TONGUE (!)

is really NOT WORTH KNOWING!!

She is a MISS BOOTH

As far as inscribed evaluation is concerned, Sayers' formatting is fairly comprehensive. Normal font is used for just nine inscriptions. Two of these could be taken as modality rather than attitude:

> you will be **anxious** to hear? [modalisation: inclination]
> I should have **liked** the window down [modalisation: inclination]

And four involve formulaic phrases for which lexicalisation has arguably bleached most of the evaluation:

> My **dear** Lord Peter
> **thanks** to your **kindness**
> my **dear** father ... !
> **Most sincerely** yours,

That leaves just five inscriptions in normal font. Four of these appear in exclamative clauses, but we cannot make too much of this since almost every sentence in Climpson's letter ends with or includes an exclamation mark (two end with two – '!!'). As with the small caps, there seems to be no pattern to these omissions.

> I had **no difficulty** in getting a comfortable room ... .
> – what a **wonderful** difference one finds today!
> **old-fashioned** people ... !
> that would **interest** an artist!
> **quite a good** description of her ... !

In order to complement our bottom up approach to the previous examples, we'll develop a more prosodic perspective here – working through the letter phase by phase as it has been organised by Sayers into paragraphs.

Evaluation in phase 1 is oriented to 'urgency' – Climpson's concern to report to Whimsey as quickly as possible.

'urgency'

> I feel sure you will be anxious to hear, at the *earliest possible* moment *how* things are *going*, and though I have only been here *one* day, I really think I have *not* done so *badly*, all things considered!;

> [italicised inscriptions]
> *not* done so *badly*; the *earliest possible* moment; *how* things are *going*; only been here *one* day

Phase 2 fills Whimsey in on Climpson's reactions to her trip, which are mainly negative (although she is careful to thank Whimsey for trying to make her journey more comfortable by insisting she go first-class). The italicised *Preston* illustrates the power of Sayers' formatting to provoke an attitudinal reading for experiential meanings we might otherwise pass over as non-evaluative. Note however that it requires some degree of specialised knowledge to know just how Preston is being evaluated, not that this would be a problem for Whimsey who is being constructed by Climpson as 'in the know' – as someone who will know what she means about Preston and share her opinion.

'a dreary journey'

My train got in quite late on Monday night, after a *most dreary* journey, with a *lugubrious* wait at *Preston*, though thanks to your kindness in insisting that I should travel *First-class*, I was not really at all tired! Nobody can realise what a *great* difference these extra comforts make, especially when one is getting on in years, and after the *uncomfortable* travelling which I had to endure in my days of poverty, I feel that I am living in almost *sinful* luxury! The carriage was *well* heated – indeed, *too much so* and I should have liked the window down, but that there was a *very fat* business man, *muffled* to the eyes in *coats* and *woolly waistcoats* who *strongly* objected to fresh air! Men are such HOT-HOUSE PLANTS nowadays, are they not, quite unlike my dear father, who would never permit a *fire* in the house *before* November the 1st, or after March 31st even though the thermometer was at *freezing-point* !

[italicised inscriptions]

a *most dreary* journey; a *lugubrious* wait; travel *First-class*; the *uncomfortable* travelling; almost *sinful* luxury; *well* heated; indeed, *too much so* [heated]

[italicised invocations]

Preston; a *great* difference [travelling first class]; a *very fat* business man; *muffled* to the eyes in *coats* and *woolly waistcoats*; *strongly* objected; never permit a *fire* in the house *before* November the 1st; even though the thermometer was at *freezing-point*.

[small caps (lexical metaphor)]

Men are such HOT-HOUSE PLANTS nowadays

Phase 3 recounts the ease with which Climpson found lodging late at night, a welcome change from the decorum of Victorian times.

'better times'

I had no difficulty in getting a comfortable room at the Station Hotel, *late* as it was. In the *old* days, an *unmarried woman arriving alone at midnight with a suitcase* would hardly have been considered *respectable* – what a wonderful difference one finds today! I am *grateful* to have lived to see such changes, because whatever old-fashioned people may say about the greater *decorum* and *modesty* of women on Queen Victoria's time, those who can remember the old conditions know how *difficult* and *humiliating* they were!

[italicised inscriptions]

would hardly have been considered *respectable*; I am *grateful*; the greater *decorum* and *modesty* of women on Queen Victoria's time; how *difficult* and *humiliating* [the old conditions]; *late* as it was; the *old* days; an *unmarried woman arriving alone at midnight with a suitcase*

In Phase 4 Climpson moves to longer term lodging, suitable for an unmarried woman and advantageous to her fact finding mission.

'suitable lodging'

Yesterday morning, of course, my *first* object was to find a *suitable boarding-house*, in accordance with your instructions, and I was *fortunate* enough to hit upon this house at the *second* attempt. It is very well run and *refined*, and there are three *elderly ladies* who are *permanent* boarders here, and are *well up* in all the GOSSIP of the town, so that nothing could be more *advantageous* for our purpose! ...

[italicised inscriptions]

a suitable *boarding-house*; I was *fortunate* enough; very well run and *refined*; nothing could be more *advantageous*

[italicised invocations]

my *first* object; the *second* attempt; three *elderly ladies*; *permanent* boarders; *well up* in all the GOSSIP of the town

[small caps]

all the GOSSIP of the town

Phase 5 brings us to the object of Climpson's inquiries, the *house* (which like Preston above is formatted for evaluation) – and what she has learned of possible relevance to the case at hand. In this connection Sayers italicises several pieces of pertinent information, only one phrase of which is intensified (***all** alone*):

the *name* of Mrs. Wrayburn's *nurse-companion*, about *sixty* years old, and she lives *all alone* in the house with Mrs. Wrayburn, except for the *servants*, and a *housekeeper*, Nobody in this house seems to *know* her *personally*, in *nurse's uniform*, to *recognise* her

These are of course the kind of details on which Whimsey depends to solve his cases and for which he values Climpson's services.

'pertinent information'

That gave me quite a *good* opportunity to ask about the *house* !! Such a *beautiful* old place, I said, and did anybody live there? (*Of course* I did not blurt this out *all at once* – I waited till they had told me of the many *quaint spots* in the district that would interest an artist!) Mrs. Pegler, a very *stout*, FUSSY old lady, with a LONG TONGUE (!) was able to tell me *all* about it. My dear Lord Peter, what I do *not* know now about the *abandoned wickedness* of Mrs. Wrayburn's early life is really NOT WORTH KNOWING!! But what was *more to the point* is that she told me the *name* of Mrs. Wrayburn's *nurse-companion*. She is a MISS BOOTH, a retired nurse, about *sixty* years old, and she lives *all alone* in the house with Mrs. Wrayburn, except for the *servants*, and a *housekeeper*. When I heard that Mrs. Wrayburn was so *old*, and *paralysed* and *frail*, I said was it not very *dangerous* that Miss Booth should be the only attendant, but Mrs. Pegler said the housekeeper was a *most trustworthy* woman who had been with Mrs. Wrayburn for many years, and was *quite* capable of looking after her any time when Miss Booth was out. So it appears that Miss Booth does go out sometimes! Nobody in this house seems to *know* her *personally*, but they say she is often to be seen in the town in *nurse's uniform*. I managed to extract quite a good description of her, so if I should happen to meet her, I daresay I shall be *smart* enough to *recognise* her! ...

[italicised inscriptions]

a *good* opportunity; a *beautiful* old place; the many quaint spots; *not* know now about the *abandoned wickedness* of Mrs. Wrayburn's early life; what was *more to the point*; so *old*, and *paralysed* and *frail*; not very *dangerous*; a *most trustworthy* woman; *quite* capable; I shall be *smart* enough to *recognise* her

[italicised invocations]

the *house*; *Of course* I did not blurt this out *all at once*; *all* about it; the *name* of Mrs. Wrayburn's *nurse-companion*; about *sixty* years old; and she lives *all alone* in the house with Mrs. Wrayburn; except for the *servants*; and a *housekeeper*; Nobody in this house seems to *know* her *personally*; in *nurse's uniform*; to *recognise* her

[small caps]

a very *stout*, FUSSY old lady, with a LONG TONGUE (!); is really NOT WORTH KNOWING!!; She is a MISS BOOTH

The letter concludes with Phase 6, resuming the urgency prosody with which it began.

'urgency'
I will let you know as *soon* as I get the *least bit* more information.

Overall the text develops attitudinally, negotiating a complex of personal and professional understandings between Climpson and Whimsey as it unfolds. The urgency of Phases 1 and 6 tunes us in to the professional zeal with which Climpson enacts an unusual job for a woman (early on in the twentieth century). Phases 2 and 3 negotiate a more personal relationship, as Climpson shares her attitudes to changing times – her ability to travel first-class (thanks to Whimsey), and her new-found independence in post-Victorian times. In Phases 4 and 5 she is on the case as it were, following Whimsey's instructions and functioning as his eyes and ears in contexts he could not engage with quite so auspiciously as a man.

Phase 1	urgency	'professional zeal'
Phase 2	a dreary journey	'personal – dependence'
Phase 3	better times	'personal – independence'
Phase 4	suitable lodging	'professional competence'
Phase 5	pertinent information	'professional acuity'
Phase 6	urgency	'professional zeal'

Prosodically then the text functions to construe the interpersonal relationship between Climpson and Whimsey. Ideational meanings are selected which enable this telos, as Sayers' formatting makes explicit – alongside their role in pushing the plot of the mystery along.

We won't attempt an item by item reading of **attitude** in Sayers' text here, leaving it to readers to try their hand at materialising the prosodies reviewed above in the attitudinal lexis of each phase. Of note in passing is the near absence of inscribed **affect** in italics (just *I am grateful*) in a text that is otherwise so packed with feeling. Of the remaining italicised inscriptions, **appreciations** (mainly of the journey and housing) outnumber **judgements** (all concerning women – Climpson, Wrayburn and Pegler):

appreciation
   a *most dreary* journey; a *lugubrious* wait; travel *First-class*; the *uncomfortable* travelling; *well* heated; indeed, *too much so* [heated]; how *difficult* and *humiliating* [the old Victorian conditions]; a *suitable boarding-house*; very well run

90　*The Language of Evaluation*

and *refined* [boarding-house]; nothing could be more *advantageous* [than the boarding-house]; a *good* opportunity; a *beautiful* old place; the many *quaint spots* what was *more to the point;* I said was it not very *dangerous* [that Miss Booth should be the only attendant]

judgement

not done so *badly;* almost *sinful* luxury; would hardly have been considered *respectable;* the greater *decorum* and *modesty* of women on Queen Victoria's time; I was *fortunate* enough; *not* know now about the *abandoned wickedness* of Mrs. Wrayburn's early life; so *old,* and *paralysed* and *frail;* a *most trustworthy* woman; *quite* capable; *I shall be smart enough to recognise her*

This, then, concludes our overview of the resources of **affect**, **judgement** and **appreciation**. In the next chapter we explore the meanings by which the authorial voice is positioned with respect to these attitudinal assessments.

Notes

1. Including relational agnates such as *I'm pleased that* …, *It's pleasing that* … .
2. However, as Suzanne Eggins has often demonstrated for us, laughter is usually provoked by wrinkles in an interaction, not happiness; in the following example provided to us by Lynn Mortensen, the laughter has nothing to do with good cheer: '… even Dr Broe told me when I left, left Lidcombe, anytime you want me, he said, you can contact me; so it's always nice to know I've got a problem there's something wrong with me … I can always go and a see him so … I don't think there'd be much chance of doing that these days (**laugh**) he could be anywhere, anywhere in the world …'.
3. In general, throughout this monograph, Jim and Peter have attempted to analyse texts compliantly as male, middle-aged, middle-class, anglo/celtic, able-bodied readers wherever texts naturalise them to do so.
4. Jim originally read *poor* as affectual sympathy; but the co-text in fact naturalises an experiential reading (people too poor to afford residential property as a result of the new zoning law).
5. We need to keep in mind of course that it is the speaker or writer who tells us what someone else feels, and so continues to function as an 'ultimate' source of appraisal.
6. Australians opposed to Prime Minister John Howard's policies around the turn of the millennium wore protest T-shirts inscribed with 'Not Happy John', engaging with him through grammatical negation (*I'm not happy with your policies* …); note that an inscription 'Unhappy John', with morphological negation, would not have had the same challenging effect.
7. We've used the symbol '∞' to indicate that Partridge is appreciating what he'd like Quoyle's lead to be, not what it is.

8. Treated as inscription since newsworthiness is a positive attribute of certain information in journalism.
9. Collins Cobuild defines *bellow* as 'shout **angrily** in a loud, deep voice', so we've included it as an inscription here.
10. Experience tells him that it's fathers who keep mothers in bed while children cry themselves to sleep, not the other way round.
11. Jim's resistant reading is of course coloured by his own experience of co-parenting; for differently positioned social subjects, complementary readings will be found.

3
Engagement and Graduation: Alignment, Solidarity and the Construed Reader

3.1 Introduction: a dialogic perspective

This chapter is concerned with the linguistic resources by which speakers/writers adopt a stance towards to the value positions being referenced by the text and with respect to those they address. The chapter provides a framework for characterising the different possibilities for this stance-taking which are made available by the language, for investigating the rhetorical effects associated with these various positionings, and for exploring what is at stake when one stance is chosen over another. Our approach locates us in a tradition in which all utterances are seen as in some way stanced or attitudinal. Thus we share with Stubbs the view that 'whenever speakers (or writers) say anything, they encode their point of view towards it' (Stubbs 1996: 197). More specifically, our approach is informed by Bakhtin's/Voloshinov's now widely influential notions of dialogism and heteroglossia under which all verbal communication, whether written or spoken, is 'dialogic' in that to speak or write is always to reveal the influence of, refer to, or to take up in some way, what has been said/written before, and simultaneously to anticipate the responses of actual, potential or imagined readers/listeners. As Voloshinov states,

> The actual reality of language-speech is not the abstract system of linguistic forms, not the isolated monologic utterance, and not the psychological act of its implementation, but the social event of verbal interaction implemented in an utterance or utterances.
> Thus, verbal interaction is the basic reality of language.
> Dialogue ... can also be understood in a broader sense, meaning not only direct, face-to-face, vocalised verbal communication between

persons, but also verbal communication of any type whatsoever. A book, i.e. a verbal performance in print, is also an element of verbal communication. ... [it] inevitably orients itself with respect to previous performances in the same sphere .... Thus the printed verbal performance engages, as it were, in ideological colloquy of a large scale: it responds to something, affirms something, anticipates possible responses and objections, seeks support, and so on. [Voloshinov 1995: 139]

Similarly, Bakhtin observes that all utterances exist

... against a backdrop of other concrete utterances on the same theme, a background made up of contradictory opinions, points of view and value judgements ... pregnant with responses and objections. [Bakhtin 1981: 281].

This dialogistic perspective leads us to attend to the nature of the relationship which the speaker/writer is presented as entering into with 'prior utterances in the same sphere' – with those other speakers who have previously taken a stand with respect to the issue under consideration, especially when, in so speaking, they have established some socially significant community of shared belief or value. Thus we are interested in the degree to which speakers/writers acknowledge these prior speakers and in the ways in which they engage with them. We are interested in whether they present themselves as standing with, as standing against, as undecided, or as neutral with respect to these other speakers and their value positions. At the same time, the dialogistic perspective leads us to attend to the anticipatory aspect of the text – to the signals speakers/writers provide as to how they expect those they address to respond to the current proposition and the value position it advances. Thus we are interested in whether the value position is presented as one which can be taken for granted for this particular audience, as one which is in some way novel, problematic or contentious, or as one which is likely to be questioned, resisted or rejected.

The framework we outline, then, is directed towards providing a systematic account of how such positionings are achieved linguistically. It provides the means to characterise a speaker/writer's interpersonal style and their rhetorical strategies according to what sort of heteroglossic backdrop of other voices and alternative viewpoints they construct for their text and according to the way in which they engage with that backdrop.

The framework's orientation is towards meanings in context and towards rhetorical effects, rather than towards grammatical forms. As a consequence, it brings together a lexically and grammatically diverse selection of locutions on the basis that they all operate to locate the writer/speaker with respect to the value positions being referenced in the text and with respect to, in Bakhtin's terms, the backdrop of alternative opinions, points of view and value judgements against which all texts operate. As already indicated in the opening chapter, this selection includes wordings which have traditionally been treated under such headings as modality, polarity, evidentiality, intensification, attribution, concession, and consequentiality.[1] The framework groups together under the heading of 'engagement' all those locutions which provide the means for the authorial voice to position itself with respect to, and hence to 'engage' with, the other voices and alternative positions construed as being in play in the current communicative context. In addition, it includes meanings which in the literature have been given such labels as 'hedges', 'downtoners', 'boosters' and 'intensifiers'[2] – for example, *somewhat, slightly, rather, very, entirely* and *sort of/kind of, true/pure* (as in *I'm kind of upset by what you said.* and *He's a true friend.*) These locutions are grouped together under the heading of 'graduation' on the basis that they are mechanisms by which speakers/writers 'graduate' either the force of the utterance or the focus of the categorisation by which semantic values are identified. This chapter explores how locutions in this second set (**graduations**) also play a dialogistic role in that they enable speakers/writers to present themselves as more strongly aligned or less strongly aligned with the value position being advanced by the text and thereby to locate themselves with respect to the communities of shared value and belief associated with those positions. We also demonstrate the ways in which categorical or bare assertions (eg *the banks are being greedy*) are just as intersubjectively loaded and hence 'stanced' as utterances including more overt markers of point of view or attitude. Our account, then, of these various sets of locutions amounts to a reanalysis, from this Bakhtinian, dialogistic perspective, of meanings and structures which have largely only been considered from the perspective of theories of language which view the individual, psychological, and self-expressive function of language as primary and as fundamental, and which, in many cases, see meaning as ultimately a matter of 'truth conditions' and not of social relationships.

In operating with such lexically and grammatically diverse groupings, we follow others who have had a similar semantic or rhetorical orientation. These include, for example, Fuller 1998, Martin 1997 whose category of 'engagement' (as a cover-all term for resources of intersubjective positioning) we have taken over and develop, and Stubbs who proposes that the category of 'modality' should be extended well beyond the modal verbs to include all wordings and formulations by which speakers/writers modulate their attachment to/detachment from the proposition (Stubbs 1996: Chapter 8).

3.2 Value position, alignment and the putative reader

The framework which we provide of these resources of intersubjective positioning is directed towards modelling the key dialogistic effects associated with these meanings. First, we are concerned with the role they play in meaning making processes by which the speaker/writer negotiates relationships of alignment/disalignment vis-à-vis the various value positions referenced by the text and hence vis-à-vis the socially-constituted communities of shared attitude and belief associated with those positions. By 'alignment/disalignment', we refer to agreement/disagreement with respect to both attitudinal assessments and to beliefs or assumptions about the nature of the world, its past history, and the way it ought to be. We note, in this regard, that when speakers/writers announce their own attitudinal positions they not only self-expressively 'speak their own mind', but simultaneously invite others to endorse and to share with them the feelings, tastes or normative assessments they are announcing. Thus declarations of attitude are dialogically directed towards aligning the addressee into a community of shared value and belief.

Secondly, we are concerned with this negotiation of alignment/disalignment as it applies to the relationship which the text construes as holding between speaker/writer and the text's putative addressee. In exploring this aspect of intersubjective meaning we, of necessity, also attend to the ways in which, by the use of various indicators, singly-constructed, mass communicative texts of the type we are considering[3] construct for themselves an 'envisaged', 'imagined' or 'ideal' reader, since it is with this putative addressee that the speaker/writer is presented as more or less aligned/disaligned.[4] Thus one of our central concerns is with the ways in which these resources act to 'write the reader into the text' by presenting the speaker/writer as, for example, taking it for granted that the addressee shares with them a particular viewpoint, or as anticipating that a given proposition will be problematic (or unproblematic) for the putative reader, or as assuming that the reader may need to be won over to a particular viewpoint, and so on.

In making the issue of alignment/disalignment central to our modelling of these resources we seek to extend our understanding of how the relationship typically termed 'solidarity' is construed in texts of this type. We should stress, however, that we are not proposing that solidarity is simply a matter of degree of ideational and/or attitudinal agreement. As many have observed before us, it is always available to the speaker/writer to bid to maintain solidarity with those with whom they disagree by indicating that they recognise this diversity of viewpoints as valid and that they are prepared to engage with those who hold to a different position. Thus solidarity can turn, not on questions of agreement/disagreement, but on tolerance for alternative viewpoints, and the communality into which the writer/speaker aligns the reader can be one in which diversity of viewpoint is recognised as natural and legitimate.

By way of a brief introductory illustration of what is at stake here interpersonally, we consider the following short extract taken from a radio interview with the then Australian Prime Minister, John Howard. The host of a current affairs program is asking Mr Howard how he views the behaviour of Australian banks in raising their fees and charges soon after they had reported earning record profits.

[3.1] – *interviewer question*
There is an argument, though, is there, the banks have been a bit greedy. I mean, their profits are high and good on them, they're entitled to have high profits, but at the same time the fees are bordering on the unreasonable now.

Here there are two value positions being advanced – (1) a view which is positively disposed towards the fact that banks make high profits and (2) a view which is negatively disposed to one particular instance of high profit taking, that resulting from this recent increase in fees. In advancing such viewpoints, the interviewer, of course, connects with well-established, ideologically-indexed communities of shared value and belief about what is and isn't appropriate and moral behaviour for banks. In his manner of formulating the proposition that, in general terms, it is right and proper for banks to make high profits, the speaker anticipates no objections to, or questioning of, such a viewpoint and therefore presents both himself and the envisaged listener as unproblematically aligned into this particular value position. In contrast, there are overt signals of anticipation that the negative view of this recent profit-making exercise is likely to be problematic and may well face objections from the envisaged listener. These take the form of devices by which the proposition that the banks are acting immorally is construed as currently subject to contestation and debate (*there is an argument though, is there ...*) and one which the speaker hesitates to align with categorically (ie ... *have been a bit greedy* rather than simply *have been greedy*, and ... *are bordering on the unreasonable* rather than simply *are unreasonable*). Thus, in this case, there is no clear-cut aligning of either the speaker or the addressee into an anti-bank community of shared value, even while the anti-bank viewpoint is being advanced. Simultaneously the speaker presents himself as potentially in solidarity with both those who hold this negative view of the banks and those who would reject it, on the basis that he recognises the validity of both viewpoints.

3.3 The resources of intersubjective stance: an overview of engagement

We turn now to considering the resources of dialogistic positioning in more detail. In this section we consider those meanings which we assign to the category of **engagement**, turning to the resources of **graduation** in section 3.16 and following sections later in the chapter. In sections devoted to individual sub-types of **engagement** and **graduation** we first identify the relevant locutions, explore their dialogistic functionality and then, where appropriate, consider potential effects with respect to putative audience construal, alignment and solidarity, as discussed above.

As indicated, we include within the category of **engagement** those meanings which in various ways construe for the text a heteroglossic backdrop of prior utterances, alternative viewpoints and anticipated responses. We begin by outlining the taxonomy within which we locate the various **engagement** meanings. The taxonomy is directed towards identifying the particular dialogistic positioning associated with given meanings and towards describing what is at stake when one meanings rather than another is employed.

Disclaim: the textual voice positions itself as at odds with, or rejecting, some contrary position:

- (deny) negation (*You don't need to give up potatoes to lose weight.*)
- (counter) concession/counter expectation (*Although he ate potatoes most days he still lost weight.*)

98 The Language of Evaluation

Proclaim: by representing the proposition as highly warrantable (compelling, valid, plausible, well-founded, generally agreed, reliable, etc.), the textual voice sets itself against, suppresses or rules out alternative positions:

- (concur) *naturally ..., of course ..., obviously ..., admittedly ...* etc.; some types of 'rhetorical' or 'leading' question
- (pronounce) *I contend ..., the truth of the matter is ..., there can be no doubt that ...* etc.
- (endorse) *X has demonstrated that ...; As X has shown ...* etc.

Entertain: by explicitly presenting the proposition as grounded in its own contingent, individual subjectivity, the authorial voice represents the proposition as but one of a range of possible positions – it thereby **entertains** or invokes these dialogic alternatives:

- *it seems, the evidence suggests, apparently, I hear*
- *perhaps, probably, maybe, it's possible, in my view, I suspect that, I believe that, probably, it's almost certain that ..., may/will/must*; some types of 'rhetorical' or 'expository' question

Attribute: by representing proposition as grounded in the subjectivity of an external voice, the textual voice represents the proposition as but one of a range of possible positions – it thereby entertains or invokes these dialogic alternatives:

- (acknowledge) *X said.., X believes ..., according to X, in X's view*
- (distance) *X claims that, it's rumoured that*

The taxonomy of options under **engagement** is represented via the system network provided at the end of this section (see Figure 3.4 on p. 134).

3.4 Engagement and the dialogistic status of bare assertions

Before we attend to the specifics of this taxonomy it is necessary to outline some broader parameters by which intersubjective positioning may vary. One of these issues was mentioned briefly in the previous section – the question of the status of the 'bare' or categorical assertion within a framework concerned with the resources of dialogistic positioning.

The barely asserted proposition has often, of course, been characterised as intersubjectively neutral, objective or even 'factual'. Lyons, for example, sets up a contrast between the supposed 'objectivity' of the bare assertion, which he terms 'factive', and the 'subjectivity' of the modalised utterance, which he terms 'non-factive' (Lyons 1977: 794). But such a characterisation does not take into the account the dialogistic functionality of such formulations, attending only to the issue of truth conditions. Once we hold the view that all verbal communication occurs against a heteroglossic backdrop of other voices and alternative viewpoints a rather different picture emerges.

The various overtly dialogistic resources we have just outlined all recognise, and engage with, that dialogistic background in some way. Each construes a particular arrangement of other voices and/or alternative viewpoints. Thus, as discussed in the earlier section, the formulation *There is an argument though, is there, the banks have been a bit greedy* construes a heteroglossic environment populated by different, competing views of whether the banks' behaviour is appropriate or not. The view that they have been 'greedy' is represented as but one view among a range of possible views. Following Bakhtin, we give the label 'heteroglossic' to all locutions which function in this way to recognise that the text's communicative backdrop is a diverse one.

Bare assertions obviously contrast with these heteroglossic options in not overtly referencing other voices or recognising alternative positions. As a consequence, the communicative context is construed as single voiced or, in Bakhtin's terms, 'monoglossic' and 'undialogised', at least for the brief textual moment taken up by the utterance. By this, the speaker/writer presents the current proposition as one which has no dialogistic alternatives which need to be recognised, or engaged with, in the current communicative context – as dialogistically inert and hence capable of being declared categorically. Such a monoglossic style is demonstrated by the following extract,

> Two years on, the British government has betrayed the most fundamental responsibility that any government assumes – the duty to protect the rule of law.
> It is a collusion in an international experiment in inhumanity, which is being repeated and expanded around the world.

In broad terms, then, we can categorise utterances accordingly to this two-way distinction, classifying them as 'monoglossic' when they make no reference to other voices and viewpoints and as 'heteroglossic' when

100 *The Language of Evaluation*

Table 3.1 The monoglossic and the heteroglossic

Monoglossic (no recognition of dialogistic alternatives)	Heteroglossic (recognition of dialogistic alternatives)
The banks have been greedy.	There is the argument though that the banks have been greedy.
	In my view the banks have been greedy.
	Callers to talkback radio see the banks as being greedy.
	The chairman of the consumers association has stated that the banks are being greedy.
	There can be no denying the banks have been greedy.
	Everyone knows the banks are greedy.
	The banks haven't been greedy.
	etc.

they do invoke or allow for dialogistic alternatives. See, for example, Table 3.1.

It must be acknowledged, however, that the precise effects as to dialogistic positioning associated with the use of bare assertions (monoglossing) are complex. There is, in fact, a set of potential effects where the precise nature of positioning will be determined by a range of factors. These include the communicative objectives being pursued by the text as a whole (for example, whether it argues, explains, narrates, recounts, records, etc.), the proposition's role with respect to these communicative objectives, and the nature of the proposition itself (for example, the degree to which it foregrounds evaluative versus experiential/ informational meanings).

One key distinction within monoglossic assertions turns on whether the disposition of the text is such that the proposition is presented as taken-for-granted or whether, alternatively, it is presented as currently at issue or up for discussion. There are various textual arrangements by which taken-for-grantedness can be construed. One is via constructions which fall within the category often termed 'presupposition' (see, for example, Kempson 1975). This taken-for-grantedness is exemplified in the following extract.

[3.2] After nine years of the government's **betrayal** of the promised progressive agenda, Canadians have a gut feeling that their country is slipping away

Engagement and Graduation 101

from them. [Canadian Hansard, http://www.parl.gc.ca/ 37/2/parlbus/chambus/house/debates/002_2002-10-01/han002_ 1215-E.htm]

Here the proposition that the government has betrayed its progressive agenda is construed as something which is no longer at issue, which is not up for discussion and which accordingly can be treated as a 'given'. Taken-for-grantedness thus has the strongly ideological effect of construing for the text a putative addressee who shares this value position with the writer/speaker and for whom the proposition is, likewise, not at issue.

Alternatively, the disposition of the text may be such that the categorical, monoglossically asserted proposition is presented as very much in the spotlight – as very much a focal point for discussion and argumentation. Such a disposition is demonstrated in the following extract taken from an editorial in *The Sun* newspaper concerned with the case of Maxine Carr, the partner of Ian Huntley who notoriously murdered two British schoolgirls in 2003. The editorial was written after it was announced that, having served a prison term for obstructing police inquiries, Maxine Carr was to be given a new identity and her anonymity was to be protected by law. This followed a campaign of hatred towards the woman by the tabloid press and after she had received numerous death threats while in jail.

[3.3] THE cloak of secrecy thrown around Maxine Carr sets a dangerous legal precedent.
Now every supposedly 'notorious' criminal will demand a new life shielded from public scrutiny once they leave jail.
Why does Carr gets this unique protection, which is not justified by any facts laid before the court?
She is just a common criminal who lied to give her murdering boyfriend an alibi.
What if she gets a job at a school?
What if she chooses to live with another Svengali-like criminal?
But the media cannot tell you anything about Carr from now on.
[*The Sun*, leading article, 15/5/04]

Here, even while the proposition that this legal decision 'sets a dangerous legal precedent' is monoglossically declared, it is not taken-for-granted. The fact that the writer then goes on to supply a series of arguments in support of the value position construes it as very much at issue and the focus of a debate. As a consequence, the texts construes a reader who does not necessarily share the writer's views on Maxine Carr's right to anonymity – who is perhaps undecided and looking for further guidance, or who, while already leaning in the writer's direction, is still interested in further argumentation. The text might even be read as anticipating that the reader may hold to a diametrically opposed position, and hence will need to be won over, although this reading is less plausible given the lack of indicators elsewhere in the text that the writer anticipates objections or resistance by the reader to the arguments being advanced.

3.5 Heteroglossia: dialogic contraction and expansion

We turn now to overtly dialogistic locutions and to the different orientations to heteroglossic diversity which they indicate. Before we set out a more detailed account of individual options, we observe that these heteroglossic resources can be divided into two broad categories according to whether they are 'dialogically expansive' or 'dialogically contractive' in their intersubjective functionality. The distinction turns on the degree to which an utterance, by dint of one or more of these locutions, actively makes allowances for dialogically alternative positions and voices (**dialogic expansion**), or alternatively, acts to challenge, fend off or restrict the scope of such (**dialogic contraction**).

Since this is a distinction not elsewhere identified in the literature we begin by briefly demonstrating it. Consider the following two contrastive text extracts by way of exemplification.

[3.4] (*dialogic contraction*)
Follain punctures the romantic myth that the mafia started as Robin Hood-style groups of men protecting the poor. He **shows** that the mafia began in the 19th century as armed bands protecting the interests of the absentee landlords who owned most of Sicily. He also **demonstrates** how the mafia has forged links with Italy's ruling Christian Democrat party since the war. [Cobuild Bank of English]

[3.5] (*dialogic expansion*)
Tickner said regardless of the result, the royal commission was a waste of money and he would proceed with a separate inquiry into the issue headed by Justice Jane Matthews. His attack came as the Aboriginal women involved in the case demanded a female minister examine the religious beliefs they **claim**

are inherent in their fight against a bridge to the island near Goolwa in South Australia. [Cobuild Bank of English]

Both extracts are obviously dialogistic in that they explicitly reference the utterances and viewpoints of external voices. This follows from the fact that they employ the grammar of reported speech. But there is more at stake here than the simple multiplying of voices. The first extract [3.4], exemplifies a formulation in which a special type of reporting verb has been used (*show, demonstrate*) – one which adopts a particular stance towards the attributed proposition, holding it to be true. (Reporting verbs of this type have been widely discussed in the literature in the context of notions of 'factivity' – see for example, Kiparsky & Kiparsky 1970 – and in the literature on attribution and direct and indirect speech. See, for example, Hunston 2000 or Caldas-Coulthard 1994). By such 'endorsing' formulations, the authorial voice presents the proposition as 'true' or 'valid' and thereby aligns itself with the external voice which has been introduced as the source of that proposition. By indicating in this way a heightened investment by the author and by co-opting some authoritative second party to the current rhetorical cause, such formulations set themselves against, or at least fend off, actual or potential contrary positions. Thus in the above instance, *show* and *demonstrate* are employed as the textual voice sets itself against the discredited alternative view of the Mafia as *Robin Hood types*. Such wordings, then, can be construed as **dialogically contractive** – they close down the space for dialogic alternatives.

The second text [3.5], has the opposite effect. Here the textual voice distances itself from the proposition framed by *claim*, representing it as, if not doubtful, then as still open to question. The effect is to invite or at least entertain dialogic alternatives and thereby to lower the interpersonal cost for any who would advance such an alternative. Accordingly, such **distancing** formulations can be seen as **dialogically expansive**, as opening up the dialogic space for alternative positions.

It must be stressed that it is not proposed that the verb *to claim* necessarily has this function in all cases. The rhetorical potential of such a word, for example, may vary systematically under the influence of different co-textual conditions, and across registers, genres and discourse domains. Our concern is, in fact, not specifically with *to claim* as a lexeme but with the dialogistic positioning exemplified in the above text extract – the dialogistic position which we have labelled **distancing**.

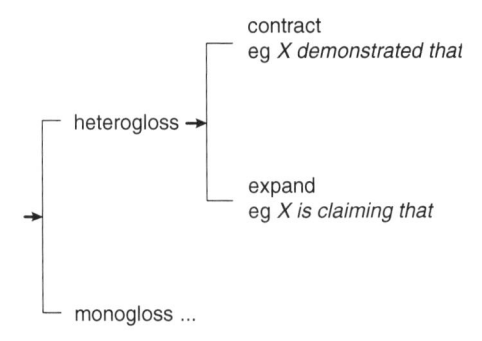

```
                            contract
                            eg X demonstrated that
             heterogloss →
                            expand
                            eg X is claiming that

             monogloss ...
```

Figure 3.1 Engagement: contract and expand

Whether or not all uses of *claim* are **distancing** in this way is an open question. The same point applies in all the exemplifications of dialogistic resources which follow.

In this distinction, then, between modes of **attribution** which **endorse** the proposition in this way and those which **distance** the authorial voice from the proposition, we see this fundamental contrast between dialogic **contraction** and **expansion**.

The **engagement** system as outlined to this point is set out in Figure 3.1.

3.6 Entertain: the dialogistic expansiveness of modality and evidentiality

We turn now to considering individual options within the **engagement** system in more detail. We will begin by exploring formulations which, are in our terms, **dialogically expansive**.

We begin with what we term 'entertain' – those wordings by which the authorial voice indicates that its position is but one of a number of possible positions and thereby, to greater or lesser degrees, makes dialogic space for those possibilities. The authorial voice **entertains** those dialogic alternatives. This is a semantic domain which has traditionally be covered in the literature under the headings of 'epistemic modality' (eg Palmer 1986 or Coates 1983) and 'evidentiality' (eg Chafe & Nichols 1986). Within the systemics tradition it is dealt with under the heading of 'modals of probability', 'reality phase' and certain types of 'interpersonal metaphor' (see Chapter 1, section 1.2.2 and Halliday 1994). It encompasses meanings by which speaker/writer makes assessments of likelihood via modal auxiliaries (*may, might, could, must*, etc.) via modal adjuncts (*perhaps, probably, definitely*, etc.), via modal attributes (*it's possible that ..., it's likely that ...* etc.), via circumstances of the *in my view* type, and via certain mental verb/attribute projections (*I suspect that ..., I think, I believe, I'm convinced that, I doubt*, etc.). In including this final subset of mental verb projections we follow Halliday who has argued convincingly that such structures are 'modal' rather than experiential or informational in their communicative functionality.[5] This view is shared by Palmer who, for example, holds that formulations such as *I think* act to indicate 'epistemic judgement' (Palmer 1986: 168). This sub-category of **entertain** also includes evidence/appearance-based postulations (*it seems, it appears, apparently, the research suggests ...*) and certain types of 'rhetorical' or 'expository' questions (those which don't assume a specific response but are employed to raise the possibility that some proposition holds).[6]

When viewed dialogistically (rather than from the perspective of a truth-functional semantics, as is often the case), such locutions are seen actively to construe a heteroglossic backdrop for the text by overtly grounding the proposition in the contingent, individual subjectivity of the speaker/writer and thereby recognising that the proposition is but one among a number of propositions available in the current communicative context. Consider by way of illustration, the use of the modal adjunct *probably* in the following extract:

[3.6] It was not a great speech. It reads like a sixth-form essay answering the question: 'Imagine you ruled the world. What would you do?' It was not the answer of a statesman, not of a realist. In fact it was **probably** the most immature, irresponsible, disgraceful and misleading address ever given by a British Prime Minister. It was all bluster, all bluff. [*Sunday Express*, 7/10/01]

More traditional accounts of modality might have interpreted such a locution as indicating 'lack of commitment to the truth value' of the proposition (for example, Palmer 1986, Lyons 1977 or Coates 1983). But the dialogistic perspective shifts our focus so that such a concern with 'epistemic status' and 'reliability of knowledge' is seen to be not always and not necessarily the primary, determining communicative motive. In this extract, for example, 'informational reliability' is not at issue. The writer is interested in advancing an entirely subjective, entirely opinion-based negative assessment of the Prime Minister's address – namely that, not only was his speech *immature, disgraceful*, and so on, but that it was more so than other similarly deplorable political addresses. He employs *probably*, and hence stops short of categoricality, in order to mark the proposition as contentious and to signal recognition that there may well be some who will not precisely share the writer's views on this matter. Tellingly, the utterance is organised in such a way that the alternative positions which are being allowed for, or **entertained**, are not those which would reject the overall negativity of the writer's viewpoint, but rather those which might quibble about whether this was, in fact, the worst speech ever given by this prime minister or by other prime ministers. Thus the speaker makes space in the text's heteroglossic backdrop for those who share his negative view of the speech but may hold that this prime minister has made even worse ones, or that some other prime minister has given an even worse address. The authorial voice presents itself as invested in this proposition while at the same time acknowledging that the value position being advanced is contingent and hence but one of a number of potential dialogistic alternatives. In this, then, we see that the primary functionality of the modal is dialogistic. It acts to acknowledge a heteroglossic backdrop for the proposition by presenting it as potentially at odds with some dialogistic alternative.

Interestingly, this sense that the writer is highly invested in the proposition would have been substantially maintained even had low intensity modalising options been employed. Thus,

> In fact this was **possibly** the most immature, irresponsible, disgraceful and misleading address ever given by a British Prime Minister.

> In fact it **may** have been the most immature, irresponsible, disgraceful and misleading address ever given by a British Prime Minister.

This points to the role of the co-text in conditioning the meanings which are conveyed by such locutions. Here the assertiveness of the *in fact*, the use of the superlative *most* and the vigour of the negative evaluation all act to indicate a strong investment in the proposition by the writer which is not greatly moderated by the use of low-intensity modal forms such as *possibly* and *may*. (For further discussion of the variability of the meanings of such modals under co-textual conditioning, see Hunston in press.)

The fundamentally dialogistic functionality of such 'modalising' locutions is perhaps most transparently apparent in cases where a mental-verb projection is employed (what Halliday terms the explicitly subjective option for assessments of probability – Halliday 1994). For example,

[3.7] The sad aspect of all this is that by giving support to this invasion Blair will be destroying the UN and **I believe** will have betrayed the British people.

Here the maximally explicit grounding of the value position in the writer's own subjectivity acts to construe a heteroglossic backdrop by which speakers/writers can be strongly committed to a viewpoint while, nonetheless, being prepared to signal a recognition that other's may not share this value position.

In some contexts, of course, such formulations can convey a sense of uncertainty or lack of commitment to truth value on the part of the speaker/writer. We observe such a context in the following extracts:

[3.8] Many things (as the notes to this extremely well prepared catalogue show quite clearly) had an aristocratic provenance which showed that Gibbs has an acute sense of tradition and fine workmanship. The organ screen in the stables was **possibly** designed by Thomas Chippendale and came from the Earl of Harewood's sale at Harewood House, Yorkshire in 1988. But Chippendale is only half the story. A pair of Moroccan painted doors – **probably** 18th century – were evocative things in their own right and indicate the eclectic nature of this collection. [*Birmingham Post* 30/09/2000: 50]

[3.9] In modern times, humans have caused extinctions of individual species by destroying their environment or by overhunting. But before humankind came on the scene, mass extinctions **may** have been caused by major changes in sea level or disruptions in the food chain. [Bank of English]

In each of these cases it is available to the reader to interpret the modalising locutions as a sign by the writer that their knowledge of the matters under consideration is to some degree limited and therefore not sufficient to allow for a categorical formulation of the proposition (eg *The organ screen was designed by Thomas Chippendale / mass extinctions were caused by major changes in sea level*). This potential 'epistemic' effect is not at odds with the fundamentally dialogistic role of such locutions. In all of these instances the proposition is grounded in an explicit subjectivity and is thereby construed as but one position among a range of alternative positions. Dialogistic alternatives to the proposition are thereby 'entertained'. However, the 'epistemic' effect is a contingent one, dependent upon the presence of particular co-textual and contextual factors by which it becomes available for the reader/listener to interpret

108 *The Language of Evaluation*

such locutions as signs of a lack of certain knowledge on the part of the speaker/writer.

This dialogistic functionality of modals and related meanings has previously been noted by those analysts who have identified what is often termed the 'pragmatic' aspect of these locutions. Myers, for example, has observed that one purpose of such locutions, at least as they operate in academic discourse, is not to mark knowledge claims as uncertain, but rather to mark the claim as 'unacknowledged by the discourse community' (Myers 1989: 12). Similarly, Hyland argues that 'hedges' (which include low intensity modals) sometimes act to convey 'deference, modesty or respect' rather than to convey uncertainty (Hyland 2000: 88). More specifically, in their analyses of *I think*, Aijmer (1997) and Simon-Vandenbergen (2000) observe that the locution has a variable functionality according to whether, in their terms, it is employed with 'factual' propositions (eg ***I think*** *Mary teaches French*) or an 'opinion' (eg *Mr President, once again* ***I think*** *we are being denied as a parliament the opportunity to make our opinions known concerning the recommencement of whale hunting* (Simon-Vandenbergen 1998: 301). For them, while the 'factual' uses of *I think* are to be interpreted as pointing to some degree of tentativeness or uncertainty on the part of the speaker, the 'evaluative' uses, in contrast, have a 'deliberative' function, expressing authority. While we are reluctant to operate with a taxonomy which so abruptly separates 'fact' from 'opinion' in this way, we nevertheless share with these researchers the view that the 'meaning' of such locutions will vary systematically according to co-textual conditioning. And we would certainly want to allow that the epistemic effect (signalling uncertainty of knowledge) is typically in operation when the proposition foregrounds experiential/informational rather than evaluative/interpersonal meanings.

3.6.1 Entertain and writer–reader relationships

The primary functionality, then, of such modalising locutions is to make allowances for, and hence to make space for, alternative voices and value positions in the ongoing colloquy within which the text is located. They construe a heteroglossic backdrop for the text in which the particular point-of-view is actually or potentially in tension with dialogistic alternatives. By this, they project for the text an audience which is potentially divided over the issue at stake and hence one which may not universally share the value position being referenced. By recognising and thus, to greater and lesser degrees, dialogistically validating alternative viewpoints they thus provide for the possibility of solidarity with those who hold to alternative positions, at least to the extent that those who hold to contrary positions are recognised as potential participants in the on-going colloquy.

The degree to which values of entertain function in this way to signal authorial anticipation that the proposition may be problematic for the intended addressee will vary under certain co-textual conditionings. This functionality is most likely to be in operation where the value position is one which obviously relates to some ideologically-significant, established axiological formation (eg *The sad aspect of all this is that by giving support to this invasion Blair will be destroying the UN and I believe will have betrayed the British people*). The functionality is less likely to be in operation when the value position at issue is one which is not so obviously ideologically connected, when, perhaps, it can be seen as more 'private' than 'public'. Consider by way of example the following:

> [3.10] [Your correspondent] suggests that MPs 'should talk to and be advised by those who know best' [about the issue of euthanasia]. As a nurse with more than 50 years experience including 10 years caring for the terminally ill I feel it appropriate to respond.
> It has been my privilege to have cared for **possibly** several hundred terminally ill patients. [letter to the editor, *Bolton Evening News*, 16/02/04]

Here there is no immediately obvious connection between the question of how many patients the writer cared for and any axiological community with which the reader might be affiliated. Accordingly, the formulation is less likely to be interpreted as anticipating the possibility of some dissent over this viewpoint on the part of those addressed and is more likely to be interpreted as a sign by the writer that this is not meant to be taken as a precise figure and accordingly that she herself might have set the figure slightly higher or slightly lower.

3.6.2 Further values of entertain

To this point we have confined our discussion to modals of probability. As indicated above, the grammar of **entertain** is more diverse than this. It also includes 'evidentials'. For example:

> [3.11] One obvious failing in Britain is the gap between the skills the workforce offers and those employers want. That mismatch **seems** worse than it was ten years ago. [Bank of English – *Economist* sub-corpus]

110 *The Language of Evaluation*

> [3.12] One persistent idea has been that the two main moderate right-wing parties, the Rassemblement pour la Republique and the Union pour la Democratie Francaise, must get together if they are to have any chance of regaining power. But each time this has been tried, it comes up against the **apparently** irreconcilable rivalries of the three figures who have dominated the French right for the past 15 years – Jacques Chirac, Valery Giscard d'Estaing. [Bank of English – *Economist* sub-corpus]
>
> [3.13] His defensive behaviour **suggests** he feels ashamed and guilty that you've discovered his habit. [Bank of English – *Sun* sub-corpus]

In each of these cases, the proposition is construed as contingent and subjectively based as a consequence of being derived via a process of deduction or surmise on the part of the speaker/writer. To present a proposition as surmised is obviously to present it as but one proposition among a range of potential alternatives and thereby to open up dialogic space for any such alternatives.

The category of **entertain** also includes a particular type of 'pseudo' question which is frequently employed in singly-constructed, non-interactive texts to **entertain** rather than to assert some proposition. These may perhaps be termed 'rhetorical questions', although this term is often restricted to those 'pseudo' questions where the addressee is positioned to supply a particular answer (see, for example, Sadock 1974). In contrast, this type of question is open-ended and has been given the label 'expository question' by Goatly (2000). The following headline to a news report on British 'celebrity', Tara Palmer-Tomkinson exemplifies this option:

> [3.14]
> **Is Tara on a downhill spiral to her bad old ways?**
> A drunken night out for Britain's favourite IT girl has set alarm bells ringing [*Daily Express*, 19/10/04: 10]

Here an expository question is employed to put the proposition into play as one possible view of Ms Palmer-Tomkinson's behaviour.

3.6.3 Directives and the modality of permission/obligation

We also include within this category of **entertain** locutions concerned with permission and obligation, traditionally the category of 'deontic' modality (for example, *You **must** switch off the lights when you leave*.). Obviously we are concerned here with a fundamentally different type of dialogic relationship – relationships of control and compliance/

resistance rather than of the offering of information and viewpoints. Despite this fundamental difference, deontic modals still construe the communicative setting as heteroglossic and open up the dialogic space to alternatives. The contrast is between the imperative (*Turn out the lights before you leave*) and the modal formulation (*You must turn out the lights before you leave*). The imperative is monoglossic in that it neither references, nor allows for the possibility of, alternative actions. The modal, in contrast, explicitly grounds the demand in the subjectivity of the speaker – as an assessment by the speaker of obligation rather than as a command. The 'directive' is thus construed as contingent, as individually based and accordingly the speaker's role as a participant in a dialogic exchange is acknowledged.

3.7 Dialogistic expansion through the externalised proposition – attribution

Under the heading of 'attribution', we deal with those formulations which disassociate the proposition from the text's internal authorial voice by attributing it so some external source.[7] This is most typically achieved through the grammar of directly and indirectly reported speech and thought. We are concerned, therefore, with the framing of propositions by means of communicative process verbs (eg *Mr. Mandela said the Group of Eight nations have a duty to help battle the scourge of AIDS*), or verbs which reference mental processes such as *believe* and *suspect*, (eg *Dawkins believes that religion is not an adaptive evolutionary vestige, but in fact a cultural virus*). The category similarly includes formulations which involve nominalisations of these processes (eg *Indonesia rejects United Nations assertion that bird flu is spreading, Chomsky's belief that language is for individuals rather than groups*) and various adverbial adjuncts such as *according to* (eg *He now poses little threat to the world, according to Halliday*) and *in X's view*.

We notice in passing that in a few cases the same lexemes crop up in both this category and that of the previously discussed **entertain** – specifically mental process verbs such as *believe*, *suspect* and circumstantials such as *in X's view*. In context, however, the two categories are easy to distinguish in that **entertain** values present the internal voice of the speaker/writer as the source (eg *I believe, in my view*) while **attributing** values present some external voice (eg *many Australians believe, in Dawkin's view*).

112　*The Language of Evaluation*

This category also includes instances of **attribution** where no specific source is specified – formulations which are sometimes categorised as 'hearsay', for example,

> the government's serologist *reportedly* lied about his qualifications
>
> Williams retired in 1932, when he was 46. *It is said that* he lied about his age as he grew older ...

and the instance discussed previously,

> there is an argument that. ...

3.7.1　Attribute: acknowledge

Within **attribution** there are two sub-categories. The first of these we term 'acknowledge' – those locutions where there is no overt indication, at least via the choice of framer, as to where the authorial voice stands with respect to the proposition. This is the domain of reporting verbs such as *say, report, state, declare, announce, believe* and *think*. For example:

> [3.15] A bishop today describes the Church of England's established status as indefensible, in a pamphlet arguing that the church should lose its political ties to the state.
> The Rt Rev Colin Buchanan, Bishop of Woolwich, says: 'In this, as in so many other things, the Church of England prefers to live by fantasy rather than look coolly at the facts.' [*The Guardian*, 21/06/04]

In identifying certain **attributions** as instances of **acknowledge** we attend narrowly only to the semantics of the framing device (typically the reporting verb) – specifically whether or not it acts to disassociate the authorial voice from the current proposition. It may well be, of course, that there are indicators elsewhere in the text that the writer/speaker more globally supports or rejects the value position being advanced. This, however, is a separate issue which needs to be dealt with elsewhere in the analysis. We will discuss this issue further below when considering the consequences for addresser–addressee rapport of **attribution**.

Acknowledgements are obviously dialogic in that they associate the proposition being advanced with voices and/or positions which are external to that of the text itself and present the authorial voice as engaging interactively with those voices. In this way they overtly construe the communicative setting as heteroglossic. This aspect of **acknowledgement** has been widely attended to in the extensive literature on reported speech and citation, especially as it operates within academic discourse. But equally importantly, such formulations are dialogic for the same reasons that values of **entertain** are dialogic – they ground the viewpoint conveyed by the proposition in an explicit subjectivity thereby signalling that it is individual and contingent and therefore but one of a range of possible dialogic options. In this sense they are anticipatorily (as opposed to retrospectively) dialogistic, making space in the ongoing dialog for those who might hold alternative views.

3.7.2 Attribute: distance

The second sub-category of **attribution** involves formulations in which, via the semantics of the framer employed, there is an explicit distancing of the authorial voice from the attributed material. For obvious reasons we give the label 'distancing' to this sub-category. It is most typically realised by means of the reporting verb, *to claim* and by certain uses of 'scare' quotes. The contrast here is with **acknowledging attributions** where the semantics of the framer (eg *say, report, believe, according to*) is such that there is no specification as to where the authorial voice stands with respect to the proposition, thus leaving it open to the co-text to present the authorial text as either aligned/disaligned with respect to the position being advanced, or as neutral or disinterested. Caldas-Coulthard has observed that the author, by the use of *claim*, 'detaches him/herself from responsibility for what is being reported' (Caldas-Coulthard 1994: 295). We would put this in slightly different terms, since values of **acknowledge** also potentially have this rhetorical effect, and observe, rather, that *claim* acts to mark explicitly the internal authorial voice as separate from the cited, external voice. We demonstrate both this functionality of values of **distancing** and how they are dialogistically different from values of **acknowledge** by means of the extract which we considered briefly above in section 3.5. We repeat it here for ease of reference and indicate instances of both **acknowledge** and **distance**.

[3.16] Tickner **said** [*acknowledge*] regardless of the result, the royal commission was a waste of money and he would proceed with a separate inquiry into the issue headed by Justice Jane Matthews. His attack came as the Aboriginal women involved in the case **demanded** [*acknowledge*] a female minister examine the religious beliefs they **claim** [*distance*] are inherent in their fight against a bridge to the island near Goolwa in South Australia. [Bank of English – *OzNews* sub-corpus]

To demonstrate what is at stake here in the author choosing to **distance** rather than **acknowledge**, we provide a rewriting of the paragraph in which the values have been reversed:

> [3.16] (rewritten) Tickner **has claimed** [*distance*] that regardless of the result, the royal commission was a waste of money and he would proceed with a separate inquiry into the issue headed by Justice Jane Matthews. His attack came as the Aboriginal women involved in the case **demanded** [*acknowledge*] a female minister examine the religious beliefs which they **say** [*acknowledge*] are inherent in their fight against a bridge to the island near Goolwa in South Australia. [Cobuild Bank of English – *Australian News* sub-corpus]

In the original version the writer is neutral with respect to the reported assertions of Tickner (then Federal Minister for Aboriginal Affairs in an Australian Labor government) but steps back from the reported assertions of the Aboriginal women. It is not that the women's propositions are overtly presented as doubtful or unreliable, but rather that the writer explicitly indicates that they are not taking responsibility for the proposition's reliability. The situation is exactly reversed in the rewritten version where the authorial voice is neutral or unspecified with respect to where it stands on the Aboriginal women's position but is overtly disassociated from the propositions of the Minister.

Distancing formulations are dialogistically expansive on the same basis as **acknowledgements**. They explicitly ground the proposition in an individualised, contingent subjectivity, that of some external source. They go somewhat further than **acknowledgements** in that, in presenting the authorial voice as explicitly declining to take responsibility for the proposition, they maximise the space for dialogistic alternatives.

3.7.3 Attribution, alignment and writer–reader relationships

There is obviously rather more to the dialogistic functionality of these **attributions** than simply that of indicating a dialogistically expansive stance on the part of the speaker/writer. For a comprehensive analysis of the rhetorical effects of these meanings in context it is necessary to do more than simply classify them as either **acknowledging** or **distancing**. The very extensive literature on citation, referencing and intertextuality in academic discourse attends to this domain of enquiry. We confine ourselves to just a couple of key questions – those which relate most directly to our central concerns with alignment and solidarity.

Some texts operate under a regime by which it is assumed that it is possible for the speaker/writer to remain aloof from, and unimplicated in, any of the value positions which are contained in attributed material. Such a regime operates in the 'hard news' reporting of the 'highbrow' or 'broadsheet' news media and was illustrated by extract [3.15] above. Such texts present a relatively 'impersonalised' or 'impartial' façade to the reader, at least when compared with more explicitly evaluative texts. To the degree that the reader interprets the writer in such instances as having nothing invested in the position being advanced in the reported material (neither acting to advance it or to undermine it), such **acknowledgements** allow the writer to remain aloof from any relationships of either alignment or disalignment. They present the writer as some sort of 'informational fair trader' who simply conveys the views of others and who is therefore unimplicated in any relationship of solidarity which the reader may enter into with the quoted source whose viewpoint is being reported. Of course, there are all manner of ways in which such texts may indirectly indicate that the writer either supports or is opposed to the attributed value position. In which case, greater to lesser degrees of alignment (either for or against the value position) will be indicated and the text may be interpreted as more or less forthrightly aligning the reader into a particular value position.

Such alignment-neutral attributions, however, are in the minority. It is more typical, particularly in argumentative texts such as media commentaries, political speeches or academic articles, for **attribution** to be much more obviously implicated in issues of alignment and solidarity. In such texts it is available to the speaker/writer to announce overtly where they stand with respect to the attributed material via some inscribed attitudinal assessment either of the attributed material itself or of its source. For example:

> There were no slip-ups in the powerful speech – finally silencing the critics who **falsely** claim Bush is no more than a Texas cattle-rancher. [Bank of English]

> The Archbishop of Canterbury **rightly** describes the mass killing of children as 'the most evil kind of action we can imagine'. [*The New Statesman*, editorial, 13/09/04: 6]

> Banerji, of course, was not among those recession deniers. Rather, he has **compellingly** argued that those so-called New Economists were a major contributor to the excesses of the bubble, as detailed here last week. [www.thestreet.com, accessed 07/31/02]

In such cases the monoglossia of the attitudinal assessment (for example that the assertions of Bush's critics are 'false') over-rides the heteroglossia of the **attribution** to present the speaker/writer as categorically aligned with a given value position and thereby bidding to align the reader into this point of view.

Other more indirect methodologies are also available by which it is possible for attributed material to be implicated in the alignment strategies at work in the text. These are mechanism by which the reader is covertly positioned to regard the attributed material as either highly credible and warrantable, or alternatively, as dubious and unreliable. High credibility can be implied via the use of sources who have high status in the field (for example, *Mr. Mandela said the Group of Eight nations have a duty to help battle the scourge of AIDS*) or, as Hood 2004 has observed, via the assembling of a multiplicity of sources in support of the attributed material. For example:

> [3.17] **Most linguists believe that** linguistic structure is most productively studied in its own terms, with its communicative use(s) considered separately. [Online linguistics lecture – LING 001: Introduction to Linguistics, Department of Linguistics, University of Pennsylvania: http://www.ling.upenn.edu/courses/Fall_1998/ling001/ com_phil.html]

An assessment of low credibility can be invoked via the use of sources who have low social status or who are shown to be in the minority. For example:

> [3.18] NATURE WILL SORT OUT THE PROBLEMS – WON'T IT?
> **Only a few scientists believe** it will. [Bank of English – British ephemera sub–corpus]

Although in such cases it is some external source, rather than the speaker/writer, who is presented as advancing the proposition, there is a strong sense that the speaker/writer is implicated in the value position and hence there is clear signalling of the value position into which the reader is being aligned.

Of course, it will be rare in such argumentative texts for the speaker/writer to leave it up to attributed material to advance core value positions. Writers/speakers will themselves announce in categorical terms where they stand on the key issues, typically only bringing in the external source to lend support to their argument. In which case, the potential of **attribution** to allow for alternative dialogic positions will be over-ridden

Engagement and Graduation 117

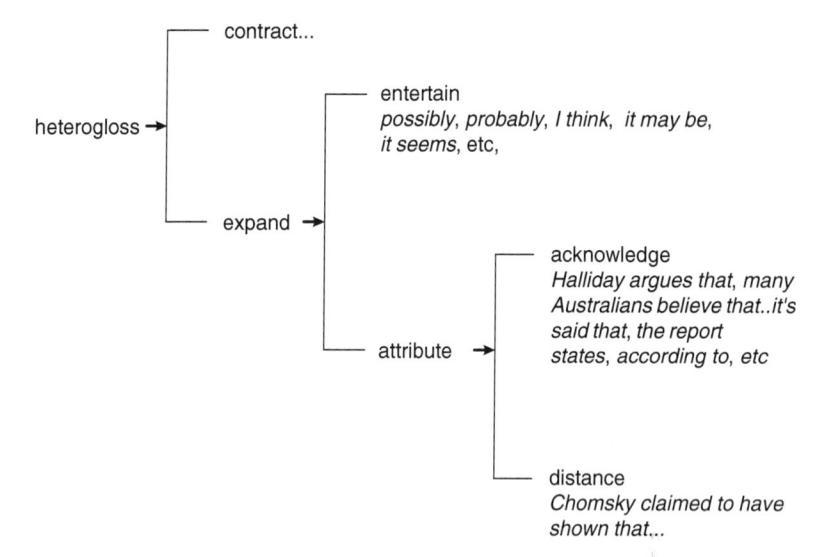

```
heterogloss →┬── contract...
             │
             └── expand →┬── entertain
                         │    possibly, probably, I think, it may be,
                         │    it seems, etc,
                         │
                         └── attribute →┬── acknowledge
                                        │    Halliday argues that, many
                                        │    Australians believe that..it's
                                        │    said that, the report
                                        │    states, according to, etc
                                        │
                                        └── distance
                                             Chomsky claimed to have
                                             shown that...
```

Figure 3.2 Engagement – dialogic expansion

(when the text is viewed as a rhetorical whole) by the monoglossia of the speaker/writer's own assertions.

The system of **engagement** (focussing on heteroglossic resources) as outlined to this point is set out in Figure 3.2.

3.8 The resources of dialogic contraction – overview: disclaim and proclaim

We turn now to those meanings which, in contrast to the values of **entertain** and **attribution** we have just considered, act to contract the dialogic space rather than to open it up. These are meanings which, even while they construe a dialogistic backdrop for the text of other voices and other value positions, are directed towards excluding certain dialogic alternatives from any subsequent communicative interaction or at least towards constraining the scope of these alternatives in the colloquy as it henceforth unfolds. These contractive meanings fall into two broad categories. The first of these we term 'disclaim' – meanings by which some dialogic alternative is directly rejected or supplanted, or is represented as not applying. The second of these we term 'proclaim' – meanings by which, through some authorial interpolation, emphasis or intervention, dialogic alternatives are confronted, challenged, overwhelmed or otherwise excluded. We consider each of these options in turn.

Under **disclaim** we cover those formulations by which some prior utterance or some alternative position is invoked so as to be directly rejected, replaced or held to be unsustainable. Obviously to deny or reject a position is maximally contractive in that, while the alternative position has been recognised, it is held not to apply. This is the domain of negation and concession/counter-expectation. We distinguish two sub-types within this **disclaim** category.

3.9 Disclaim: deny (negation)

From the dialogistic perspective, negation is a resource for introducing the alternative positive position into the dialogue, and hence acknowledging it, so as to reject it. Thus in these dialogistic terms, the negative is not the simple logical opposite of the positive, since the negative necessarily carries with it the positive, while the positive does not reciprocally carry the negative, or at least not typically.[8] This aspect of the negative, though perhaps at odds with common-sense understandings, has been quite widely noted in the literature – see for example, Tottie 1982, Leech 1983: 101, Pagano 1994 or Fairclough 1992: 101.[9] Consider, for example, the following extract from an advertisement placed in magazines by the British Heart Foundation.

> [3.19] We all like something to grab hold of. But sometimes you can have too much of a good thing. And a man whose table diet consists of double cheeseburgers and chips can end up looking like a tub of lard. <u>There's nothing wrong with meat, bread and potatoes</u>. But how about some lean meat, wholemeal bread and jacket potatoes?

Here the **denial**, *There is nothing wrong with meat, bread and potatoes*, is dialogic in that it invokes, and presents itself as responding to, claims/beliefs that 'there IS something wrong with meat, bread and potatoes'.

3.9.1 Denial, alignment and writer–reader relationships

Denial is a variable mechanism with respect to alignment and putative reader positioning. We only have the space here to consider a couple of instances of this variability. On some occasions in mass-communicative texts of the type we are considering, the denial is directed outwards and away from the current writer–reader relationship as the writer indicates a disalignment with some third party. Consider the following extract by way of example,

[3.20] Sir, Your report ('Anthrax vaccine refused by half Gulf personnel', February 12), recorded comments by Paul Keetch MP who claimed that the Ministry of Defence was 'sowing confusion' among troops by making this programme voluntary and that by doing so it was abdicating leadership. May I repeat my assurances that this is **not the case**. Anthrax represents a real threat to our armed forces and we seek to protect our troops through detection systems, individual physical protection and medical countermeasures (immunisation and antibiotics). But the best single protection against anthrax is immunisation.
While we strongly advise personnel to accept the vaccine for their own protection, the programme is a voluntary one. That is entirely consistent with long-standing medical practice in the UK to offer immunisations only on the basis of voluntary informed consent. ... [*The Times*, letters to the editor, 21/02/03, from Lewis Moonie, MP, Parliamentary Under-secretary of State for Defence and Minister for Veterans Affairs]

Here, obviously, the writer indicates a disalignment with the views of 'Paul Keetch MP' and in so doing aligns the reader into a position of opposition to Keetch's views. The denial is constructive of the putative reader to the extent that it presents that reader as potentially susceptible to the 'false' views of Keetch. This is conveyed, not so much by the **denial** itself, but by the fact that the writer supplies so much argumentative material in what follows by way of support for the denial, thus construing the putative reader as possibly still needing to be convinced, or at least as still needing more information on the subject.

In other cases, the **denial** will be against the putative addressee, specifically against beliefs which they speaker/writer assumes that at least some members of his/her mass audience will be subject to. This was the case in [3.19] above and also in the following instance.

[3.21] The gas we use today, natural gas, contains more than 90 per cent methane, and was known long before the discovery of coal gas. Natural gas burns with twice the heat of coal gas, is **not** poisonous and has **no** odour. [Bank of English – US academic sub-corpus]

Tottie 1987 and Pagano 1994 employ the term 'implicit negation' in connection with **denials** of this type and Pagano makes the point that they act to project 'existential paradigms' onto this intended audience (1994: 254). **Denials** such as those exemplified by [3.21] present the addresser as having greater expertise in some area than the addressee and as, on that basis, acting to correct some misunderstanding or misconception on the addressee's part (for example, that natural gas *would* be poisonous). Thus they are corrective rather than confrontational, presenting the addresser as sensitively attending to the addressee's level of knowledge and seeking to adjust their communication accordingly. As such they will enhance solidarity as long as the reader is not resistant to having this particular lack of knowledge projected onto them, and as long as they have no reason to reject the particular viewpoint being advanced.

3.10 Disclaim: counter

The second sub-type of **disclaim** includes formulations which represent the current proposition as replacing or supplanting, and thereby 'countering', a proposition which would have been expected in its place. For example, in

> [3.22] **Even though** we are getting divorced, Bruce and I are still best friends,

the proposition that Bruce and the writer *are still best friends* is in a countering relationship with the proposition that they are getting divorced. That Bruce and the writer are still best friends is presented as defeating what would otherwise be the 'normal' expectation arising from their divorce, namely that they wouldn't be on friendly terms.

Such formulations are often given the label 'adversative' while Tottie (1987) classifies them as a type of negation. They are dialogistic in the same way as **denials** in that they invoke a contrary position which is then said not to hold. They often operate in conjunction with **denials**, with the **denying** proposition in direct contradistinction with the expectation which is assumed to arise from an immediately prior or an immediately posterior proposition. For example,

> [3.23] Even though he had taken all his medication, his leg didn't look any better. [Bank of English – US academic sub corpus]

The **countering** is typically conveyed via conjunctions and connectives such as *although, however, yet* and *but*. It may also be realised via a small set of comment adjuncts/adverbials. For example:

> [3.24] Only ten tonnes or so have been sold. Most of the stockpile is 'scrap', and since almost everybody bans ivory imports there is no longer a legal market. <u>Surprisingly</u>, there seems to have been little smuggling through Hong Kong. [Cobuild Bank of English – *Economist* sub-corpus]

Adjuncts such as *even*, *only*, *just* and *still* also have a counter-expectational aspect to their meaning. Thus,

> They <u>even</u> organised a car for you at the airport.

indicates that more services are being provided here than would normally be expected.

3.10.1 Countering, alignment and writer–reader relationships

These **counters** are similar to **denials** such as [3.21] above in that they project on to the addressee particular beliefs or expectations, or, to modify Pagano's term slightly (Pagano 1994), particular axiological paradigms. Thus in [3.23] above, the text construes an audience which has the expectation that to take all one's medication is typically to ensure that healing will follow. Frequently, such **counters** are aligning rather than disaligning in that they construe the writer as sharing this axiological paradigm with the reader. The writer is presented as just as surprised by this 'exceptional' case as it is assumed the reader will be. Solidarity, of course, will be at risk for any actual addressee who doesn't happen to subscribe to the taken-for-granted axiological paradigm. Thus any reader who happens to regard it as perfectly natural for divorcing couples to remain on good terms will be alienated by [3.22], the more so because the viewpoint which they object to is taken for granted.

The engagement system as outlined to this point is set out in Figure 3.3.

3.11 Proclaim: concur, pronounce and endorse

We group together under the heading of 'proclaim' those formulations which, rather than directly rejecting or overruling a contrary position, act to limit the scope of dialogistic alternatives in the ongoing colloquy. We identify three sub-types of **proclamation** which we now consider in turn.

122 *The Language of Evaluation*

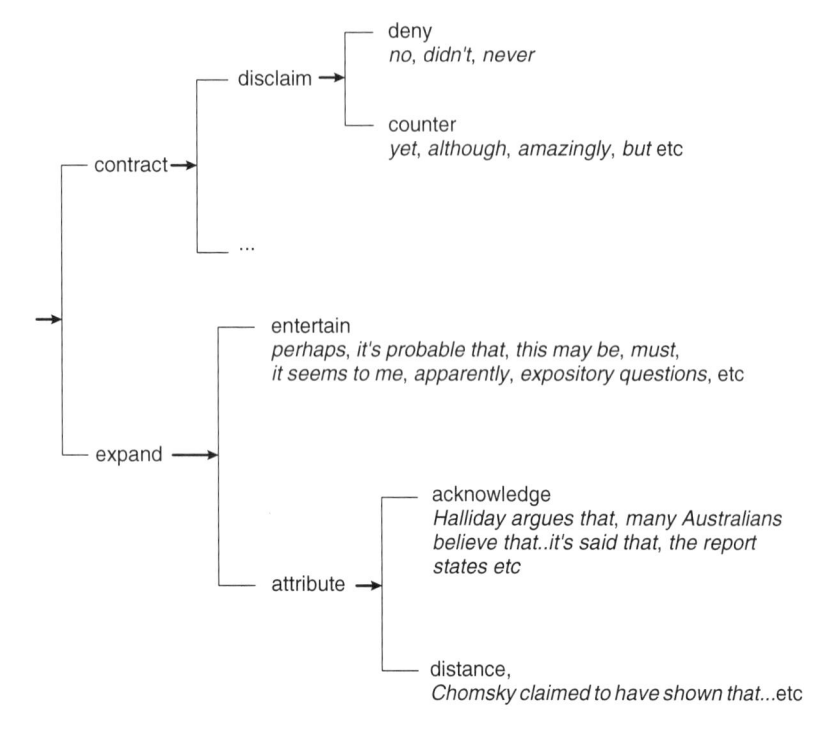

```
                    ┌─ deny
                    │  no, didn't, never
         ┌─ disclaim ─┤
         │          └─ counter
         │             yet, although, amazingly, but etc
contract ┤
         │
         └─ ...

        ┌─ entertain
        │  perhaps, it's probable that, this may be, must,
        │  it seems to me, apparently, expository questions, etc
expand ─┤
        │            ┌─ acknowledge
        │            │  Halliday argues that, many Australians
        │            │  believe that..it's said that, the report
        └─ attribute ┤  states etc
                     │
                     └─ distance,
                        Chomsky claimed to have shown that...etc
```

Figure 3.3 Engagement – contract: disclaim

3.12 Proclaim: concur

The category of 'concur' involves formulations which overtly announce the addresser as agreeing with, or having the same knowledge as, some projected dialogic partner. Typically, this dialogic partner is the text's putative addressee. This relationship of **concurrence** is conveyed via such locutions as *of course, naturally, not surprisingly, admittedly* and *certainly*. Consider by way of example the following transcription from an interview by Abu Dhabi television with the monarch of Jordan, King Abdullah.

> [3.25] **Abu Dhabi TV:** Why do these groups resort to violence Your Majesty, despite the contradiction between violence and Islam?
> **HM King Abdullah:** <u>Naturally</u>, we understand the state of anger and frustration from which Arabs and Muslims suffer as a result of their feelings of the

absence of justice, or of injustice being levied against them. [www.jordanembassyus.org/hmka01212003.htm, accessed 18/03/04]

Here the speaker's use of the locution *naturally* construes for the text an audience which shares with the speaker the view that the anger and frustration of Arabs and Muslims is understandable.

Similarly, in the following,

[3.26] When, belatedly, their selectors chose Paul Adams, who would assuredly have won them the second Test in Johannesburg, their attack became 'very good' in the opinion of Trevor Bailey, who has seen a few in his time. Bailey, **of course**, was that rarity, a cricketer who at his best was world-class with both bat and ball. [Bank of English – *OzNews* sub-corpus],

the writer's use of *of course* construes an audience for the text which shares the writer's highly-positive estimation of the celebrated English cricketer, Trevor Bailey.[10]

This relationship of **concurrence** may also be realised via certain types of rhetorical or 'leading' questions – those by which the writer/speaker is presented as assuming that no answer needs to be supplied for a particular question on account of that answer being so 'obvious'. (There is a contrast here with 'expository' questions of the type discussed in section 3.6.2 above which don't assume a given reply on the part of the addressee and which, accordingly, are dialogically expansive rather than contractive.) Addresser and addressee are thus presented as so thoroughly in alignment, and the proposition at issue so 'commonsensical', that agreement can be taken for granted. Consider by way of example the following leading question from the front cover of the 25 March 2002 edition of the *New Statesman* magazine. A full-page coloured picture depicts a group of young, friendly and happy Iraqi children in close-up. Looking up towards the camera, they wave bunches of flowers and with welcoming smiles directly engage with the viewer. The text of a headline superimposed over the picture reads.

Iraq: Should we go to war against these children?

Here the question leads the reader to an 'unavoidable' answer. The text operates under the assumption that the reader will inevitably supply, 'No, of course we shouldn't go to war with these children.'

These various **concurring** formulations, then, are dialogistic in that they present the speaker/writer as 'in dialogue' with the text's audience generally. Such formulations are contractive in that they represent the shared value or belief as universally, or at least as very widely, held in the current communicative context. Thus they have the effect of excluding any dialogistic alternatives from the ongoing colloquy in that they position any who would advance such an alternative as at odds with what is purportedly generally agreed upon or known. Accordingly, they construe for the text a backdrop which is heteroglossic in that it contains multiple voices (the authorial voice and those it is purportedly in concord with), but from which dissident voices and positions are excluded.

3.12.1 Some complications for writer–reader relationships – interactions between concur and counter

The functionality of values of **concur** is complicated by the fact that they often occur as a precursor to a **countering**. This arrangement is illustrated in the following.

> [3.27] [Robert Maxwell was] the eternal outsider, a man who had fought Establishment prejudice and pettifogging bureaucracy to get where he was. **Sure** [*concur*], he broke rules. **Yes** [*concur*], he ducked and dived. **Admittedly** [*concur*], he was badly behaved. **But** [*counter*] look at what he achieved. From nothing, he had become a multinational businessman with an empire stretching across the world, the confidant of statesmen and just as famous himself. [Bank of English – UKMags sub-corpus]

There are two interlinked rhetorical moves here (a rhetorical pair) by which the authorial voice first presents itself as agreeing with the construed reader with respect to a proposition, only to step back, so to speak, and to indicate a rejection of what are presented as the natural assumptions arising from that initial proposition. In the above instance, for example, the authorial voice acknowledges the validity of certain strongly negative assessments of Robert Maxwell, only then to dismiss these as not sufficient to prevent an over-ridingly positive regard for Maxwell. The writer thus acknowledges an anti-Maxwell community of shared value, even recognising that it has some validity, only then to indicate disalignment from that community and membership in the contrary pro-Maxwell point of view. In the literature such pairings are characterised as 'concessions', pointing to the strategy which is in play here by which argumentative ground is given up initially (the initial **concurring** concession), only for that ground to be retaken in the subsequent **counter** move. In such contexts there is often a sense that the **concurrence** is in some way reluctant, grudging or qualified on the part of the speaker/writer, and in this there is a contrast with the **concurrence** moves considered above (ie those employing *naturally* or *of course*) where typically there is no such sense of holding back or distancing. In more delicate analyses, then, it may be useful to distinguish between conceding **concurrence** (the type we are currently considering – eg <u>Admittedly</u> ... *but*; <u>I accept that</u> ... *however* ...) and affirming **concurrence** (as discussed in the previous section – *naturally, obviously, of course*, etc.).

We note, as well that conceding **concurrence** can indicate higher or lower degrees of reluctance:

> [more reluctant] **Admittedly** he was badly behaved, but look at what he has achieved.

> [less reluctant] **Certainly** he was badly behaved but look at what he has achieved.

In the case of the less reluctant formulations there is an indication of a relatively high degree of commitment by the speaker to the conceded proposition. We note as well that it is only as elements in a **concede + counter** pairing that terms such a *certainly* have this conceding functionality. It is important to note that there are two uses of *certainly* – the concessional meaning just discussed and an alternative meaning where agreement with some dialogic partner is not implied. In this second instance, the locution simply construes high commitment to the proposition on the part of the speaker/writer via an assessment of high probability, and hence is classified as an instance of *entertain*. Such a use is exemplified in the following.

> In my view, whether or not Mr. French broke the law in publicly corroborating evidence of which he had no personal knowledge, he has **certainly** disgraced the Attorney General's office in lending credence to the assertions of the Swift Boat veterans for Truth. [http://talkleft.com/new_archives/007655.html]

By such **concede + counter** pairings, the writer construes a putative reader who is presumed to be to some degree resistant to the writer's primary argumentative position. Thus in [3.27] above the reader is presumed to be resistant to the writer's ultimately positive view of Robert Maxwell. The pairings occur as the writer bids to win the reader over. By the concessional first step, the writer validates the reader's contrary viewpoint by acknowledging that it is understandable and has a rational basis. A point of solidarity is thus established. It is only in then holding

126　*The Language of Evaluation*

that the usual or expected implications do not arise from the conceded proposition(s) that the authorial voice sets itself against the putative reader. Thus such pairings can be seen as gestures towards solidarity in contexts where the writer anticipates, at least initially, disagreement on the part of the reader.

3.13　Proclaim: endorsement

By the term 'endorsement' we refer to those formulations by which propositions sourced to external sources are construed by the authorial voice as correct, valid, undeniable or otherwise maximally warrantable. This construal is achieved indirectly by the use of verbal processes (or their nominalised equivalents) which portray certain acts of semiosis as providing the grounds for the speaker/writer to presuppose this warrantability. The verbs in question include *show, prove, demonstrate, find* and *point out* and have been discussed in the literature in terms of notions of 'factivity' (see for example Kiparksy & Kiparsky 1977). For example:

> [3.28] Five of the studies examine the effects of economic dependence on economic inequality. All five **show that** dependence is associated with greater inequality. More specifically, five studies **demonstrate that** investment dependence – investment by foreign firms in a society's domestic economy – increases economic inequality. [Bank of English – US academic sub-corpus]
>
> [3.29] Complaints about the treatment of the 'Al Qaida' detainees should subside now that Downing Street has released details from a report which **shows that** the British prisoners have 'no substantial complaints' about their conditions.

The dialogism of such formulations is obvious enough, at least in its retrospective aspect. In both referencing and endorsing the utterances of a prior speaker, the authorial voice enters into a dialogic relationship of alignment with that speaker. However, the situation is, perhaps, not quite so straightforward when we consider the anticipatory dialogistic aspect. These dialogistically contractive **endorsements** are like dialogistically expansive **attributions** (see section 3.7) in that, through the grammar of reported speech (what in SFL is termed 'projection'), they ground the proposition in an individual, and hence contingent subjectivity. However, while **attributions** exploit the grammar of reported speech to unambiguously disassociate the proposition from the internal authorial voice, at least momentarily, no such authorial disassociation operates with **endorsements**. Here the internal voice takes over responsibility for the proposition, or at least shares responsibility for it with the cited source. The subjectivity at issue, then, is a multiple one – that of both the external source and the inner authorial voice. And crucially it is the inner authorial voice which does the rhetorical heavy lifting, so to speak, intervening in the meaning making to construe the proposition as 'proven', 'shown', 'demonstrated' and so on.

Endorsements, therefore, associate the proposition with an individual subjectivity, and primarily with the subjectivity of the authorial voice. And since individual subjectivities are always in alternation and in tension with other subjectivities, **endorsements** act to construe a heteroglossic backdrop of potential alternative viewpoints for the proposition. However, simultaneously, the **endorsement** functions to exclude any such alternatives from the ongoing colloquy via the speaker/writer's adjudgement of the proposition as maximally warrantable. For this reason they are, as we have already indicated, **dialogistically contractive** and by dint of this contractiveness they clearly align the reader into the value position which is being advanced at this point by the text.

3.14 Proclaim: pronounce

The category of **pronounce** covers formulations which involve authorial emphases or explicit authorial interventions or interpolations. For example: *I contend ..., The facts of the matter are that ..., The truth of the matter is that ..., We can only conclude that ..., You must agree that ...,* intensifiers with clausal scope such as *really, indeed,* etc. and, in speech, appropriately placed stress (eg *The level of tolerance IS the result of government intervention*).

Pronouncement is demonstrated in the following extract taken from a speech by US president John F. Kennedy in which he announced his government's plans to land an astronaut on the moon.

> [3.30] Now it is time to take longer strides – time for a great new American enterprise – time for this nation to take a clearly leading role in space achievement, which in many ways may hold the key to our future on earth. I believe we possess all the resources and talents necessary. **But the facts of the matter are that** we have never made the national decisions or marshaled the national resources required for such leadership.

The formulation, *the facts of the matter are that*, constitutes an overt intervention into the text by the authorial voice – an interpolation of the authorial presence so as to assert or insist upon the value or warrantability of the proposition. The authorial voice makes more salient its subjective role through this effort at 'vouchsafeing' the proposition that the US had *never made the national decisions or marshalled the national resources required for such leadership*. Such insistings or emphasisings imply the presence of some resistance, some contrary pressure of doubt or challenge against which the authorial voice asserts itself. It is only necessary to insist when there is some counter viewpoint against which the insistence is directed. Accordingly, while such formulations acknowledge the heteroglossic diversity of the current communicative context, they set the authorial voice against that diversity, presenting that voice as challenging or heading off a particular dialogistic alternative. Thus the interpersonal cost to any who would advance such a contrary position is increased and the dialogic space for this alternative in any upcoming dialogic interaction is reduced.

Consider, by way of further example, the following sequence taken from a letter by the *Guardian* newspaper's features editor to readers of the UK Chinese community's www.dimsum.co.uk web site. The letter was a response to anger by members of the Chinese community over a review published in the *Guardian* of the movie, *Crouching Tiger, Hidden Dragon*. The members of the community felt that the review was racist and perpetuated anti-Chinese stereotypes. The **pronouncement** which is at issue here is indicated in bold:

[3.31] Dear (angry) readers,

I apologise for not replying to all of you personally, but since most of you have made similar points about Charlotte Raven's column, I hope you don't mind if I address them together.

Broadly most of you have written or mailed me to say that you thought Charlotte's column about Crouching Tiger Hidden Dragon was racist because it invoked the old stereotype of the Chinese being inscrutable. Some of you made more specific points about Charlotte's lack of appreciation for Chinese cinema, and someone went as far as to suggest that by using the phrase 'it seemed to contain multitudes' to describe the performance of the cast, Charlotte was alluding to Western images of 'Chinese masses'.

In e-mail correspondence and conversations with some of you I have defended Charlotte's column quite robustly.

It is absolutely clear to me that what Charlotte was arguing was that Crouching Tiger was a bad film to which liberal audiences imputed a significance shaped by their own prejudices about Chinese cinema and the Chinese in general.

Here we observe the writer interpolating himself explicitly into the text in order to indicate his maximal investment in the current proposition. More crucially, the textual voice doesn't indicate this heightened personal investment in the proposition in a communicative vacuum. Rather it does so against some opposed dialogic alternative – against a contrary view of what the *Guardian's* reviewer ('Charlotte') was arguing in her reviewing.

By way of further illustration consider the following two extracts:

[3.32] Andrew B. Lewis of Burlington, Vermont, wrote, 'There was a lot of talk during Daniel Schorr's spot on "Weekend Edition" about George Bush's not having a coherent postwar policy for Iraq. **I contend that** Bush and King Fahd do, indeed, have a policy that entails the destruction of the Kurds and the Shiites.' [Bank of English]

[3.33] ... many birdkeepers who have been robbed complain of lack of police interest. The police respond by countering that they have more pressing priorities with which to contend. This may be true, but **I contend that** a telephone call to a person who has been robbed takes only a couple of minutes and shows that someone cares. [Bank of English]

Once again these authorial interventions are directed towards confronting and defeating a contrary position.

We identify, then, as instances of **pronouncement** formulations which involve authorial interpolations and emphases which are directed against some assumed or directly referenced counter position. Such formulations are dialogistic in that they acknowledge the presence of this counter view in the current communicative setting and are contractive in that they challenge, confront or resist this particular dialogistic alternative. In being directed in this way against a contrary value position they have some kinship with the two sub-systems of **disclaim – deny** and **counter**.

3.14.1 Pronouncement, alignment and writer–reader relationships

The consequences for writer-reader relationships associated with the use of **pronouncements** will vary according to whether the challenge is to a value position which the text directly or indirectly presents as being held, or likely to be held, by the addressee (eg [3.31]), or whether, alternatively, the challenge is to the value position of some alternative third party. This latter situation applied in [3.33] above which is taken from the 'club news' section of the journal of the (British) National Council

130 *The Language of Evaluation*

For Aviculture and which accordingly has an intended audience of birdkeepers. The writer's challenge is to the police on behalf of this target audience, many of whom have apparently been writing to the journal complaining that police do not take appropriate action in the event of their prize birds being stolen.

When the **pronouncement** confronts the addressee (as in [3.31]), there is an obvious threat to solidarity since the authorial voice overtly presents itself as at odds with this construed addressee. Where such a confrontation does take place, the speaker/writer will often employ further dialogistic resources by which additional grounds will be supplied by which solidarity may obtain, even in the face of this apparent disalignment.

When the **pronouncement** confronts some third party (eg the police as in [3.33]) on behalf of the putative addressee, the opposite situation applies. Here the text obviously builds solidarity in that the speaker/writer is presented is standing with the addressee in opposition to some axiologically alien third party. This strategy (the addresser standing with the addressee against some dialogic adversary) is frequently exploited in political rhetoric and journalistic commentary.

3.14.2 Pronouncement – lexicogrammatical realisations

As the previous discussion has indicated, **pronouncement** is a rhetorically, discourse-semantically motivated category and its realisations are lexico-grammatically diverse. Nevertheless, it is still possible to provide an account of the typical grammar of **pronouncement**. We notice, in fact, that the range of options is in some way analogous with the range of options which are available for the realisation of the modal values which we outlined in Chapter 1 (see sections 1.2.2 and 1.2.4) and considered again in our discussion of **dialogistic expansiveness** (see section 3.6 above). Recall that in English there are two axes of variation by which modal assessments can be construed: subjective versus objective and explicit versus implicit. The subjective–objective distinction turns on whether the speaker/writer's subjective role in making the assessment is overtly announced (eg *I believe that he's lying*; *He may be lying* = 'subjective') or is in some way obscured, backgrounded or impersonalised (eg *It's probable he's lying*; *Probably he's lying* = 'objective'). The explicit–implicit distinction turns on whether the modal assessment is given prominence through being encoded by means of a matrix clause (eg *I believe that*; *It's probable that* ... = 'explicit') or whether it is

Table 3.2 Realisation options for pronouncement

	subjective (*explicitly grounded in the speaker/writer's subjectivity*)	objective (*subjectivity obscured or impersonalised*)
explicit (*emphasis via a matrix/top level clause*)	I contend it's the worst address by a British Prime Minister	The facts of the matter are that it was the worst address ... .
implicit (*emphasis via a sub-clausal element*)	It **WAS** the worst address ...	Really, it's the worst address ...

but one element of the clause (eg *He's probably lying; He may be lying* = 'implicit').

The same optionality and proportionalities can be observed across many of the realisations of **pronouncement**. See, for example, Table 3.2.

In the previous discussion we exemplified two of these options: objective explicit (*the facts of the matter are ...*) and subjective explicit (*I contend that ...*). The objective, implicit option is exemplified by the following:

[3.34] Contrary to what one might expect, unhappy couples reported many occasions of feeling happy when together. The beeper found them enjoying themselves watching their child's baseball game, having a barbecue with neighbors, even going out to a movie alone with each other. ... What **really** differentiates cool from warm couples is greater frequency of negative experiences, rather than fewer positive experiences when together. The distressed couples in our study reported twice as many times together that both were in negative moods. [Bank of English]

Here the *really* is employed as the authorial voice sets itself against the commonsense assumption that dysfunctional couples are those which experience few happy interactions.

The subjective, implicit option is realised via formulations in which there is some added emphasis on the finite auxiliary – eg *I **DID** turn out the lights before I left*. This is obviously more a feature of speech than of writing. Nevertheless, we do observe the same option in written language, where formatting (for example all capitals) is employed to

132 *The Language of Evaluation*

Table 3.3 A taxonomy of pronouncement realisations

	subjective (*explicitly grounded in the speaker/writer's subjectivity*)	**objective** (*subjectivity obscured or impersonalised*)
explicit (*emphasis via a matrix/top level clause*)	It is absolutely clear to me that what Charlotte was arguing was that Crouching Tiger was a bad film to which liberal audiences imputed a significance shaped by their own prejudices	the facts of the matter are that we have never made the national decisions or marshaled the national resources required for such leadership.
	we have to remember that bobbies move around – and slowly. And when they're busy with one person, they're not available to others	
	I contend that Bush and King Fahd do, indeed, have a policy	
	I contend that a telephone call to a person who has been robbed takes only a couple of minutes and shows that someone cares	
implicit (*emphasis via a sub-clausal element*)	Bobbies on the beat are NOT the real answer	Conservatives do not really want states to spend more, in order to compensate for reduced federal spending
	A terrifying new probe yesterday revealed Saddam Hussein WAS secretly preparing for chemical, biological and even nuclear war	What really differentiates cool from warm couples is greater frequency of negative experiences

indicate the emphasis. This is a device favoured by tabloid newspaper headline writers.

Examples of the various options within **pronouncement** grouped according to this taxonomy are provided in Table 3.3.

3.14.3 Pronouncement and assessments of high probability

There is one further aspect of the functionality of these **pronouncing** meanings which requires a brief mention. It is sometimes the case in the hedging and meta-discourse literature (see for example, Hyland 2000) that emphasising formulations of this type are grouped together with assessments of high probability (eg *He must be lying; I'm convinced he's lying*) under a heading such as 'booster' or 'up-toner'. There are certainly grounds for such a grouping on the basis that assessments of high probability and the authorial interpolations which we classify as **pronouncement** both indicate heightened investment or involvement in the proposition by the speaker/writer – both types of locution do 'boost' in this way. Nevertheless, alongside this point of communicative similarity, there is also an important dissimilarity. Despite the speaker/writer's upscaled investment, assessments of high probability are nevertheless still dialogistically expansive, and are classified as instances of **entertain**. Thus *he must be lying* construes the proposition as one which has been derived by the speaker via some process of deduction and hence one which is presented as defeatable should new, counter evidence become available. Accordingly, there is nothing rhetorically untoward about *He must be lying, don't you think?* In formulations involving explicitly subjective modal assessments such as *I'm convinced he's lying*, the explicit grounding of the proposition in the speaker/writer's own cognitive processes presents the proposition as but one view among a range of potential alternative views, even while the speaker/writer signals that they are strongly committed to this particular viewpoint. Halliday has made a similar point in observing that we only explicitly declare ourselves to be 'certain' when, in fact, there is some question or debate as to certainty (Halliday 1994: 362). Accordingly, as assessments of probability, such modals are dialogically expansive – they still 'entertain' the possibility of dialogistical alternatives. Pronouncements, in contrast, do not 'entertain' alternative positions in this way but, as we have demonstrated, are directed towards challenging and dismissing an alternative viewpoint. They, therefore, are dialogistically contractive rather than expansive. As a consequence of this analysis we are able to distinguish between two sub-types of 'boosters' – those which are dialogistically expansive (eg *I am convinced that ...*) and those which are contractive (eg *I contend that ...*).

An overview of the **engagement** system is provided by the system network set out in Figure 3.4.

3.15 Engagement, intertextuality and the grammar of reported speech

By way of clarification we briefly note that under this framework, reported speech (what in systemic linguistics is termed 'projection') is

134 *The Language of Evaluation*

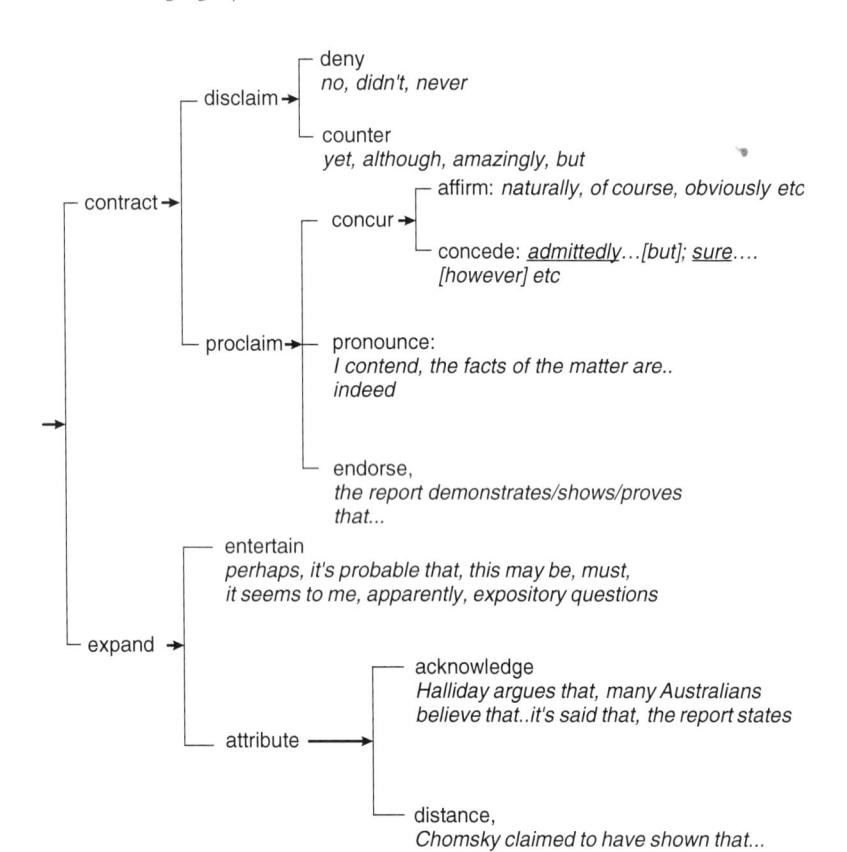

```
                    ┌─ disclaim ─┬─ deny
                    │            │   no, didn't, never
                    │            │
                    │            └─ counter
                    │                yet, although, amazingly, but
      ┌─ contract ──┤
      │             │            ┌─ concur ──┬─ affirm: naturally, of course, obviously etc
      │             │            │           │
      │             │            │           └─ concede: admittedly…[but]; sure….
      │             │            │              [however] etc
      │             └─ proclaim ─┤
      │                          ├─ pronounce:
      │                          │   I contend, the facts of the matter are..
──────┤                          │   indeed
      │                          │
      │                          └─ endorse,
      │                              the report demonstrates/shows/proves
      │                              that…
      │
      │             ┌─ entertain
      │             │   perhaps, it's probable that, this may be, must,
      │             │   it seems to me, apparently, expository questions
      └─ expand  ───┤
                    │                        ┌─ acknowledge
                    │                        │   Halliday argues that, many Australians
                    └─ attribute ────────────┤   believe that..it's said that, the report states
                                             │
                                             └─ distance,
                                                 Chomsky claimed to have shown that…
```

Figure 3.4 The engagement system

diversified across the system. This follows from the fact that the structure

   matrix clause + projected clause

can variously realise **attribute: distance**, eg:

   They are claiming he can't tell the wood from the trees.

attribute: acknowledge, eg:

   They have stated that he can't tell the wood from the trees

as well as **proclaim: endorse**, eg:

They demonstrated that he can't tell the wood from the trees.

This follows from our dialogistic perspective under which the issue of who/what is the primary source of the proposition is secondary to the issue of how the authorial voice is positioning itself with respect to the anticipated reactions and responses of the audience which is being construed for the text. Thus it is the semantics of dialogistic **contraction/expansion**, orientated as this is towards such anticipation, which takes precedence over whether the purported source of the proposition is external or internal to the text. Frameworks which give preference to sourcing (for example, Sinclair's notion of 'attribution' and 'averal' – Sinclair 1986) have a retrospective orientation in that they look backwards to the origin of the proposition in some prior utterance. Our framework has a prospective or anticipatory orientation in that we are concerned with they way in which the text builds for itself an audience and presents itself as engaging in various ways with this audience.

The distinction captured by Sinclair's notions of 'attribution' and 'averal' (as he defines these terms) is, of course, a highly significant one rhetorically. It is almost always vital in the sort of text analyses we conduct to establish who is being presented as the source of the proposition and whether or not the speaker/writer has sought to shift responsibility for the proposition to some external source. White (1998, 2004b) has used the terms 'extra-vocalisation' and 'intra-vocalisation' to cover the distinction.

3.16 Graduation: an overview

We turn now to the second major sub-system of meanings with which we are concerned in this chapter – those concerned with up-scaling and down-scaling.

As we indicated briefly in Chapter 2, a defining property of all attitudinal meanings is their gradability. It is a general property of values of **affect**, **judgement** and **appreciation** that they construe greater or lesser degrees of positivity or negativity. See for example, Table 3.4.

Gradability is also generally a feature of the **engagement** system. Here the meaning which is scaled will vary from sub-system to sub-system, though, more broadly, **engagement** values scale for the degree of the

136 *The Language of Evaluation*

Table 3.4 The gradability of attitudinal meanings

	low degree			high degree
judgement	competent player reasonably good player	good player quite good player	very good player	brilliant player extremely good player
affect	contentedly slightly upset	happily somewhat upset	joyously very upset	ecstatically extremely upset
appreciation	a bit untidy attractive	somewhat untidy beautiful	very untidy	completely untidy exquisite

Table 3.5 The gradability of engagement values

	lower		higher
entertain	I suspect she betrayed us possibly she betrayed us she just possibly betrayed us	I believe she betrayed us probably she betrayed us she possibly betrayed us	I am convinced she betrayed us definitely she betrayed us she very possibly betrayed us
attribute	She suggested that I had cheated	She stated that I had cheated	She insisted that I had cheated
pronounce	I'd say he's the man for the job	I contend he's the man for the job	I insist that he's the man for the job
concur	admittedly he's technically proficient (but he doesn't play with feeling)		certainly he's technically proficient (but ... .)
disclaim	I didn't hurt him		I never hurt him

speaker/writer's intensity, or the degree of their investment in the utterance. See for example, Table 3.5.

The semantics of **graduation**, therefore, is central to the appraisal system. It might be said that **attitude** and **engagement** are domains of **graduation** which differ according to the nature of the meanings being scaled. This section provides an outline of the lexicogrammatical resources by which **graduation** is realised and a discussion of some of the key dialogistic effects associated with this up-scaling/down-scaling.

3.16.1 Force and focus

Graduation operates across two axes of scalability – that of grading according to intensity or amount, and that of grading according to prototypicality and the preciseness by which category boundaries are drawn. Graduation according to intensity/amount has its natural domain of operation over categories which involve inherently scalar assessments – for example the attitudinal assessments just exemplified (gradable along clines of positivity/negativity) but also assessments of size, vigour, extent, proximity, and so on. The term 'force' references graduations of this type. We explore the semantics of **force** in detail in sections 3.18 to 3.20 below.

Graduation according to prototypicality operates as phenomena are scaled by reference to the degree to which they match some supposed core or exemplary instance of a semantic category. Via locutions such a *true, real, genuine* (ie *He's a true friend*) the phenomenon is assessed as prototypical and via locutions such as *kind of, of sorts, effectively, bordering on*, and the suffix *-ish* (ie *It was an apology of sorts, we'll be there at five o-clock-ish*) the phenomenon is assessed as lying on the outer margins of the category. The term 'focus' references graduation of this type and we explore the semantics and dialogistic functionality of this resource in the following section.

3.17 Graduation: focus

Graduation according to prototypicality (**focus**) applies most typically to categories which, when viewed from an experiential perspective, are not scalable. These are the clearly bounded, either–or categories which operate in experiential taxonomies where category membership is more or less precisely determined by some combination of sufficient and necessary conditions. In this case, **graduation** operates to reconstrue these categories in such a way that they participate in scalable clines of prototypicality. For example,

> They don't play **real** jazz.
> They play jazz, **sort of**.

From the experiential perspective, jazz music is a distinct category, within a taxonomy of music types, defined by various properties (for example, according to one commonly-applied definition, it involves improvisation and certain 'swung' rhythms). However, in the above instances, it is reconstrued according to an interpersonal semantic by

138 *The Language of Evaluation*

which some types of musical performances are assessed as prototypical of the jazz category and others as being only marginal exemplars. Membership in the 'jazz music' category is no longer an either–or proposition but a matter of degree. **Graduation** which operates in this way is termed 'focus'.

Under **focus** it is possible to up-scale, or 'sharpen', the specification so that prototypicality is indicated (eg *a real father, a true friend*) or to downscale, or 'soften', the specification so as to characterise an instance as having only marginal membership in the category (eg *they sort of play jazz, they are kind of crazy, it was an apology of sorts*). **Softening** values have been explored in the literature under such headings as 'hedges' (see for example Lakoff 1973) and 'vague language' (see Channell 1994) and the sharpening of values has been considered under the heading of intensifiers, boosters and amplifiers (see, for example, Labov 1984 and Hyland 2000).

Graduation according to prototypicality, however, is not confined to such 'experiential' categories. Some inherently scalar categories (generally gradable according to intensity) are also gradable according to prototypicality. For example, we encounter both *a **very** red carpet* [*intensity*] and *a piece of **genuinely** red carpet* [*prototypicality*]. Similarly it is possible to graduate an attitudinal, and hence naturally scalable, term such as *upset* not only by reference to intensity (*slightly upset, very upset*), but also by reference to prototypicality – *I'm feeling kind of upset / I'm feeling upset, sort of*. In this last instance, *kind of / sort of*, construes the speaker's feelings as lying on the borderline of *upset-ness*, as having only a marginal/non-prototypical membership in the category.

The **graduation** network as demonstrated to this point is illustrated in Figure 3.5.

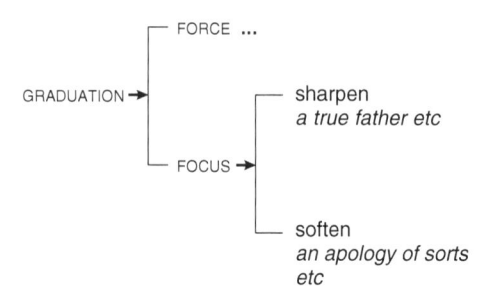

GRADUATION →
— FORCE ...
— FOCUS →
  — sharpen
    a true father etc
  — soften
    an apology of sorts etc

Figure 3.5 A preliminary outline of graduation

3.17.1 Focus and attitude – experiential categories

When the term being graduated under **focus** is an otherwise non-attitudinal term (eg *jazz music, husband, father*) there is a strong tendency for the cline of prototypicality to be invested with attitudinality. Instances of **sharpening** often strongly flag a positive attitudinal assessment (eg *a real husband, a true husband*) while instances of purported marginality flag a negative assessment (eg *jazz of sorts, it provides a sanctuary of a kind*). The nature of the **attitude** evoked will be determined by the specific semantics of the graduated category and will also be subject to co-textual influences such as, for example, attitudinal prosodies established by inscribed attitudinal values elsewhere in the text.

3.17.2 Focus, inscribed attitude and writer–reader relationships

When the term being graduated according to prototypicality is already explicitly attitudinal (eg *a real brat, a real wonder, kind of upset, kind of crazy, bordering on the unreasonable, kind of marvellous*) the rhetorical effect varies according to whether the value is **sharpening** or **softening**. Under sharpening (*a real brat, a genuine hero*), the effect is to indicate maximal investment by the authorial voice in the value position (either negative or positive) being advanced and hence to strongly align the reader into the value position being advanced.

When the **softened** term is a negative one, the effect is to indicate a lessening of the speaker/writer's investment in the value position and hence to offer a conciliatory gesture directed towards maintaining solidarity with those who hold contrary views. We considered an instance of such a **softening** in our discussion of *bordering on the unreasonable* in the introductory section of the chapter.

The effect is not so straightforward when the **softened** term is a positive one. Consider by way of example the following extract from a New York Film Academy review of actor Meryl Streep's performance in the movie *Adaptation*. In the movie, Streep portrays a real-life, still living New York celebrity and author, Susan Orlean. The movie is notable in that it is makes very clear that the characterisation of Orlean is not intended to be true-to-life but, rather, is fancifully fictional. It is particularly relevant for our current concerns that in this 'fictionalised' characterisation, Orlean is portrayed in very negative terms as, according to the review, an 'orchid-obsessed, drug-snorting, Lady Macbethish adulteress'. (**Softenings** of positive attitudinal terms have been underlined.)

[3.35] Maybe the language isn't precise, but her [Streep's] faux Susan Orlean is flawless – a smartly assayed embodiment of yearning (intellectual, artistic, spiritual) that's very funny and even **kind of sexy**. And what's the real-life Orlean's review? 'It's the funniest concept you can imagine: Meryl Streep, greatest actress in the world, is me,' says the author. 'It's **kind of marvelous**.' [www.ew.com/r0/ew/ – accessed 29/08/03]

The first softening (*kind of sexy*) occurs as the writer, via the counter-expectational *even* (*even kind of sexy*), construes a putative reader for whom it will be surprising that such a negatively-evaluated character could be portrayed as 'sexy'. The precise communicative effect of the softening is difficult to articulate precisely. The strategy seems to be one in which the writer indicates reserve towards the positively evaluative 'sexy' so as to maintain solidarity with those for whom such positivity towards a 'drug-snorting, Lady Macbethish adulteress' would be untoward. The second softening (*kind of marvellous*) occurs in a quote from the real-life author, Susan Orlean, herself. Once again the precise communicative effect is difficult to pin down but it seems to us to act as a display of modesty on the part of Orlean. Presumably appearing to take too much pleasure in being portrayed by the 'greatest actress in the world' may come across as gloating or smug and hence the expression of this pleasure is attenuated (*kind of marvellous* rather than just *marvellous*). In general, then, softening of positive values occurs when the positive assessment is being construed as potentially problematic for writer–reader solidarity.

3.18 Graduation: force – intensification and quantification

We turn now to the second major sub-category of **graduation** – that of **force**.

As indicated, **force** covers assessments as to degree of intensity and as to amount. Assessments of degree of intensity can operate over qualities (eg *slightly foolish, extremely foolish; it stopped somewhat abruptly, it stopped very abruptly*), over processes (eg *This slightly hindered us, This greatly hindered us*), or over the verbal modalities of likelihood, usuality, inclination and obligation (eg *it's just possible that, it's very possible that*). We employ the term 'intensification' to refer to this scaling of qualities and processes.

Engagement and Graduation 141

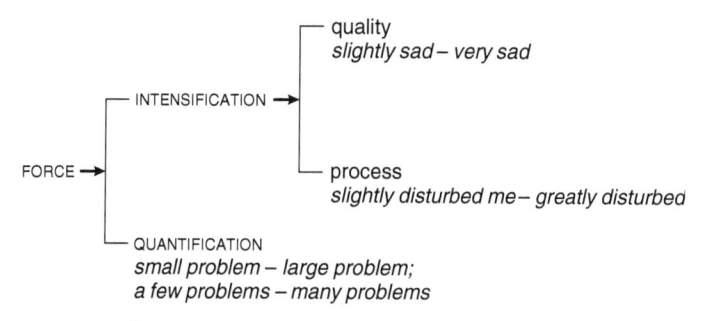

```
                       ┌── quality
                       │   slightly sad – very sad
          ┌── INTENSIFICATION →┤
          │            │
          │            └── process
FORCE →  ┤                 slightly disturbed me – greatly disturbed
          │
          └── QUANTIFICATION
              small problem – large problem;
              a few problems – many problems
```

Figure 3.6 Force: intensification – quality and process

Assessments of amount apply to entities, rather than to qualities and processes. We term such assessments, 'quantification'. These provide for the imprecise measuring of number (eg a *few* miles, *many* miles) and imprecise measuring of the presence or mass of entities according to such features as their size, weight, distribution or proximity (eg <u>small</u> *amount*, <u>large</u> *amount*; <u>nearby</u> *mountain*, <u>distant</u> *mountain*).

A preliminary network for the resources of **force** is provided in Figure 3.6.

3.19 Force: intensification

3.19.1 Modes of intensification – isolating

The assessment of degree of intensity of qualities and processes is termed 'intensification'. **Intensifications** divide into two broad lexico-grammatical classes – 'isolating' and 'infusing'. The distinction turns on whether the up-scaling/down-scaling is realised by an isolated, individual item which solely, or at least primarily, performs the function of setting the level of intensity, or whether the sense of up/down-scaling is fused with a meaning which serves some other semantic function. Isolating realisations are exemplified by the following:

Up/down-scaling of qualities

[*pre-modification of an adjective*]

<u>a bit</u> miserable, <u>somewhat</u> miserable, <u>relatively</u> miserable, <u>fairly</u> miserable, <u>rather</u> miserable, <u>very</u> miserable, <u>extremely</u> miserable, <u>utterly</u> miserable

[pre-modification of an adverb]

<u>slightly</u> abruptly, <u>somewhat</u> abruptly, <u>fairly</u> abruptly, <u>quite</u> abruptly, <u>rather</u> abruptly, <u>very</u> abruptly

Up/down-scaling of verbal processes

[adverbially modified verbal group]

this upset me <u>slightly</u>, this upset me <u>a bit</u>, this upset me <u>somewhat</u>, this upset me <u>greatly</u>

Up/down-scaling of modalities

<u>just</u> possible, <u>somewhat</u> possible, <u>quite</u> possible, <u>very</u> possible

<u>reasonably</u> often, <u>quite</u> often, <u>very</u> often, <u>extre</u>mely often

Localised or relative scaling with respect to intensity is realised via comparatives and superlatives – for example,

<u>less</u> miserable, <u>least</u> miserable, <u>more</u> miserable, <u>most</u> miserable

<u>more</u> probable, <u>most</u> probable

happi<u>er</u>, happi<u>est</u>

3.19.2 Maximisation

At the upper-most end of the scale of intensification are located value which have been termed 'maximisers' (eg Quirk, Greenbaum, Leech & Svartivik 1985) – locutions which construe the up-scaling as being at the highest possible intensity. There is a proliferation of options at this maximising end of the intensity spectrum. For example,

<u>utterly</u> miserable, <u>totally</u> miserable, <u>thoroughly</u> miserable, <u>absolutely</u> miserable, <u>completely</u> miserable; <u>perfectly</u> happy

These maximizers also include the highest value for the modal assessments of usuality – ie *always*. This value often operates hyperbolically to convey strong writer/speaker investment in the proposition, rather than any 'literal' sense of constancy or uninterrupted repetition. For example,

When I'm on a diet I'm <u>always</u> thinking about food; This gate in <u>constant</u> use.

3.19.3 Lexicalisation

Intensifiers of this type (eg *slightly, very, rather*) are typically classed as 'grammatical' items on the grounds that they are a closed set and that they have no referential meaning. However, intensification is also carried out by isolated modifiers which are 'lexical' rather than 'grammatical'. These are locutions which are either figurative in some way,

<u>ice</u> cold,
<u>crystal</u> clear
<u>dirt</u> poor

or which convey an attitudinal overtone,

<u>reasonably</u> happy,
<u>amazingly</u> happy, <u>deliriously</u> happy, <u>perfectly</u> happy
<u>dreadfully</u> cold,
<u>ridiculously</u> easy

We note, however, that such formulations involve what Sinclair has termed 'delexicalisation'. They are collocations which are so fixed and formulaic that the intensifying premodifying epithet no longer carries its full semantic load. As Sinclair observes,

> The meaning of words chosen together is different from their independent meanings. They are at least partly delexicalized. This is the necessary correlate of co-selection. If you know that selections are not independent, and that one selection depends on another, then there must be a result and effect on the meaning which in each individual choice is a delexicalization of one kind or another. It will not have its independent meaning in full if it is only part of a choice involving one or more words. [Sinclair 1994: 23]

Thus, in practice, there is nothing semantically untoward about the fact, for example, that *ice cold Coke* is, in fact, virtually never *ice cold*. Similarly, to characterise someone as *deliriously happy* is not to characterise them as *delirious* (a negative **judgement** of **capacity**), and is only subtly different from characterising them as *extremely happy*.

3.19.4 Modes of intensification – infusion

As indicated, with **infused** intensification there is no separate lexical form conveying the sense of up-scaling or down-scaling. Rather the scaling is conveyed as but one aspect of the meaning of a single term. For example,

Quality

contented, happy, joyous

(she performed) competently, skilfully, brilliantly

warm, hot, scalding

Process

this <u>disquieted</u> me, this <u>startled</u> me, this <u>frightened</u> me, this <u>terrified</u> me

the water <u>trickled</u> out of the tap, <u>flowed</u> out of the tap, <u>poured</u> out of the tap, <u>flooded</u> out of the tap

the price <u>inched up</u>, the price <u>rose</u>, the price <u>shot up</u>

she <u>ambled</u>, she <u>walked</u>, she <u>strode</u>

I <u>glanced over</u> the manuscript, I <u>looked over</u> the manuscript, I <u>scrutinised</u> the manuscript

The clouds <u>drifted</u> across the sky. The clouds <u>raced</u> across the sky.

Modality

possible, probable, certain

rarely, occasionally, sometimes, often, always

Here, then, degree of intensity is conveyed as individual terms in a sequence of semantically related terms contrast in degree of intensity with the other members of that sequence.

3.19.5 Modes of intensification – repetition

Intensification can also be realised via repetition – either by the repeating of the same lexical item,

It's hot hot hot.

We laughed and laughed and laughed.

or by the assembling of lists of terms which are closely related semantically. For example,

In fact it was probably the most <u>immature</u>, <u>irresponsible</u>, <u>disgraceful</u> and <u>misleading</u> address ever given by a British Prime Minister.

3.19.6 Intensification and verbal processes – some additional issues

Above we demonstrated the up/down-scaling of verbal processes by means of 'grammatical' intensifiers such as *slightly* and *greatly* (eg *This slightly troubles me / This greatly troubles me*). However, **intensification** as it applies to processes is somewhat more complex grammatically than this initial outline may suggest. While qualities (as realised by adjectives and adverbs) are very generally scalable by means of grammatical intensifiers (eg via *slightly, rather, very*), this is not the case with processes. Only a relatively small subset is scalable via such 'grammatical' means. This grammatically-scalable group includes verbs of **affect** (as demonstrated in the previous examples) as well as several other semantic subsets (Matthiessen 1995, section 4.8.2.5). For example:

[*processes conveying attitudinal assessments*]

You slightly misled me. You completely misled me.

We have been somewhat betrayed by the government. We have been utterly betrayed by the government.

This slightly improves its appearance. This greatly improves its appearance.

[*processes of transformation*]

They have slightly reduced the deficit. They have greatly reduced the deficit.

[*processes of conation*]

This hindered us slightly. This greatly hindered our progress.

She helped us slightly. She helped us a great deal.

Many other types of processes are not scalable by these means. Thus, by way of just a few examples, it is not typically possible to scale the intensity of the action depicted by a motion verb by means of such grammatical adverbs. English does not allow for,

*The water slightly flowed. *The water greatly flowed.

Nor does it provide 'grammatical' means for up-scaling/down-scaling the intensity of most verbs of perception. Thus the non-occurrence of,

*He slightly watched the passing parade. *He greatly watched the passing parade.

Rather, as Hood 2004 demonstrates, English provides for the up-scaling/down-scaling of such processes via lexical means, specifically by means of lexical adverbs which scale by reference to a notion of vigour.[11] The precise semantics of this up-scaling/down-scaling will vary according to the specific semantics of the verb. We illustrate a range of these lexical intensifications with respect to 'vigour' below:

The water flowed slowly. The water flowed swiftly

She brushed it gently. She brushed it vigorously.

She held it loosely. She held it firmly

The light shone dimly across the valley. The light shone brightly across the valley.

She slept lightly. She slept deeply/soundly

She watched desultorily. The watched intently.

He casually observed those around him. He closely observed those around him.

Here the 'vigour' which is being scaled up or down is variously a matter of speed (*slowly/swiftly*), physical force (*gently/vigorously, loosely/firmly*), illumination (*dimly/brightly*), consciousness (*lightly/deeply*) or concentration (*desultorily/intently; casually/closely*).

These lexicalised realisations of degree of intensity take us to a point in the grammar which is marginal between interpersonal meaning and experiential meaning in that such values combine a subjective assessment of degree of 'vigour' with a depiction of some condition in the external world – the 'manner' in which the process took place. Traditionally within systemic functional linguistics, such adverbs have been classified as 'circumstances of manner' and treated as experiential meanings (see Halliday 1994: 150–1). We follow Stillar, who has argued for separating circumstances/adverbials of manner from other circumstantial meanings (such as those of time, location, cause) on the basis that manner is not an aspect of the material world, since there is no 'inherent way' in which processes are enacted. Accordingly circumstances of manner always implicate the speaker/writer's subjectivity – the speaker's selection of particular manner adverb leaves a trace of their own attitudes and point-of-view (Stillar 1998: 37).

Scaling for degree of 'vigour' is not, of course, confined to 'isolating' formulations of this type. In exemplifying the infused **intensification** of verbal processes above, we offered several instances where the intensification is likewise by reference to degree of vigour. Thus,

> The clouds <u>drifted</u> across the sky (*down-scaled 'vigour' with respect to motion*)

is the analogue of

> The clouds <u>moved slowly</u> across the sky

while

> The clouds <u>raced</u> across the sky (*up-scaled 'vigour' with respect to motion*)

is the analogue of

> The clouds <u>moved rapidly</u> across the sky.

Similarly,

> I <u>glanced</u> over the work (*down-scaled 'vigour' of perception*)

is the analogue of

> I <u>casually looked</u> over the work

while

> I <u>scrutinised</u> the work (*up-scaled 'vigour' of perception*)

is the analogue of

> I <u>looked closely</u> at the work.

3.19.7 Intensification of processes – metaphor

Figurative meanings (metaphor and simile) are also occasionally employed in the intensification of processes. These occur both under isolation, for example,

> He came out <u>like a jack in a box</u> (*high degree of vigour*)

and under infusion, for example,

> Prices have <u>sky-rocketed</u> (*high degree of vigour*)
> The water <u>dribbled</u> from the tap (*low degree of vigour*)

Such metaphors typically involve de-lexicalisation. In the terms employed in the literature on metaphor they are, to greater or lesser degrees, 'dead', 'dormant', 'inactive' or 'conventionalised'.

3.19.8 The grammar of intensification – summary

In summary, then, the semantics of intensification is one by which:

- the **intensification** (up-scaling/down-scaling) applies to either qualities (*slightly greedy, very greedy*) or verbal processes (*reduced it slightly, reduced it greatly*);
- the **intensification** is realised either via an isolated lexeme (*slightly, very, greatly*), via semantic infusion (*happy ^ ecstatic; trickled ^ poured*) or via repetition (*laughed and laughed and laughed*);
- the realisation is either figurative (<u>crystal</u> *clear, came out* <u>like a jack in box</u>, *prices* <u>sky-rocketed</u>) or non-figurative (<u>very</u> *clear,* <u>greatly</u> *reduced, moved* <u>rapidly</u>);
- in the case of isolated **intensifications**, the realisation is either grammatical (<u>very</u> *easy,* <u>greatly</u> *reduced*) or lexical (<u>amazingly</u> *easy,* <u>crystal</u> *clear, moved* <u>rapidly</u>);
- lexical **intensifications** of qualities are typically attitudinal – for example, *amazingly, dreadfully, ridiculously*, though at least some figurative locutions are less so – for example, <u>ice</u> *cold*;
- lexical **intensifications** of processes are not typically attitudinal – for example, *moved* <u>swiftly</u>, *stared* <u>intently</u>, with a few exceptions – for example, *prices fell* <u>dramatically</u>.

The combinations of these features which operate for the scaling of qualities is demonstrated in Table 3.6, and for the scaling of processes in Table 3.7 following.

3.20 Force: quantification

Quantification involves scaling with respect to amount (eg size, weight, strength, number), and with respect to extent, with extent covering

Table 3.6 Feature combinations for quality intensifications [Qualities]

repetition	infusion	isolation		
		grammatical	lexical	
			non-figurative	figurative
a deplorable, disgraceful, despicable act	contended ^ happy ^ joyous	slightly greedy ^ relatively greedy ^ very greedy	dreadfully poor (attitudinal)	dirt poor (attitudinal); ice cold (non-attitudinal)

Table 3.7 Feature combinations for process intensifications [Processes]

repetition	infusion		isolation		
	non-figurative	figurative	grammatical	lexical	
				non-figurative	figurative
we laughed and laughed and laughed	likes ^ loves ^ adores; trickles ^ flows, gushes	prices inched up ^ prices sky-rocketed	slightly reduce ^ greatly reduce	move slowly ^ move rapidly (non-attitudinal); fell dramatically (attitudinal)	came out like a jack in a box (non-attitudinal); wander about like Brown's cows (attitudinal)

scope in time and space (ie how widely distributed, how long lasting) and proximity in time and space (ie how near, how recent).

The semantics of this sub-system are complicated by the fact that the quantified entity can be either concrete (eg *large shark, many sharks, nearby sharks*) or abstract (eg *a large problem, many problems; a few anxieties, a slight fear; a great success, her many betrayals*). Often these abstract entities will convey attitudinal meanings. For example:

(affect) I have <u>many</u> worries about your performance. / A <u>huge</u> sense of relief overwhelmed me. / I have a <u>tiny little</u> concern as regards her design sense

(judgement) There is <u>vast</u> corruption in this government. / His one <u>small</u> moral weakness is towards ... / He's got a <u>great</u> talent for playing the guitar / I do seem to have a <u>small</u> talent for explaining things to people of all ages

(appreciation) The <u>many</u> beauties of the Nile valley. / There is a <u>slight</u> problem with your essay / There are a <u>few</u> problems with your essay.

The abstractions, of course, construe as entities values which might otherwise have been construed either as qualities or as processes. For example.

a slight concern [quantified entity] <u>versus</u> *slightly concerned* [intensified quality/process]

a huge success [quantified entity] <u>versus</u> *very successful* [intensified quality]

her many betrayals [quantified entity] <u>versus</u> *frequently betrayed* [process with high value of usuality]

Following Halliday, such formulations are classified as 'grammatical metaphors' in that they involve one category (a quality or a process) being presented as if it were another category (a thing/entity). (See Chapter 1 section 1.2.2 for further discussion.) Accordingly, such formulations construe semantically complex categories in which one layer of meaning (the semantic status of the category as quality or process) is laid over another layer of meaning (the lexicogrammatical status of the category as noun).

What this means is that formulations such as *a huge disappointment/ a slight concern* involve **quantification** when viewed from the perspective of the lexicogrammar (reckonings of the size of 'entities') but **intensification** from the perspective of the discourse semantic meanings being made. We give preference to the lexicogrammar and classify such as instances of graduation: **quantification** (rather than of **intensification**) in recognition of the fact that there is a subtle difference of meaning between the assessment of some behaviour as, for example, *a huge disappointment* (quantification) rather than as *hugely disappointing* (**intensification**). However, it is still necessary to recognise the special 'grammatically metaphorical' nature of this type of **quantification**. In some analyses it may be useful to identify them as instances of **intensification** via **quantification**, or **intensification** as **quantification**.

3.20.1 Modes of quantification: number, mass and extent

Quantifications graduate with respect to imprecise reckonings of number (eg *a few, many*), imprecise reckonings of mass or presence (eg *small,*

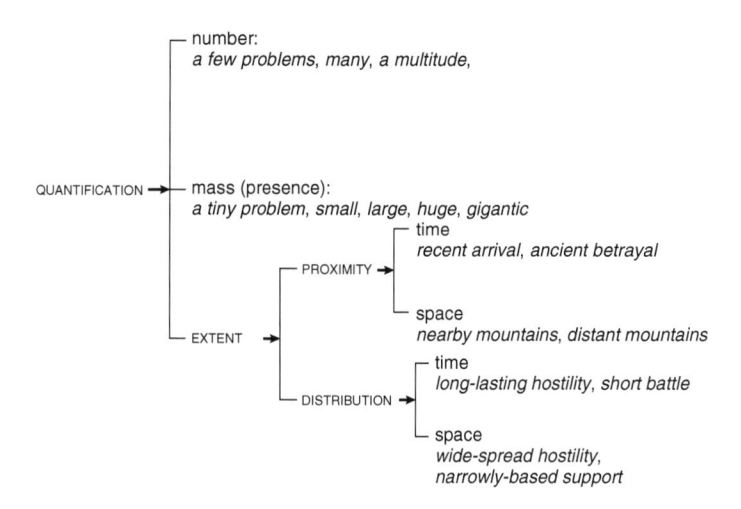

```
                    ┌─ number:
                    │  a few problems, many, a multitude,
                    │
QUANTIFICATION ──┤── mass (presence):
                    │  a tiny problem, small, large, huge, gigantic
                    │                        ┌─ time
                    │         ┌─ PROXIMITY ──┤  recent arrival, ancient betrayal
                    │         │              │
                    │         │              └─ space
                    └─ EXTENT ┤                 nearby mountains, distant mountains
                              │                ┌─ time
                              │                │  long-lasting hostility, short battle
                              └─ DISTRIBUTION ─┤
                                               └─ space
                                                  wide-spread hostility,
                                                  narrowly-based support
```

Figure 3.7 Force: quantification

large; thin, thick; light, heavy; dim, bright) and imprecise reckonings of extent in time and space, with time and space being measured with respect to proximity (eg *near, far; recent, ancient*) or distribution (eg *long-lasting, short-term; wide-spread, sparse*). A system network for quantification is provided in Figure 3.7.

3.20.2 Quantification: isolation and infusion

Quantification is typically via an isolated term acting as a modifier of the graduated entity – eg *many, large, heavy, near, recent, long-lasting*. Nevertheless, there are locutions which are analogous with the infusing formulation we observed under **intensification** in that the estimation of quantity is carried, not by a modifier, but by the noun head itself. For example:

> [*number*]
>
> Canon unveils **a throng of** digital imaging products (versus <u>many</u> digital imaging products)
>
> **The trickle of** enquiries rapidly became **a stream** (versus 'a <u>few</u> enquiries soon became <u>many</u> enquiries')

[*mass – size*]

he's a **mountain** of a man (versus 'he's a <u>large</u> man.')

she's a **slip** of a girl (versus 'she's a <u>small</u> girl')

[*extent*]

I see a **paucity** of talent in this country

There was a **profusion** of pink at the Alexandra Blossom Festival

3.20.3   Quantification: metaphor

As the examples just listed demonstrate, these infusions often involve metaphor which, once again, is to greater or lesser degrees delexicalised (eg *a trickle of enquiries, a mountain of a man*). But metaphor is also to be found in isolating locutions. For example,

> Very shortly we were struggling through **mountainous seas**

The combinations of these features which operate for quantification are set out in Table 3.8.

3.21   Force (intensification and quantification), attitude and writer–reader relationships

As already outlined briefly in the opening chapter (see Chapter 1, section 1.2.5), **force** (both **intensification** and **quantification**) interacts with attitude to either increase or decrease the 'volume' of that attitude as evaluative prosodies are set up across the text. There are associated effect with respect to alignment and solidarity. Upscaling of attitude frequently acts to construe the speaker/writer as maximally committed to the value position being advanced and hence as strongly aligning the reader into that value position. Thus, in the following extract,

Table 3.8   Feature combinations for quantification

isolated		infused	
non-figurative	figurative	non-figurative	figurative
small ^ large ^ huge, a few ^ many	mountainous seas	a crowd of party-goers, a profusion of pink	mountain of a man, a trickle/stream of enquiries

for example, the up-scaling of *unwise* construes the writer as maximally committed to the community of shared value which regards the legislature negatively:

> [3.36] The legislature's **extremely unwise decision** to remove the cap on tuition increases at Ohio's colleges was accompanied by an even more reckless act. [www.cleveland.com/livelines/index.ssf?/livelines/ more/060801.html]

Downscaling frequently has the obverse effect of construing the speaker/writer as having only a partial or an attenuated affiliation with the value position being referenced.

Force plays another important attitudinal role in frequently acting to flag that meanings which are not explicitly attitudinal are, nevertheless, evaluatively charged. Thus **force** is one of the mechanisms by which attitudinal tokens (as opposed to inscriptions) are construed. This functionality was briefly noted at several points previously. Thus in Chapter 2 we observed that the infused intensification conveyed by *smashed* in,

> We took the traditional lands and **smashed** the traditional way of life.

acts to signal to the reader/listener that ethical issues are at stake here. And as we noted in section 3.7.3 above, via upscaled quantification of the sources to whom some proposition is attributed (eg *most linguists believe that* ...), it is possible to construe indirectly that proposition as highly warrantable. (For further detail and discussion of this effect see Hood 2004.)

A full system-network for **graduation** is supplied in Figure 3.8.

3.22 Analysing intersubjective positioning

With this we conclude our outline of the resources of **engagement** and **graduation**. In this final section we provide a brief exploration of how these meanings interact with each other and with values of **attitude** as evaluative orientations are built across the unfolding text. Although the text we employ for this purpose is a short one (a free-standing snippet from a newspaper column made up of five similar such snippets), it nevertheless demonstrates some of the key effects which are to be observed as **engagement**, **graduation** and **attitude** interact in context. The text is concerned with two popular British television police dramas, *Inspector*

154 *The Language of Evaluation*

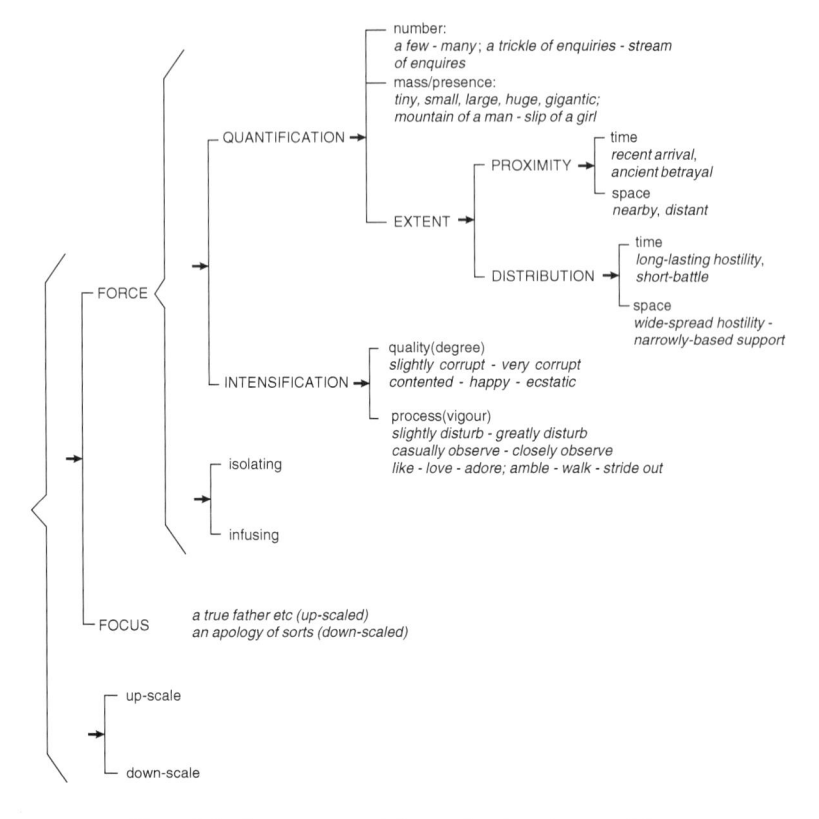

```
                        ┌─ number:
                        │   a few - many; a trickle of enquiries - stream
                        │   of enquires
         ┌─ QUANTIFICATION ─┤
         │              │   mass/presence:
         │              └─  tiny, small, large, huge, gigantic;
         │                  mountain of a man - slip of a girl
         │                                    ┌─ time
         │                                    │   recent arrival,
         │                      ┌─ PROXIMITY ─┤   ancient betrayal
         │                      │             └─ space
         │                      │                nearby, distant
         │         ┌─ EXTENT ───┤
         │         │            │             ┌─ time
         │         │            │             │   long-lasting hostility,
┌─ FORCE ─┤        │            └─ DISTRIBUTION ─┤ short-battle
│         │        │                          └─ space
│         │        │                             wide-spread hostility -
│         │        │                             narrowly-based support
│         │                       ┌─ quality(degree)
│         │                       │   slightly corrupt - very corrupt
│         │                       │   contented - happy - ecstatic
│         └─ INTENSIFICATION ─────┤
│                                 │   process(vigour)
│                                 └─  slightly disturb - greatly disturb
│                                     casually observe - closely observe
│                                     like - love - adore; amble - walk - stride out
│
│         ┌─ isolating
│
│         └─ infusing
│
│                    a true father etc (up-scaled)
└─ FOCUS             an apology of sorts (down-scaled)

   ┌─ up-scale
   │
   └─ down-scale
```

Figure 3.8 System network for graduation: force and focus

Morse and *The Sweeney*, both of which featured the actor John Thaw in the lead role. *Inspector Morse* was screened in the 1990s and *The Sweeney* in the 1970s. The latter was renowned for its warts-and-all portrayal of its police detective characters (played by Thaw and Denis Waterman) who were beloved by viewers on account of their fallibility and the fact that they often cut corners in their efforts to apprehend the guilty. It also makes reference to the British 'Police and Criminal Evidence Act' a major 1984 reform to the codes of practice by which police officers in the UK stop, search, detain and arrest suspects.

> I KNOW Inspector Morse was supposed to be the pinnacle of the late John Thaw's career, but to my mind he never did anything better than Detective

Inspector Jack Regan in The Sweeney. I still occasionally watch reruns on satellite TV. Even now, 25 years on, they remain wonderful – not least in their depiction of a proper police force in the days before the twin blights of the Police and Criminal Evidence Act and political correctness. [From a weekly column by Simon Heffer, *Daily Mail* – 23/02/02]

In such analyses we are interested in whether key propositions are formulated monoglossically or heteroglossically and, if the proposition is monoglossically formulated, in whether it is 'taken-for-granted' or treated as 'at issue'. If heteroglossically formulated, we are interested broadly in whether the author's stance is dialogistically contractive or expansive, and then more narrowly in the sub-type of **engagement**, the nature of any alignments construed, and the responses being anticipated. With respect to **graduations**, we are interested in which meanings they are applied to and whether they act to indicate increased or decreased investment in the value position.

In the following we provide a proposition by proposition analysis attending to these issues:

> <u>I know</u> [*contract*: *concur*] Inspector Morse was <u>supposed</u> [*expand*: *distance*] to be the <u>pinnacle</u> [*attitude*: *intensified* +ve *appreciation*] of the late John Thaw's career ...

By *was supposed to be* the writer attributes the proposition (that Inspector Morse was the pinnacle of John Thaw's career) to some unspecified, but presumably quite broadly-based, external source, while at the same time **distancing** himself from that proposition. (The contrast here is between *Inspector Morse is supposed to be the pinnacle* [distancing] and *Inspector Morse is seen as the pinnacle* [acknowledging].) By *I know*, he presents himself as sharing with the reader, not a positive assessment of Inspector Morse, but the knowledge that there are many people (those who do the 'supposing') who hold this view. As indicated previously, **concurrences** of this type are often precursors to a **counter**, in which case they present the writer as conceding a point to a contrary value position, only then to step back and to more broadly confront that dialogic alternative. This is the case here – the *I know* is likely to be read as concessive, especially as it operates in conjunction with the **distancing** effect of *supposed*. By this combination of dialogistically expansive and contractive meanings, the writer construes a heteroglossic backdrop for the text in which there is divided opinion as to which of the John Thaw police dramas is the best, anticipates that at least some of his readers will hold *Inspector Morse* to be Thaw's best work, while foreshadowing that he himself does not share this view. He thus anticipates disalignment between himself and at least some members of his construed audience over this issue.

> but [*contract: counter*] to my mind [*expand: entertain*] he never [*contract: deny / intensify: heightened negation*] did anything better [*attitude +ve appreciation / intensify: heighten = 'the best'*] than Detective Inspector Jack Regan in The Sweeney.

The connective *but* supplies the foreshadowed **counter**, thereby signalling that the writer's own preference for *The Sweeney* over *Inspector Morse* is somehow counter-expectational. He thus makes dialogic space for those who prefer *Inspector Morse* in his acknowledgment that his own taste is 'abnormal'. By the **denial** (*never*) he, of course, explicitly declares his disalignment with those who believe that Thaw did, in fact, do things which were better than *The Sweeney*. We note the use of the intensifying *he never did* (contrasting with *he didn't do*) in order to signal the strength of his alignment with this particular value position. Crucially, this intensified declaration of disalignment with at least some of his projected audience is framed by the dialogistically expansive *to my mind*. He thereby acknowledges that this is but one of a range of possible views of Thaw's various performances, by this simultaneously signalling an anticipation that those he is addressing may not share his view and making space for any such dialogistic alternatives in the ongoing colloquy in which he places the text.

> I still [*contract: counter*] occasionally [*intensify: down-scaled usuality*] watch reruns on satellite TV.

The *still* here construes the writer's occasional watching of such reruns as in some way counter-expectational – it counters the expectation that an individual such as the celebrated columnist Simon Heffer would not watch such programs, given their age or perhaps given that they are now only shown on 'satellite' television. The sentence is only incidental with respect to the text's central evaluative concerns. Nevertheless it acts to construe as natural, and to project onto the audience, particular expectations about the viewing of old television programs and the viewing habits of the writer. It constructs the writer and reader as sharing certain assumptions about what is 'normal' behaviour in this regard.

Even now, [contract: counter] 25 years on, they remain wonderful [attitude +ve appreciation]

Here the writer references, and projects onto the audience, a paradigm of aesthetic evaluation by which the value of television programs is assumed to decline with age. The *even* presents *The Sweeney's* 'wonderfulness' as an unexpected exception to this 'rule' and thereby intensifies the positivity of the writer's assessment. At the same time, Heffer acknowledges the somewhat untoward nature of his high estimation, thus opening up a line of possible rapport with those who are not quite so positively disposed.

not least in their depiction of a proper [*graduation/focus: (sharpen), token of attitude: +ve normality*] police force in the days before the twin blights [*attitude −ve appreciation (valuation = unhealthy)*] of the Police and Criminal Evidence Act and political correctness. [*for this writer, attitude: −ve propriety*]

The crucial propositions here are that previously the UK had a 'proper' police force, but this is no longer the case, and that this is because the Police and Criminal Evidence Act and political correctness have 'blighted' law enforcement in the UK. The proposition that policing has been ruined in this way is monoglossed and, by means of the nominalisation *the twin blights of*, formulated as 'taken-for-granted'. This taken-for-grantedness acts to present this highly negative view of policing policy as unproblematic and self-evident for the reader for whom the text is intended, thus construing both writer and the intended reader as having categorical membership in this particular attitudinal community. Via the monoglossia, the writer construes the value positions of those who have a different view of these changes to policing practices (presumably those who implemented them and keep them in place) as not needing to be recognised or engaged with in any way. As a consequence, those who might hold to such a dissenting view are excluded from any possible solidarity with the writer since, not only are they very obviously at odds with the writer, but theirs is a viewpoint which places them outside the discursive community which the text constructs for itself.

This analysis is demonstrated diagrammatically in Table 3.9. Instances of upscaling **graduation** are indicated by SMALL CAPS and attitudinal inscriptions are boxed. (Notice that these inscriptions often also involve graduation.) The table should be read downwards, following the numbering (not from left to right), zigzagging across columns as required.

158 *The Language of Evaluation*

This short text, then, provides examples of two rather different configurations of alignment/disalignment. The first is primarily a dyadic arrangement between writer and audience as the writer presents himself as potentially at odds with at least some of his readers over which is the best John Thaw police drama series, while at the same time providing grounds by which solidarity may be maintained in the face of this disagreement. The second alignment configuration is a triadic one. Writer and reader are presented as standing together in their negativity towards these 'politically correct' changes against the alien, 'otherness' of those who implemented them and/or who might now speak in their favour. In the first instance the relationship of disalignment is construed via values of **distance**, **counter** and **denial** while the grounds for solidarity, in the face of this disalignment, are provided via instances of **concur** and

Table 3.9 Engagement analysis of Heffer text

heterogloss		monogloss
expand	**contract**	
	(1) I know [*concur*]	
(2) Inspector Morse was supposed [*distance*] to be the PINNACLE of the late John Thaw's career		
	(3) but [*counter*]	
(4) to my mind [*entertain*]		
	(5) he NEVER [*deny*] did anything BETTER than Detective Inspector Jack Regan in The Sweeney	
	(6) I still [*counter*] occasionally watch reruns on satellite TV ...	
	(7) Even now [*counter*], 25 YEARS ON, they remain WONDERFUL not least [*deny*] in their depiction of	
		(8) a proper police force in the days before the twin BLIGHTS of the Police and Criminal Evidence Act and political correctness

entertain. In the second instance, total alignment between writer and reader is construed via the monoglossic, taken-for-grantedness of the writer's negativity towards the Police and Criminal Evidence Act and 'political correctness'.

Analyses of this type clearly demonstrate the point that appraisal meanings do not operate as isolated values but rather as elements in integrated complexes of meaning where the ultimate rhetorical effect is an artefact of which meanings have been chosen, in which combinations and in which sequences.

Notes

1. For modality see Palmer 1986, and for evidentiality see Chafe & Nichols 1986.
2. For hedging/boosting see Jakobson 1957, Myers 1989, Meyer 1997, Hyland 1996, and for intensification see Labov 1984.
3. Since our focus is upon typically written, singly-constructed texts directed at a mass audience, we must, of necessity, leave as an open question whether or not the positioning effects we describe also apply in immediately interactive, person-to-person text types where, of course, any construal of addresser-addressee relationships is usually subject to immediate challenge, rejection or compliance by the addressee. For discussion of the negotiation of alignment in the context of person-to-person verbal interaction see Clark, Drew & Pinch 2003 or Eggins & Slade 1997.
4. This notion of a 'putative', 'ideal' or 'imagined' reader/audience has, of course, been widely explored in the literature. See, for example, Eco 1984, Coulthard 1994 or Thompson 2001.
5. The now widely accepted argument is that *I think* in structures such as *I think we should leave now* or *I think Rupert cheated* is not the main clause and does not carry full ideational/informational weight. Rather it functions in much the same way as modal adjuncts such as *possibly* or *probably* would – thus *I think we should leave now* is close in its communicative functionality to *Probably we should leave now*. For the details of this argument see Halliday 1994: 254.
6. For further discussion of this type of 'expository question' see White 2003.
7. Although there is some overlap between our use of the term 'attribute' and the use that is made of the term in the Birmingham school of Sinclair, Tadros and Hunston (see for example Sinclair 1986, Tadros 1993, Hunston 2000), ours is, nevertheless, a somewhat different formulation directed towards analysing dialogistic functionality rather than towards identifying the primary source of the proposition.
8. There are some contexts where the positive can invoke the negative – for example, a sign at the verge of a wide expanse of neatly mown lawn by a footpath in Toronto, Canada, carried the following: 'Please Walk On The Grass'. Certain assertions of obligation or entitlement also may involve the positive invoking the negative. Thus, 'Class 4A must work quietly' may suggest that someone, somewhere has been suggesting that Class 4A has

NOT been working quietly. This is especially the case with counter-factuals – for example, 'You should have helped your mother with the groceries'.
9. Leech makes essentially this point when he states, 'In fact, the [Co-operative Principle] will predict that negative sentences tend to be used precisely in situations when ... [the speaker] wants to deny some proposition which has been put forward or entertained by someone in the context (probably the addressee).'
10. We note that some instances of *of course* are less highly charged rhetorically in that they perform more of a text organisational function. In order to develop a particular description, explanation or argument, the author needs to state some information which will almost certainly be known by the intended reader because, for example, it is part of the established 'knowledge' operating in that field. This type of *of course* acts almost as an apology, conveying a meaning along the lines of, 'I know you know this, but I still need to state it in order to make my point clearly.'
11. We are indebted to Sue Hood for this insight and specifically for this notion of intensification via degrees of 'vigour'. For an extended discussion see Hood 2004.

4
Evaluative Key: Taking a Stance

4.1 Introduction

Our purpose in previous chapters has been to provide a general account of the resources of evaluation and intersubjective positioning as these operate within English. In this chapter we shift from this global perspective to a more local one. We are concerned with patterns in the use of evaluative resources within texts by which certain types of evaluation and stance are favoured or foregrounded while others occur infrequently, only in restricted settings, or not at all. We report on preliminary findings which suggest that such patterns of use reoccur across groupings of related texts, and postulate the operation of certain conventionalised 'styles' or 'regimes' of evaluative positioning. We conclude that these styles or regimes can be related to particular rhetorical effects and construct particular authorial identities or personas. We demonstrate that in some discourse domains – for example that of mainstream 'broadsheet' journalism – particular text compositional conventions operate to strongly condition the evaluative styles employed by writers.

Before we begin our discussion proper, it is necessary to briefly clarify the status of such 'styles' or 'regimes' as linguistic phenomena. In this we rely on the view of language as socio-semiotic system which has developed within systemic functional theory. We supplied a brief outline of the SFL framework in Chapter 1. Here we focus more specifically on aspects relevant to this notion of evaluative style.

SFL holds language to be a communally-based system of meaning-making possibilities or options (a meaning-making potential), with those possibilities actualised or instantiated by individual texts. (See, for example, Martin 1992b, or Halliday & Matthiessen 1999.) Individual texts exploit only a sub-set of the options made available by the language and hence texts will vary in which of the meaning-making possibilities they take up. This variability is conditioned by key aspects of the social context in which the text operates, namely the social roles and relationships of those involved in the communication, the nature of the text as a communicative process and the domain of human activity or experience it references or enacts. Particular settings for these aspects of social context condition which linguistic options are likely to be taken up by the text. Configurations of these aspects of social context tend to reoccur and accordingly so do the configurations of linguistic options taken up by texts as they reflect a particular social setting. Thus the stylistic similarities which have been observed, for example, in the language doctors use with their patients can be related to consistencies in the power relations which operate in such consultations, the subject matter of illness/medical treatment, and the spoken, spontaneous, face-to-face nature of the communication. Such contextually conditioned configurations of linguistic options are termed 'registers'. A register, therefore, can be thought of as a meaning-making sub-potential – a particular setting of the meaning-making options available to the speaker by which they will be more likely to take up certain options and less likely to take up others, to the point that some options will occur repeatedly while others will be significantly constrained in their use or will not be taken up at all.

The SFL approach, then, leads us to look at linguistic phenomena variably from the perspective of language as meaning making potential and from the perspective of the instantiation of that potential in individual texts. It leads us to identify what Halliday and Matthiessen (1999) have termed a 'cline of instantiation'. At one end of this cline is language viewed as a generalised system of meaning-making potential and at the other extreme is language viewed as the instantiation of that meaning-making potential in individual texts. Between these two extremes are vantage points by which we observe situation-based settings for that generalised potential (sub-potentials) which can be observed across texts of the same text-type or register. Thus, as shown in Table 4.1, we can locate our analytical perspective at any of a number of points along the system/instance cline.

Notice that, following Martin & Rose 2003, we do not see textual instances as the end point of instantiation. While texts are often highly constraining in terms of the meanings which are to be taken up, it is, nevertheless, only through the act of reader/listener interpretation in a given context that meaning actually occurs. And this final 'reading' may, of course, vary between readers/listeners according to

Table 4.1 Cline of instantiation – from system to reading

1. system (the global meaning making potential provided by the language)
2. register (contextual variants or sub-selections of the global meaning-making potential – involving more fully institutionalised reconfigurations of the probabilities for the occurrence of particular meaning-making options or for the co-occurrence of options)
3. text type (groups of texts with comparable configurations of the probabilities of occurrence of options – involving less fully institutionalised configurations of the probabilities)
4. instance (individual texts – the actualisation of the global meaning making potential, typically in conformity with the sub-potential settings of a given register)
5. reading (the uptake of meanings in a text according to the listener/reader's subjectively determined reading position.)

the assumptions, knowledge and value systems they bring to the text and the use they are making of the text. (See Chapter 2, section 2.6 for a fuller account of different orientations to 'reading'.) Thus a text can be seen as providing for a set of possible meanings (though some will be significantly more favoured and hence more probable than others), with particular possibilities only instantiated by a given reading. For one text there can be a range of instantiations and hence interpretations.

The styles of evaluative language which are our concern in this chapter can be understood by reference to this framework, with the appraisal resources we have outlined up to this point operating at the level of generalised systemic potential and the evaluative styles with which we are currently concerned operating at the level of register and of text-type. We outline the cline of potential/instantiation as it applies for evaluation in Table 4.2.

You will notice that we propose two analytical vantage points in the instantiation cline falling between the extremes of system and instance/reading, namely those of 'key' and 'stance'. Through this we identify two ways of looking at the communicative/rhetorical effect we have, to this point, been terming evaluative style. The notion of 'style' always involves degrees of generalisation. In some cases, that generalisation may be across the utterances which constitute a relatively large number of texts, whose voice recurs very generally in institutional settings. We refer to this kind of generalisation of evaluative options as 'key'. Within key, we are also interested in more delicate distinctions among voices

164　*The Language of Evaluation*

Table 4.2　Cline of instantiation – evaluation

1. appraisal (system) – the global potential of the language for making evaluative meanings, eg for activating positive/negative viewpoints, graduating force/focus, negotiating intersubjective stance
2. key (register) – situational variants or sub-selections of the global evaluative meaning making potential – typically reconfiguration of the probabilities for the occurrence of particular evaluative meaning-making options or for the co-occurrence of options
3. stance (text-type) – sub-selections of evaluative options within text; patterns of use of evaluative options within a given 'key' associated with particular rhetorical objectives and the construction of authorial personae
4. evaluation (instance) – instantiation of evaluative options in text
5. reaction (reading) – the take-up of evaluative meanings in a text according to the listener/reader's subjectively determined reading position; the attitudinal positions activated by the reader as a result of their interaction with the text

based on generalisations about relatively smaller numbers of text. We refer to these sub-keys as 'stance'.

4.2　Evaluative key in journalistic discourse – the 'voices' of news, analysis and commentary

We will begin by exploring the notion of evaluative 'key'. We conduct our discussion firstly in the context of journalistic discourse and then briefly by reference to patterns of use of evaluative language in secondary-school-level history text books and student writing. We propose that there are three evaluative keys operating within news and current affairs journalism in the English language, so-called 'high-brow' or 'broadsheet' print media (for example, broadsheets such as *The New York Times*, *The Times*, *The Guardian*, *The Sydney Morning Herald*, the international wire services such as Reuters and Associated Press and the online output of the British Broadcasting Corporation). We term these keys 'reporter voice', 'correspondent voice' and 'commentator voice'. We then demonstrate the operation of analogous configurations of evaluative meanings in secondary-school history, relying on the research of Coffin. Finally we turn to the question of 'stance' and explore the patterns of use of evaluative resources which can be observed in several commentary articles.

In observing print media news reporting texts in their usual context of publication in newspapers, we notice that some taxonomy of journalistic styles or modes seems already to be in operation among journalists themselves. These divisions are indicated by such labels as 'news', 'analysis', 'opinion' and 'comment', with the labels attached either to individual news items or to divided-off sections within the newspaper. It is customary for sections designated as 'news' to precede those designated as 'comment/opinion', although the distinction is not always maintained absolutely. Texts with the label 'analysis' tend to occur in both 'news' and 'comment/opinion' sections.

Previous research by Iedema, Feez and White (see Iedema *et al.*,1994, White 1997 and White 1998) and our own continuing work has demonstrated that while these journalistic labels are not consistent with respect to linguistic features, it is possible, nevertheless, to relate the labels in an informal way to regularities in the use journalistic texts make of the resources of appraisal. It is possible to identify evaluative keys within journalistic writing which can be loosely linked with the journalistic categories of 'news', 'analysis' and 'comment/opinion'. These keys have been given the labels mentioned above – 'reporter voice', 'correspondent voice' and 'commentator voice'.

In outlining this taxonomy of journalistic evaluative styles we rely on the previous work of Iedema *et al.* 1994, and White 1998 mentioned above, but also on our own close textual analysis of a small-scale corpus of journalistic texts. The corpus is made up of the following items:

1. Police rounds reporting (accident and misadventure)
    - 10 news-page items (wire service, BBC online and broadsheets)
2. Crime and Court reporting
    - 10 news-page items (wire service, BBC online and broadsheets)
3. War reporting
    - 10 news-page items (wire service, BBC online and broadsheets)
4. Political Coverage
    - 30 news-page items; 10 items from 'analysis' sections or with 'political editor', 'correspondent' or similar by-lines (wire service, BBC online, and broadsheets)
    - 15 comment/opinion/editorial page items (broadsheets)

In the analysis, all instances of values of **attitude**, **engagement** and **graduation** were recorded, with each identified value being tagged for its sub-type and for its source (whether the author or some external, cited source).

This analysis revealed two types of patterning. First there were highly regular patterns involving the presence/absence of a sub-set of evaluative meanings by which the texts in the corpus could be divided into clear-cut groupings – the 'keys' to which we referred above. These regularities involved the absence/presence of unmediated (authorially-sourced) inscribed **judgement**, and, in those texts where unmediated, inscribed **judgement** did occur, the absence/presence of the **judgement** subcategories of **veracity** and **propriety**. Specifically, the texts in the corpus divided into the following groupings: (1) those in which there was no unmediated inscribed **judgement**; (2) those in which there was unmediated, inscribed **social esteem** (**normality, capacity, tenacity**) but no **social sanction** (**veracity, propriety**); and (3) those in which there was both unmediated **social esteem** and **social sanction**. For the data in our corpus the probabilities associated with these patternings were close to 1 or to 0, according to key type. Thus we found that 36 of our texts had no instances of unmediated inscribed **judgement**, while a further six had only one or two instances. Similarly, there were 11 texts which made regular use of unmediated inscribed **social esteem** but had no instances of unmediated inscribed **social sanction**, and a further three which were similarly oriented towards **social esteem** but which had only the one instance of unmediated, inscribed **social sanction**. Additionally, there were two contingencies associated with these patterns. Unmediated (authorially-sourced) assessments of obligation (eg *they should/must; it's necessary that*) and the reporting of the author's own affectual responses only occurred in those texts which also included instances of unmediated, inscribed **social sanction**. Accordingly, in our corpus, the absence of unmediated inscribed **social sanction** is a definitive predictor that there will be no instances of unmediated assessments of obligation or the reporting of the author's own affectual responses.

The second type of pattern involved, not a categorical difference between keys, but rather a scaling of probabilities by which a given evaluative meaning occurs less frequently or more frequently according to key type. Here frequency is both a matter of whether or not any instances of the meaning occur in a text of a given key, and of the number of instances of that meaning in a given text. This second type of patterning involved values of the attitudinal subtype of **appreciation** and of **graduation** and **engagement**. For reasons of space we will focus primarily on the pattern involving **appreciation** as an exemplar of this second type of patterning and will only present a brief summary of our findings with respect to patterns of **graduation** and **engagement**.

4.2.1 Journalistic keys – patterning with respect to attitude

An analysis of the occurrence of inscribed (explicit) **judgement** across our corpus indicates the following broad distinction:

1. (grouping 1) texts where there are no instances of authorially-sourced (unmediated) inscribed **judgement** – any such judgement is attributed to some external, cited source (36 texts in our corpus, all 'news page' items);
2. (grouping 2) texts where authorially-sourced inscribed **judgement** occurs with some regularity (33 texts).

The following extracts exemplify these two groupings. (Instances of inscribed **judgement** have been underlined and emboldened.)

[4.1] – *grouping 1 (no explicit, authorially-sourced judgement)*
The families of British detainees at Guantanamo Bay are to take their fight for the men's release to the US with the help of the foremost American civil liberties group, they announced yesterday.

Politicians, campaigners and lawyers joined relatives of the prisoners to launch the Guantanamo Human Rights Commission at the House of Commons.

Nine Britons and three British residents are among the 660 men who have been held at the American naval base in Cuba for more than two years without charge or access to lawyers. Another 11 Europeans, several from France, Sweden and Germany, are also detained at Camp Delta.

'We have to speak not only to the courts of law but to the court of public opinion,' Nadine Strossen, the president of the ACLU, said. She said there was growing concern over the Bush administration's actions in the 'war on terror'. ...

'It is plain and clear that the treatment of these 660 being held without charge, without access to a lawyer, without access to a court, **violates the most fundamental of human rights**,' said Philippe Sands QC, professor of law at University College, London. [*Guardian*, 21/01/04: 4]

[4.2] – *grouping 2 (explicit authorial judgement)*
Two years ago today, Feroz Abbasi, a British citizen arrested in Afghanistan, was one of the first detainees to be transferred hooded, shackled and manacled by the US military to Camp X-Ray in Guantanamo Bay. His mother, Zumrati, who lives in Croydon, was informed about five days later – by the media. It took a further six days for a British government official to contact her. Significantly, she was assured that her son did not need a lawyer. Two years on, the British government has **betrayed the most fundamental**

168   *The Language of Evaluation*

responsibility that any government assumes – the duty to protect the rule of law. **This abnegation of the essence of democratic government** goes much further than **a failure to protect the nine British citizens** who are incarcerated in this **legal black hole**. It is nothing less than a **collusion** in an **international experiment in inhumanity**, which is being repeated and expanded around the world. [*Guardian*, 10/01/04: leader pages – 24]

In the first category, then, those values of **judgement** which occur are always mediated through attribution (the journalistic author is never their immediate source). This is demonstrated in the final paragraph of extract [4.1] where the evaluative proposition that the treatment of the detainees *violates the most fundamental of human rights* is attributed to *Philippe Sands QC, professor of law at University College, London*.

In contrast, category 2 texts make regular use of unmediated (authorially-sourced) **judgement** – that is to say, in unattributed contexts where responsibility for the proposition is unambiguously being taken by the journalistic author. This is demonstrated by extract [4.2] above where it is the author who passes the judgement that the government has *failed to protect* its people (an instance of negative **judgement: capacity**) and that it has *betrayed the most fundamental responsibility* and has colluded *in inhumanity* (instances of negative **judgement: propriety**).

Tokens of **judgement** (indirect invocations) are not implicated in this pattern – they occur freely in both textual groupings. Thus in extract [4.1], the journalistic author provides a depiction which has a clear potential, given the appropriate reading position, to trigger an assessment of negative **propriety** on the part of the US authorities. S/he offers the 'factual' information that nine Britons and three British residents are being held without charge or access to lawyers. Tellingly s/he also characterises the length of their detention as in some way contrary to expectation – *more than two years*. There are a number of similar tokens of **judgement** in the first paragraph of [4.2], where, for example, the journalistic author assembles the 'facts' so as to depict the detained Mr Feroz Abbasi, as being lead away, *hooded, shackled and manacled*.

Our preliminary study indicates that the absolute prohibition on unmediated explicit **judgement** (grouping 1) operates more frequently in certain journalistic domains than in others – for example it typically operates in police-rounds and court reporting but significantly less frequently in the context of political coverage. Thus in our corpus, 9 out

Evaluative Key: Taking a Stance 169

of the 10 police rounds reports had no instances of unmediated explicit **judgement**, while only 12 out of the 30 political reports conformed to this pattern. We use the term 'reporter voice' (following Iedema *et al.* 1994 and White 1998) for this evaluative key. The choice of the label is motivated by the strong association between this voice and the journalistic role of 'general reporter' – the journalistic function most typically associated with 'hard news' coverage.

The second category, where there is a regular occurrence of unmediated **judgement**, has been termed 'writer voice', with the labelling motivated by the common-sense distinction between the more formulaic 'reporting' of 'hard news' coverage and the somewhat less formulaic, more individualised 'writing' associated with media 'analysis', 'commentary' and 'human interest'. This first, two-way cut between reporter and writer voice is represented diagrammatically in Figure 4.1.

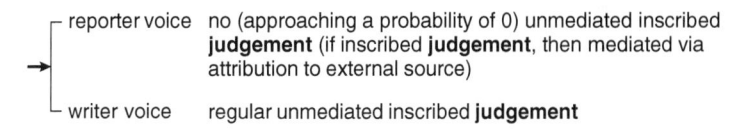

```
┌─ reporter voice   no (approaching a probability of 0) unmediated inscribed
│                   judgement (if inscribed judgement, then mediated via
→│                  attribution to external source)
└─ writer voice     regular unmediated inscribed judgement
```

Figure 4.1 Reporter and writer voices: patterns of inscribed authorial judgement

A further distinction within 'writer voice' texts is observable when we attend more delicately to the types of **judgement** values which occur. We observe a distinction between:

1. those texts where there are no constraints on any values of **judgement** – whatever the values (**social esteem** or **social sanction**), they may occur in unmediated contexts (authors are free to evaluate by means of the full range of **judgement** options); and
2. those texts where the **judgement** values of **social esteem** occur in unmediated contexts, but where any **judgement** values of **social sanction** occur only in attributed contexts (authors pass judgements of **normality, capacity** and/or **tenacity** but not of **veracity** or **propriety**).

In the first category, then, the full repertoire of attitudinal values is employed without any apparent co-textual requirements. It is, in fact, only here that we observe journalistic texts in which the author employs, on his/her own behalf, the language's full attitudinal potential. We give the label 'commentator voice' to this grouping for the obvious reason that, within the broadsheet media,[1] this evaluative style is typically only found in the context of commentary, opinion and editorials. Extract [4.2], which we discussed above, exemplifies this 'commentator voice' category. It is typical of this category in being primarily concerned with assessments of **social sanction**, but with also making some reference to assessments of social esteem. For example,

> Two years on, it is clear that the British government has **betrayed the most fundamental responsibility** [−ve *social sanction: impropriety*] that any government assumes – the duty to protect the rule of law. **This abnegation of the essence of democratic government** [−ve *social sanction: impropriety*] goes much further than **a failure to protect the nine British citizens** [−ve *social esteem: incapacity*] who are incarcerated in this legal black hole. It is nothing less than a **collusion** in an **international experiment in inhumanity** [+ve *social sanction: impropriety*] which is being repeated and expanded around the world.

Texts which fall into the second category (unmediated **social esteem** but no/minimal unmediated **social sanction**) occur most typically in the context of news page analysis and backgrounders by rounds writers and correspondents and this evaluative key has consequently been labelled 'correspondent voice'. It is also very frequently the 'voice' of news-page political coverage. These texts, then, are like commentator voice texts in that the journalistic author does pass judgement, but are unlike them in that the author is limited to a smaller repertoire of **judgemental** values. On the other hand, they are akin to reporter voice texts with respect to inscribed **social sanction** in that where such assessments do occur, they occur only in material attributed to external sources.

This 'correspondent voice' key is demonstrated by means of the following text analysis. It involves a news-page political analysis piece concerned with the release of a 'statement of personal beliefs' in early 2004 by the then newly-appointed British Conservative Party leader, Michael Howard. The Conservative Party leader's statement consisted of a series of declarations of the form, 'I believe it is natural for men and women to want health, wealth and happiness for their families.' We identify instances of inscribed authorial **judgement**, but also attend to instances of authorial **appreciation**, since they are part of the more general attitudinal environment in which the **judgements** operate. This more extended exemplification is provided here in order to demonstrate that the orientation to **social esteem**, rather than **social sanction**, is maintained across the text as a whole. On account of space limitations we do not provide the entire text but have been careful to ensure that nothing has been removed which would be significant for an analysis of evaluative style.

[4.3] – *correspondent voice (analysis of correspondent voice text)*
Key to text-analysis annotations
… indicates some of the original text has been omitted
underlined = material attributed to an external source, hence material for which the author does not take responsibility (not included in the analysis of authorial voice)
bold+Impact = authorial (non-attributed) inscribed **judgement**
Franklin Gothic small caps = **appreciation**

MOST voters, if quizzed about Michael Howard, would list his role in the poll tax, getting **kebabbed**[1] by Jeremy Paxman on Newsnight,

[1] kebbaded *–ve judgement: capacity (to 'get kebabbed' by an interviewer is to demonstrate a lack of proficiency in handling the media, hence negative capacity)*

and Ann Widdecombe's Devastating[2] putdown that he had 'something of the night' about him.

[2] devastating putdown *+ve appreciation (of 'putdown') acting as a token of +ve judgement: capacity (to 'devastatingly put-down' is to demonstrate rhetorical skill)*

But today we are treated to a new and Surprising[3] twist on the Howard image. In a 'personal credo', the Tory leader borrows the rhetorical style of John F Kennedy or Martin Luther King to set out a philosophy he says will underpin the next manifesto.

[3] surprising *appreciation (but only if 'surprising' here conveys a positive sense – otherwise un-usuality and/or impersonalised affect)*

Meanwhile, he uses his first keynote interview since becoming leader to talk about going to Beatles concerts (he saw them before they were **famous**[4] enough to top the bill),

[4] famous *+ve judgement: normality*

his early love of Elvis, and the **untimely**[5] death of his immigrant father from cancer. Mr Howard also tells how he challenged segregation in America's Deep South in the Sixties by choosing to sit beside a black person in a Greyhound bus. He invited his fellow passenger for a cup of coffee at a rest stop but was told it was impossible because blacks could not go into whites-only cafs. …

Mr Howard is a more **passionate**[6] and **INTERESTING**[7] political personality than the product of Thatcherism he is often portrayed as.

There is nothing **REMARKABLE**[8] about a politician trying to improve their public image by talking about their beliefs, tastes in films or youthful exploits.

Tony Blair **cornered the market**[9] in personality politics a decade ago, and his older **rival has a lot of catching up to do**.[10]

But what is really **REMARKABLE**[11] about Mr Howard's move is the timing.

January 2004 bears all the portents of being a MILESTONE[12] political month, with the Hutton inquiry report into the death of David Kelly and the rebellion over university fees coming in the space of four weeks.

The conventional wisdom of Tory MPs is that Mr Howard need only bare his claws in the Commons, unleash **his acid debating skills**[13] against the Prime Minister and the Tories cannot help but soar in the polls.

The Evening Standard (London) 02/01/04

[5] untimely −ve judgement: normality (the material attributed to Howard contains a number of obvious tokens of +ve judgement which, of course, have the potential to position the reader to view Howard positively)

[6] passionate +ve judgement: tenacity
[7] interesting +ve judgement: capacity

[8] appreciation

[9] +ve judgement: capacity

[10] −ve judgement: capacity

[11] remarkable +ve appreciation

[12] milestone +ve appreciation: social valuation

[13] acid skills +ve judgement: capacity

Evaluative Key: Taking a Stance 173

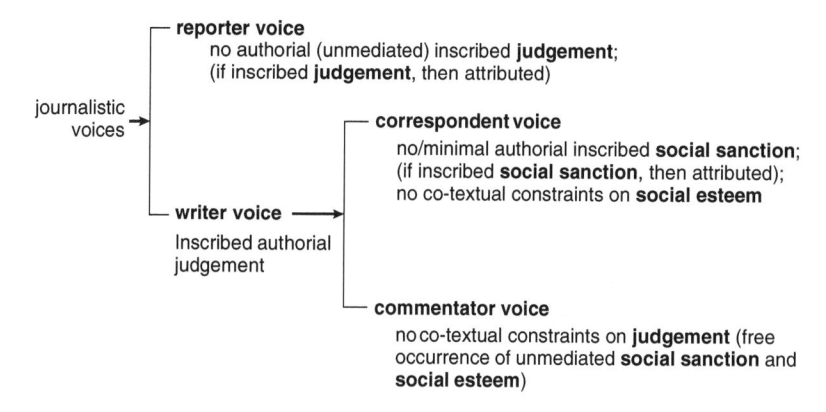

```
journalistic ─┬─ reporter voice
voices        │   no authorial (unmediated) inscribed judgement;
              │   (if inscribed judgement, then attributed)
              │
              └─ writer voice ─┬─ correspondent voice
                 Inscribed     │   no/minimal authorial inscribed social sanction;
                 authorial     │   (if inscribed social sanction, then attributed);
                 judgement     │   no co-textual constraints on social esteem
                               │
                               └─ commentator voice
                                  no co-textual constraints on judgement (free
                                  occurrence of unmediated social sanction and
                                  social esteem)
```

Figure 4.2 Elaborated system of journalistic key

This three-element taxonomy of journalistic keys is illustrated diagrammatically in Figure 4.2.

This patterning, then, suggests that within journalistic discourse there are three distinct configurations/re-configurations of the language's global potential for evaluative meaning making – three sub-potentials. Commentator voice operates under an evaluative arrangement in which the full range of **judgement** values is available to the writer, while in both correspondent and reporter voice there is a reconfiguration by which fewer options are accessible – in correspondent voice, the journalistic author has no, or only very limited, access to unmediated, explicit **social sanction**, while in reporter voice access to unmediated explicit **judgement** of all types is curtailed. From this perspective, reporter voice and correspondent voice group together as instances of attitudinal restriction. Our study suggests that these re-configurations are highly regular across 'broadsheet' journalistic discourse of this type. Our corpus provided the following breakdown:

- (reporter voice) Thirty-six texts had no instances of unmediated inscribed **judgement**, while a further six had only one or two instances. These texts were all located in sections designated as 'news'.
- (correspondent voice) Eleven texts included instances of authorially-sourced inscribed **social esteem**, but had no instances of

inscribed authorial **social sanction** – a further five texts had instances of inscribed authorial **social esteem** and only one or two instances of inscribed authorial **social sanction**. These texts were located variously in sections designated as news or as comment/opinion.
- (commentator voice) Seventeen texts made regular use of inscribed authorial **social sanction** and all of these also contained some instances of inscribed authorial **social esteem**. All these texts were either located in comment/opinion sections or were explicitly labelled 'comment' or 'analysis'.

The patternings with respect to the other attitudinal sub-systems (**appreciation** and **affect**) were of a different order. Neither authorially-sourced **appreciation** nor **affect** were subject to the same degree of curtailment as applied to inscribed **judgement** in reporter voice and inscribed **judgement: social sanction** in correspondent voice, with instances of both sub-types occurring across the three keys. Perhaps most tellingly, both unmediated **affect** and **appreciation** occur with some regularity in reporter voice texts. This pattern of occurrence is demonstrated by the following analysis of a 'hard news' misadventure report. In the text, all instances of inscribed **judgement** are mediated through attribution to external sources, while there are several instances of authorially-sourced (unmediated) **appreciation** and **affect**

[4.4]: *Reporter voice Italian ski-lift disaster report, appreciation and affect analysis*

Key to annotation

- mediated (attributed) material is underlined
- inscribed appreciation in SMALL CAPS (underlined SMALL CAPS indicates attributed appreciation)
- inscribed affect in *italics* (underlined *italics* indicates that affectual reactions are being reported by external sources)
- inscribed judgement in **bold+impact** (underlining of the **bold+impact** indicates that the judgement is attributed)

Italian PM: Plane Was FAR TOO LOW [1]

CAVALESE, Italy (AP) – The U.S. Marine jet that severed a ski lift cable, plunging 20 people to their deaths, **violated Italian air safety regulations**[2] with its "earth-shaving flight" across a snowy hillside, the prime minister of this *angry*[3] nation said Wednesday.

The defense minister said the American pilot should be prosecuted, several KEY[4] lawmakers said U.S. bases in Italy should be closed, and Italian and American investigators started looking into the accident near Trento, about 90 miles east of Milan.

'This is not about a low-level flight, but a **terrible act**,[5] a nearly earth-shaving flight, **beyond any limit allowed by the rules and laws**,'[6] Premier Romano Prodi told reporters.

Witnesses said the Marine EA-6B Prowler swooped through the valley just above the treetops on Tuesday. Its tail severed two, fist-sized, steel cables, sending a gondola full of European skiers and the operator to their deaths.

Startled by an unusually loud boom, 66-year-old Carla Naia looked up and saw the jet 'coming at me at an incredible speed.'

'I've seen lots of planes and I've often cursed them,' the Cavalese resident said. 'But this one seemed **completely out of control**,[7] far lower and faster than the others.'

[authorial evaluations indicated in bold]
[1] attributed −ve appreciation: valuation (harm): negatively construed state-of-affair, acting as token of −ve judgement (triggering assessment of negligence or incompetence on the part of the pilots)

[2] attributed −ve judge: propriety

[3] **authorial reporting of an affectual response**

[4] **authorial +ve appreciation: valuation (social significance)**

[5] attributed −ve judge: propriety (As a consequence of grammatical metaphor, 'act' is grammatically a 'thing' but emantically a 'process', specifically a human behaviour. Accordingly, 'terrible act' may be ambiguous as to the distinction between judgement and appreciation.)

[6] attributed −ve judge: propriety

[7] attributed −ve judge: capacity

176   *The Language of Evaluation*

Residents of this valley have long complained about low-flying jets out of Aviano Air Base at the foot of the Italian Alps.

'We are fed up,'[8] said Mauro Gilmozi, the mayor of this PICTURESQUE[9] town of 3,600.

[8] reporting of an affectual response by an external source
[9] authorial +ve appreciation: quality

"This '**Top Gun' stuff**[10] has got to stop."
...

[10] attributed −ve judge: tenacity (over-enthusiastic, blazé, macho, alternatively −ve propriety – criminally reckless – may be ambiguous as to judgement versus appreciation according to how the reference of 'stuff' is resolved)

Anger[11] continued to build in Italy, an IMPORTANT[12] U.S. ally and home to seven MAJOR[13] U.S. military installations. U.S. flights over Italy have increased dramatically since the international intervention in Bosnia, one of Aviano's most IMPORTANT[14] jobs. ....

[11] **authorial reporting of an observed affectual reaction**

[12, 13, 14] **authorial +ve appreciation: valuation (social significance)**

Foreign Minister Lamberto Dini *deplored*[15] the accident but said that it would not '<u>distort our alliances and our collective security structures</u>.' Defense Minister Beniamino Andreatta took a HARSHER[16] line, demanding that the pilot be prosecuted. ...

[15] reporting of an affectual response by an external source

[16] authorial −ve appreciation: quality

(Associated Press 4/2/98)

Our data does suggest, however, that values of **appreciation** occur more frequently in writer voice than in reporter voice, pointing, as we indicated above, to a clinal difference in patterns of occurrence. Specifically, we recorded the following rates of occurrence of authorially-sourced **appreciation** in our corpus:

- reporter voice: 35 of the 42 texts contained instances at rates of between 0.9 and 6.3 per 500 words

- writer voice: all texts contained instances at rates of between 1.6 and 11.3 per 500 words.

No significant patterns of difference between keys was observable in the use of values of **affect** until we attended to whether the author was describing his/her own emotional responses or was purporting to report the emotional responses of participants in the event being depicted (as was the case in [4.4] above – eg <u>Anger</u> continued to build in Italy). (Notice that we distinguish here between the writer projecting an affectual response onto some participant in the depicted event – eg *this <u>angry</u> nation* – and external sources reporting their own emotions – eg *'We are <u>fed up</u>,' said Mauro Gilmozi*. In the first instance the **affect** is unmediated, in the second mediated.) The only instances of writers reporting their own affectual responses occurred in commentator voice texts – that is to say, in texts which also included explicit authorially-sourced **social sanction**. For example,

It was, then, with <u>fury</u> that I returned home on Saturday to find my own country rumbling with the mumbles of the peaceniks.

The complete absence of such meanings from all our reporter and correspondent voice texts is strongly suggestive that there is a conventionalised re-configuration of meaning potential by which this type of **affect** is curtailed in these two voices. Curtailment of authorial **affect** goes hand-in-hand with curtailment of authorially-sourced **judgement**. However, we also note that authorial **affect** of this type was not a particularly regular feature of the commentator voice sub-grouping in our corpus – it occurred in only four out of the 17 commentator voice texts and then at only a low rate of frequency.

The profile of the three voices with respect to attitude is set out in Figure 4.3.

There is one further evaluative meaning which, in our data, co-patterns with unmediated **social sanction** and authorial **affect** – instances of unmediated assessments of obligation, eg *it's necessary that...; the government must act to ensure*. To deal with what is at stake here interpersonally we need to attend to the distinction between the informational and the actional functionality of language. Within SFL, clauses are classified according to whether they are concerned with the offering or requesting of information (statements and questions), or the offering or requesting of goods-&-services (commands and offers). Those concerned with information exchange are termed 'propositions' and those with goods-&-services exchanges 'proposals'. (See Halliday 1994: 71.) Propositions are exhaustively grounded in the linguistic domain in that,

178   *The Language of Evaluation*

```
journalistic
voices
├── reporter voice
│     no (extremely low probability of) unmediated inscribed judgement
│     no authorial affect
│     lower probability (relative to writer voice) unmediated inscribed appreciation
│     + observed affect (e.g. the angry nation)
│
└── writer voice → Inscribed authorial judgement
      ├── correspondent voice
      │     no (low probability of) unmediated inscribed social sanction
      │     no authorial affect
      │     regular unmediated inscribed social esteem
      │     higher probability (relative to reporter voice) unmediated inscribed
      │       appreciation
      │     + observed affect (e.g. the angry nation)
      │
      └── commentator voice
            no co-textual constraints on judgement (free occurrence of unmediated
              social sanction and social esteem)
            higher probability (relative to reporter voice) unmediated inscribed
              appreciation
            + observed affect (e.g. the angry nation)
            + authorial affect
```

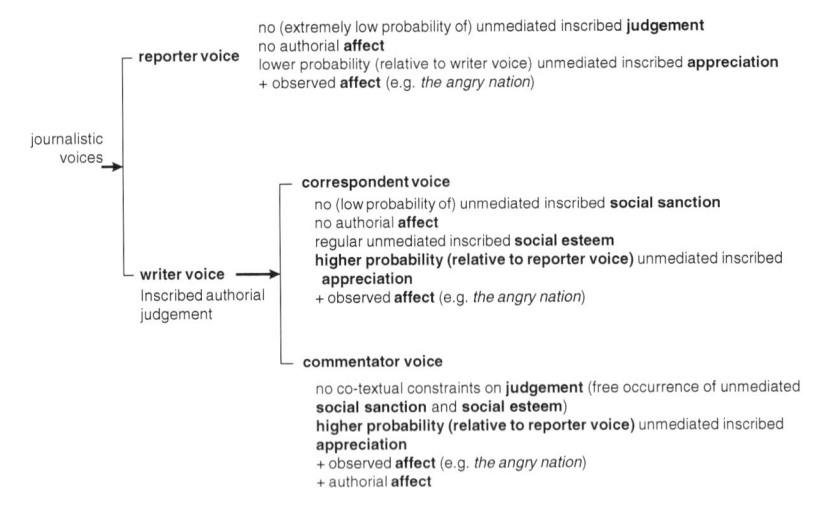

Figure 4.3   Journalistic keys – attitudinal profile

for their successful operation, they require only the exchange of verbally construed meanings. In contrast, the scope of proposals extends beyond the linguistic in that they frequently have as their objective some non-linguistic action. Thus by employing a command we seek to control the behaviour of those we address and to have them supply some good or service. Proposals in this sense are 'actional' in that they are directed towards eliciting particular actions in those addressed.

Media texts of the type we are considering very rarely contain outright commands or offers. Apart from metadiscursive directives such as *let us not forget that*, there were none in our small-scale corpus. However, media texts do occasionally include a clause type which is closely related to the command, those involving modals of obligation and related structures. For example:

> What can an ordinary person do about a world turned on its head, where governments that claim to be democratic engage in repression, coercion and even torture on an international scale? **Everyone needs to protest – peacefully, but as loudly and as persistently as they are able**. Every act counts.

While such formulations are statements in terms of their grammatical structure, in terms of their speech functionality they are indirect realisations of commands – they constitute a type of demand for some action or response on the part of the addressee or some third party. They can therefore be classified as 'actional' rather than 'informational' and

Evaluative Key: Taking a Stance 179

can be grouped with direct commands under the general heading 'directive'. (For further discussion modals of obligation see Chapter 3, section 3.6.3 and for their relationship with commands see the section on interpersonal metaphors of mood in Halliday 1994, Chapter 10.) In our data, authors propose such directives (as opposed to reporting directives by external sources) only in those texts in which they also pass **judgements** of **social sanction** – authorial directives only occur in commentator voice texts. In reporter voice and correspondent voice texts, should any directives occur, they are contained in material attributed to external sources. We demonstrate these difference patterns of occurrence/co-occurrence by means of the following two extracts – the first from the reporter voice misadventure report we analysed above (where all directives are mediated through attribution), the second from a commentator voice text in which a number of unmediated directives occur. Directives have been marked in bold and authorially-sourced **social sanction** is indicated by means of underlined SMALL CAPS. Material attributed to external sources is contained in square brackets

[4.5] – *reporter voice*

Italian PM: [Plane Was Far Too Low]

CAVALESE, Italy (AP) – The US Marine jet that severed a ski lift cable, plunging 20 people to their deaths, [violated Italian air safety regulations with its 'earth-shaving flight' across a snowy hillside], the prime minister of this angry nation said Wednesday.

The defense minister **said [the American pilot should be prosecuted]**, several key lawmakers **said [US bases in Italy should be closed]**, and Italian and American investigators started looking into the accident near Trento, about 90 miles east of Milan.

...

Foreign Minister Lamberto Dini deplored the accident but said that [it would not 'distort our alliances and our collective security structures.'] Defense Minister Beniamino Andreatta took a harsher line, **demanding that [the pilot be prosecuted.]**

[4.6] – *commentator voice*

A recent ruling by Federal District Judge Stanley Sporkin against the State Department sheds light on OFFENSIVE, racially BIASED visa policies used in the American consulate in São Paulo, Brazil, and other consular offices around the world. Instead of defending these policies, **the State Department should be working to eliminate them.**

180   *The Language of Evaluation*

The case involved a Foreign Service officer, Robert Olsen, who was dismissed because he refused to follow 'profiles' used in the São Paulo office in rejecting non-immigrant visa applications. When there is evidence of a fraud ring operating among specific groups, a profile or checklist of characteristics can help alert consular officers to <u>SHADY</u> applicants. But it is another thing entirely to enforce a standing policy that denies tourist and business visas to people based on their race, ethnic background or style of dress.

...

The Government argues that these generalized stereotypes are used to increase scrutiny, and do not necessarily lead to the denial of a visa. But even that difference places a heavy, <u>UNJUST</u> burden on some applicants that other applicants of non-suspect races do not face. Judge Sporkin ruled that [these profiles were illegal under Federal immigration law, and that the termination of Mr. Olsen for refusing to use these profiles was improper]. The case has been remanded to the Foreign Service Grievance Board, **which should reinstate Mr. Olsen to his job.**

Consulates need discretion in determining who gets a visa, but those decisions should be based on objective and fair criteria. The need for busy Foreign Service officers to rely on shorthand lists is understandable, but does not justify the <u>REPREHENSIBLE</u> use of factors like ethnic background. Foreigners have no legal recourse if they are <u>UNFAIRLY</u> denied a visa, but it <u>OFFENDS THE SPIRIT OF FAIRNESS</u> to carry out a <u>DISCRIMINATORY</u> policy in consular offices that Americans would not tolerate at home.

Within broadsheet journalistic discourse, then, there is a resetting of the probabilities of occurrence/co-occurrence under which there is a high probability that texts which contain authorial directives will also contain authorial **social sanction**, and that texts that do not contain authorial **social sanction** will not contain authorial directives. This pattern of association is perhaps in part explicable by reference to differences in rhetorical objective. Many commentator voice texts take the form of hortatory expositions. They set out to persuade the reader of the need for some action to be taken and accordingly make at least some use of authorial directives. (Extract [4.6] above exemplifies this type.) In contrast, reporter voice texts and many correspondent texts act, not to argue or persuade, but to report or depict. Accordingly, they have no need for authorial directives. However, this is only a partial explanation. Correspondent voice texts are by no means always depictions of events, which is hardly surprising given that they also evaluate these events. In extract [4.3] above, for example, we observe a correspondent voice text which both reports on the release of the Tory leader's personal statement and also provides an argument that its release points to a revival in the party's fortunes. Accordingly, there is no immediately apparent reason why hortatory argumentation (calls for certain actions to take place) should not also be conducted in correspondent voice style. There is no obvious reason why texts which are oriented towards **social esteem** (as opposed to **social sanction**) should not also include authorial directives.

An alternative explanation for this pattern of co-occurrence may be found in the underlying semantic connection between directives (as modals of obligation) and values of **social sanction**, a connection which we outlined in Chapter 2, section 2.3. As outlined there, values of **social sanction** – specifically those of **propriety** – involve the lexicalisations of an underlying modal value of obligation. There is an obvious connection, via grammatical metaphor and lexicalisation, between *The government must act in this way* and *It is right/proper/fair that the government act in this way*. Thus modals of obligation (directives) are like the attitudinal values of **propriety** and **veracity** in acting to 'sanction' behaviour (see Martin 2000b). It would seem that within broadsheet journalistic discourse, this function of 'sanctioning' – whether it be via attitudinal assessments or via directives (modals of obligation) – is confined to the one journalistic role, that of commentator. Even though the correspondent voice writer may argue and evaluate, they typically refrain from either mode of 'sanctioning'.

Figure 4.4 represents the relationship between the journalistic voices which operates by reference to this 'sanctioning' function.

4.2.2 Journalistic key – clinal distinctions

The patternings, then, with respect to inscribed authorial **judgement** and authorial assessments of obligation are re-settings of the language's global evaluative meaning making potential which operate with a high degree of probability in our data. Additionally, as we indicated above, there are patterns which, while they are associated with these three journalistic roles of 'reporter', 'correspondent' and 'commentator', operate as clinal tendencies rather than clearly-bounded distinctions. One such patterning – that associated with values of **appreciation** – was exemplified in the earlier discussion.

Our analysis identified several other similarly clinal and probabilistic patternings involving sub-types of both **graduation** and **engagement**. For reasons of space we provide only a brief outline of these below. (For a fuller account of journalistic voice see White 1998.)

```
                  non sanctioning:
                  reporter voice and
                  correspondent voice
                         │
                         │    ┌─────────────────────────────┐
                         │    │ – authorial social sanction │
                         │    │ – authorial directives      │
                         │    │   (proposals)               │
       sanction →        │    └─────────────────────────────┘
                         │
                         │
                  sanctioning:
                  commentator voice
                         │
                         │    ┌─────────────────────────────┐
                         │    │ + authorial social sanction │
                         │    │ + authorial directives      │
                         │    │   (proposals)               │
                         │    └─────────────────────────────┘
```

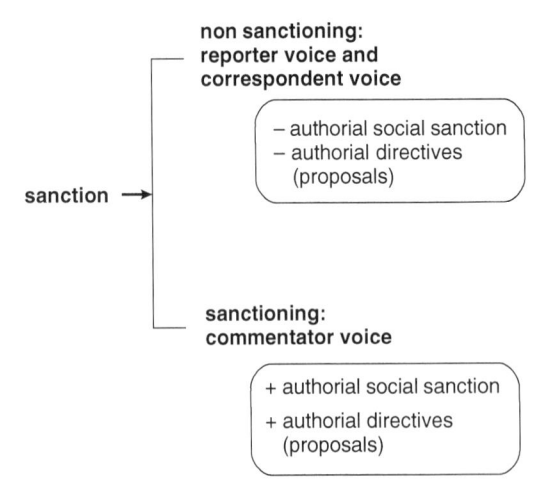

Figure 4.4 Journalistic voices and authorial sanction

- 'grammatical', 'isolating' **intensification** (eg *somewhat, slightly, quite, rather, very, fairly, extremely* and *greatly*) was less frequent in unattributed contexts in reporter voice texts than in correspondent voice and commentator voice texts.
- 'infused' intensification of processes (eg *the ski lift **plunged**, the Marine EA-6B Prowler **swooped**,* prices ***sky-rocketed***) was more frequent in reporter voice texts than in the writer voice texts.
- **Attribution** (typically **acknowledge**, but also **distance**) occurs regularly across the three voices (in association with the journalistic function of mediating other voices and discourses) but at the highest frequency in reporter voice and at the lowest frequency in commentator voice.
- Values of **entertain** (eg *may, perhaps, it seems, arguably, evidently*) occur with a significantly lower frequency in reporter voice than in writer voice (in unattributed contexts).
- **Denials** (in unattributed contexts): less frequent in reporter voice (only 14 of the 42 reporter voice texts contained instances, with rates of from 0.6 to 1.2 instances per 500 words) than in writer voice (eg in commentator voice rates of from 4.5 to 9.8 instances per 500 words.)
- No significant patterns were found with respect to values of **counter** when the meaning was realised as a logical connection between clauses (for example, by conjunctions such as *however, although, yet,*

but, etc.). A significant pattern did emerge when we considered counter-expectational particles such as *only, still, just, even*. Instances were found in only three of the reporter voice texts, where they occurred at a low rate (no more than .9 per 500 words). In contrast, they occurred in almost half of our correspondent voice texts and all but two of our commentator voice texts. In the writer voice texts the rate per 500 words was significantly higher than for the reporter voice texts.

- No instances of **pronounce** in unattributed contexts occurred in the reporter voice texts (eg *the truth of the matter, I contend ...* etc.). Here there was a clear contrast with both the writer voices, although values of **pronounce** occurred significantly more frequently in commentator than in correspondent voice texts. We also found no instance of values of **concur** (*of course, naturally, predictably*) in the reporter-voice grouping, and once again there was a clear contrast with the writer voice texts where these values occur at roughly equal rates across the two voices.
- Values of **endorse** (*'they demonstrated that ...'* etc.) occur across the three voices.

By this analysis, then, we are able to describe with some specificity the linguistic regularities and tendencies which constitute the evaluative styles or keys of journalistic discourse. We have found that the voices involve particular reconfigurations of the system's meaning-making potential, with these reconfigurations establishing clearly different probabilities for the occurrence of the different types of **attitude, graduation** and **engagement**. It is possible to relate these different configurations to different authorial presences and different potential rhetorical effects. Reporter voice, for example, can be seen as a regime of strategic impersonalisation by which the author's subjective role is backgrounded. We note with interest that, while this regime operates with a virtual prohibition on inscribed authorial **judgement** and assessments of obligation, it strongly favours **intensification** via infusion, and permits instances of inscribed authorial **appreciation**, the reporting of the **affectual** responses of third parties, assessments of counter-expectation construed as an inter clausal relationship, and the **distancing** and the **endorsement** of the viewpoints of external sources. As well, it makes frequent use of tokens of **judgement**. It thus operates ideologically by presenting itself as 'factual' and 'neutral' via this avoidance of socially sanctioning and esteeming meanings while simultaneously positioning the reader via its selective use of values of **engagement, graduation**, the other types of

attitude and **judgement** tokens. Evidence for the effectiveness of this ideology is to be found in the persistence of the commonsense view that 'quality' journalism is 'objective' and evaluatively impartial. The correspondent versus commentator voice distinction acts to naturalise a power hierarchy within mainstream media organisations by which a distinction is made between the discursive role in which the writer is authorised to employ the full range of evaluative meanings, including those which pass moral judgement, and a discursive role in which the writer, while still authorised to be explicitly evaluative, is significantly more constrained attitudinally.

4.3 Evaluative key and the discourses of secondary-school history

We turn now to a short consideration of evaluative key in history by way of opening a discussion of how key operates across institutions and discourse domains, We rely here, and report on, the work of Caroline Coffin – see Coffin 1997, 2000 and 2002. In her study of the language of the Australian secondary-school history classroom (both student writing and textbooks), Coffin found that there were several distinct (prototypical) patternings with respect to the use being made of appraisal values and that the Higher School Certificate (HSC) student texts which she examined could be clustered by reference to these patterns (Coffin 2002: 513–18). On the basis of these patternings, she concluded that there is a system of key operating in secondary-school history which quite closely correlates with that of journalistic discourse. These patternings involved the occurrence and frequency of values of unmediated inscribed **judgement** and of unmediated inscribed **appreciation**, specifically the sub-category of **appreciation: social value** by which assessments of significance, prominence, efficacy, etc. are made (eg *key, major, important*). Coffin's taxonomy of keys in history is set out in Figure 4.5.

According to Coffin, recorder key (**judgement** via tokens, not via explicit authorial attitude) operates as the writer provides what is presented as an unproblematic, 'factual' account of past events, even as the tokens of **judgement** in the text operate covertly to position the reader attitudinally and ideologically towards those events. This key, then, assumes reader alignment with the writer's world view. In contrast, in the two appraiser keys (interpreter and adjudicator), the writer is much more intrusive in terms of judging and evaluating people and

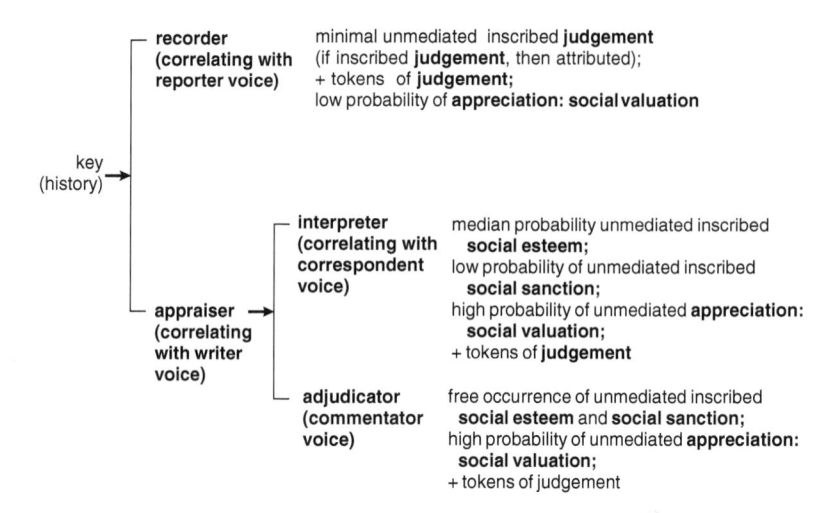

```
                    recorder            minimal unmediated inscribed judgement
                    (correlating with   (if inscribed judgement, then attributed);
                    reporter voice)     + tokens of judgement;
                                        low probability of appreciation: social valuation
    key
    (history)
                                        interpreter          median probability unmediated inscribed
                                        (correlating with      social esteem;
                                        correspondent        low probability of unmediated inscribed
                                        voice)                 social sanction;
                    appraiser                                high probability of unmediated appreciation:
                    (correlating                               social valuation;
                    with writer                              + tokens of judgement
                    voice)
                                        adjudicator          free occurrence of unmediated inscribed
                                        (commentator           social esteem and social sanction;
                                        voice)               high probability of unmediated appreciation:
                                                               social valuation;
                                                             + tokens of judgement
```

Figure 4.5 The keys of history – network again

phenomena, with the writer's worldview being 'much more in view' (Coffin 2002: 518).

Coffin found that it in the textbook examples in her corpus it was typical for the different stages of the text to be associated with a different key. Thus it was frequently the case that the opening stages of historical recounts (the 'background' and 'record of events' stages) were written in recorder key, with a key change into one of the appraiser keys (typically adjudicator) occurring in the final, rhetorically crucial 'deduction' stage (Coffin 1997: 207).

Coffin also found that there was a close correlation between the grading received by the HSC examinees and the key employed in the essays they submitted for assessment. Texts written exclusively in recorder key (without any transition into appraiser key) typically received a 'Typical Average Range' grading, while it was frequently the case that essays receiving a 'Typical Excellent Range' grading employed an appraiser key (Coffin 2002: 515–16).

Coffin's work demonstrates that the reconfiguration of the language's evaluative meaning-making potential according to conventionalised, regularised patterns is a generalised phenomenon which we can expect to observe broadly across discourse domains. It also demonstrates that, while there may well be commonalities connecting the evaluative keys of different institutional domains, the evaluative profiles of keys can be expected to vary according to their social context and the specific interpersonal concerns of that context.

For further discussion of evaluative key, especially with respect to key changes within texts, see Rothery and Stenglin's work and Macken-Horarik's work on narrative (Rothery & Stenglin 2000, Macken-Horarik 2003).

4.4 Stance

As outlined previously (see Chapter 1, section 1.2.6 and section 4.1 above), instantiation is a scale mediating the general semiotic climate of a culture in relation to textual weather. In this section we'll move down the scale from key to stance, and look at different evaluative positions that might be taken up within a commentator voice. This is not intended to be exhaustive of possibilities within this key; we currently have little idea what the range of stances associated with this key would be. All that is intended here is an illustration of different configurations of evaluative meaning, each of which is concerned in a complementary way to deal with the social sanction of behaviour.

The first two texts we'll consider come from the magazine *Granta: the magazine of new writing*, from an issue entitled 'What we Think of America: episodes and opinions from twenty-four writers.' The first is by Harold Pinter, and is reproduced below. We'll restrict our discussion for the most part to the two sections of the text we have boxed in, which deal with the American response to the events of 9/11.

[4.7] *Harold Pinter* – Britain

On September 10, 2001 I received an honorary degree at the University of Florence. I made a speech in which I referred to the term 'humanitarian intervention' – the term used by NATO to justify its bombing of Serbia in 1999.

I said the following: On May 7, 1999 NATO aircraft bombed the marketplace of the southern city of Nis, killing thirty-three civilians and injuring many more. It was, according to NATO, a 'mistake'.

The bombing of Nis was no 'mistake'. General Wesley K. Clark declared, as the NATO bombing began: 'We are going to systematically and progressively attack, disrupt, degrade, devastate and ultimately – unless president Milosovic complies with the demands of the international community – destroy these forces and their facilities and support.' Milosovic's forces, as we know, included television stations, schools, hospitals, theatres, old people's homes – and the marketplace in Nis. It was in fact a fundamental feature of NATO policy to terrorize the civilian population.

The bombing of Nis, far from being a 'mistake', was in fact an act of murder. It stemmed from a 'war' which was in itself illegal, a bandit act, in defiance of the United Nations, even contravening NATO's own charter. But the actions taken, we are told, were taken in the pursuance of a policy of 'humanitarian intervention' and the civilian deaths were described as 'collateral damage'.

> 'Humanitarian intervention' is a comparatively new concept. But President George W. Bush is also following the great American presidential tradition by referring to 'freedom-loving people'. (I must say I would be fascinated to meet a 'freedom-hating people'.) President Bush possesses quite a few 'freedom- loving people' himself – not only in his own Texas prisons but throughout the whole of the United States, in what can accurately be described as a vast gulag – two million prisoners in fact – a remarkable proportion of them black. Rape of young prisoners, both male and female, is commonplace. So is the use of weapons of torture as defined by Amnesty International – stun guns, stun belts, restraint chairs. Prison is a great industry in the United States – just behind pornography when it comes to profits.
> There have been many considerable sections of mankind for whom the mere articulation of the word 'freedom' has resulted in torture and death. I'm referring to the hundreds upon hundreds of thousands of people throughout Guatemala, El Salvador, Turkey, Israel, Haiti, Brazil, Greece, Uruguay, East Timor, Nicaragua, South Korea, Argentina, Chile and the Philippines and Indonesia, for example, killed in all cases by forces inspired and subsidized by the United States. Why did they die? They died because to one degree or another they dared to question the status quo, the endless plateau of poverty, disease, degradation and oppression which is their birthright. On behalf of the dead, we must regard the breathtaking discrepancy between US government language and US government action with the absolute contempt it deserves.
> The United States has in fact – since the end of the Second World War – pursued a brilliant, even witty, strategy. It has exercised a sustained, systematic, remorseless and quite clinical manipulation of power worldwide, while masquerading as a force for universal good. But at least now – it can be said – the US has come out of its closet. The smile is still there of course (all US presidents have always had wonderful smiles) but the posture is infinitely more naked and more blatant than it has ever been. The Bush administration, as we all know, has rejected the Kyoto agreement, has refused to sign an agreement which would regulate the trade of small arms, has distanced itself from the Anti-Ballistic Missile Treaty, the Comprehensive-Nuclear-Test-Ban Treaty and the Biological Weapons Convention. In relation to the latter the US made it quite clear that it would agree to the banning of biological weapons as long as there was no inspection of any biological weapons factory on American soil. The US has also refused to ratify the proposed International Criminal Court of Justice. It is bringing into operation the American Service Members Protection Act which will permit authorization of military force to

188 *The Language of Evaluation*

> free any American soldier taken into International Criminal Court custody. In other words they really will 'Send in the Marines'.
> Arrogant, indifferent, contemptuous of International Law, both dismissive and manipulative of the United Nations: this is now the most dangerous power the world has ever known – the authentic 'rogue state', but a 'rogue state' of colossal military and economic might. And Europe – especially the United Kingdom – is both compliant and complicit, or as Cassius in Julius Caesar put it: we 'peep about to find ourselves dishonourable graves'.

There is, however, as we have seen, a profound revulsion and disgust with the manifestations of US power and global capitalism which is growing throughout the world and becoming a formidable force in its own right. I believe a central inspiration for this force has been the actions and indeed the philosophical stance of the Zapistas in Mexico. The Zapistas say (as I understand it): 'Do not try to define us. We define ourselves. We will not be what you want us to be. We will not accept the destiny you have chosen for us. We will not accept your terms. We will not abide by your rules. The only way you can eliminate us is to destroy us and you cannot destroy us. We are free.'

> These remarks seem to me even more valid than when I made them on September 10. The 'rogue state' has – without thought, without pause for reflection, without a moment of doubt, let alone shame – confirmed that it is a fully-fledged, award-winning, gold-plated monster. It has effectively declared war on the world. It knows only one language – bombs and death. 'And still they smiled and still the horror grew.'
> [*Granta* 77: 66–9]

Pinter's stance in the two sections we're considering foregrounds **judgement** over **affect** and **appreciation**, strongly amplifies attitude and regularly proclaims his position. Rhetorically speaking it's a full-on attack on US foreign policy, including its reaction to 9/11. As far as **judgement** is concerned, it is mainly negative, focussing on **social sanction**:

> **social esteem** – poverty, disease, dared to question, brilliant, witty, sustained, systematic, quite clinical, colossal military and economic might, compliant, without a moment of doubt
> **social sanction** – humanitarian, freedom-loving, freedom-hating, freedom-loving, accurately, rape, torture, freedom, torture, degradation,

Evaluative Key: Taking a Stance 189

oppression contempt, remorseless, manipulation, masquerading, a force for universal good, more naked, more blatant, arrogant, indifferent, contemptuous, dismissive, manipulative, most dangerous power, authentic 'rogue state', 'rogue state', complicit, shame, monster

This condemnation is enhanced by several instances of **appreciation** which can be read as tokens of **judgement**:

appreciation [tokens of judgement] – great American presidential tradition ('of great Presidents'), vast gulag, great industry, breathtaking discrepancy, dishonourable graves, horror

A good deal of this criticism and condemnation is strongly amplified with respect to both **graduation: quantity** (underlined) and **graduation: intensity** (boxed in):

quite a few 'freedom-loving people', the whole of the United States, a vast gulag, two million prisoners, a remarkable proportion of them black, many considerable sections of mankind, the hundreds upon hundreds of thousands of people, in all cases, to one degree or another, the endless plateau of poverty, the breathtaking discrepancy, the absolute contempt; quite clinical, all US presidents, infinitely more naked, quite clear, no inspection, any American soldier; most dangerous, colossal military and economic might

This is further reinforced by the recurrent use of parataxis to build up rhetorical triplets, quadruplets and an even longer listing of countries undermined by the US:

- stun guns, stun belts, restraint chairs
- has rejected ..., has refused to sign ..., has distanced itself
- the Anti-Ballistic Missile Treaty, the Comprehensive-Nuclear-Test-Ban Treaty and the Biological Weapons Convention
- arrogant, indifferent, contemptuous of International Law
- a fully-fledged, award-winning, gold-plated
- poverty, disease, degradation and oppression
- a sustained, systematic, remorseless and quite clinical
- without thought, without pause for reflection, without a moment of doubt, let alone shame

190 *The Language of Evaluation*

- throughout   Guatemala, El Salvador, Turkey, Israel, Haiti, Brazil, Greece, Uruguay, East Timor, Nicaragua, South Korea, Argentina, Chile and the Philippines and Indonesia

For the most part Pinter's loud condemnation proclaims his position (employing dialogistically contractive values of **pronouncement**, **endorsement** and **concurrence**), aligning readers to his point of view. As highlighted below (contractions boxed in, expansions underlined), these are mainly used to promote his reading of American prisons as a Stalinist gulag and to affirm America's 'go it alone' policy as far as international regulations and agencies are concerned.

'Humanitarian intervention' is a comparatively new concept. But President George W. Bush is also following the great American presidential tradition by referring to 'freedom-loving people'. (I must say I would be fascinated to meet a 'freedom-hating people'). President Bush possesses quite a few 'freedom-loving people' himself – not only in his own Texas prisons but throughout the whole of the United States, in what can accurately be described as a vast gulag – two million prisoners in fact – a remarkable proportion of them black. Rape of young prisoners, both male and female, is commonplace. So is the use of weapons of torture as defined by Amnesty International – stun guns, stun belts, restraint chairs. Prison is a great industry in the United States – just behind pornography when it comes to profits.

There have been many considerable sections of mankind for whom the mere articulation of the word 'freedom' has resulted in torture and death. …

On behalf of the dead, we must regard the breathtaking discrepancy between US government language and US government action with the absolute contempt it deserves.

The United States has in fact … pursued a brilliant, even witty, strategy. It has exercised a sustained, systematic, remorseless and quite clinical manipulation of power worldwide, while masquerading as a force for universal good. But at least now – it can be said – the US has come out of its closet. The smile is still there of course (all US presidents have always had wonderful smiles) but the posture is infinitely more naked and more blatant than it has ever been. The Bush administration, as we all know, has rejected the Kyoto agreement, has refused to sign an agreement which would regulate the trade of small arms, has distanced itself from the Anti-Ballistic Missile Treaty, the Comprehensive-Nuclear-Test-Ban Treaty and the Biological Weapons Convention. In relation to the latter the US made it quite clear that it would agree to the banning of biological weapons as long as there was no inspection of any biological weapons factory on American soil. The US has also refused to ratify the proposed International Criminal Court of Justice. It is bringing into operation the

American Service Members Protection Act which will permit authorization of military force to free any American soldier taken into International Criminal Court custody. In other words they |really| will 'Send in the Marines'.
...

> These remarks <u>seem to me</u> |even more valid| than when I made them on September 10. The 'rogue state' has – without thought, without pause for reflection, without a moment of doubt, let alone shame – |confirmed| that it is a fully-fledged, award-winning, gold-plated monster. It has <u>effectively</u> declared war on the world. It knows only one language – bombs and death. 'And still they smiled and still the horror grew.' [*Granta* 77: 66–9]

It is really only in his final paragraph that Pinter expands his discourse. He appreciates his proclamations as *even more valid* than before, but individuates this as his view among others (*seems to me*). And he graduates America's declaration of war on the world as an affirmation that is not completely accurate, but a reasonable description of what is going on (*effectively*). Having met force with force in his acceptance speech, Pinter opens up in retrospect – reminding readers as he does so of his own literary pedigree (*'And still they smiled, and still the horror grew.'*) He moves from speaking to a captive audience in other words to writing for a wider readership, who might otherwise dismiss his views as unreasonably extreme. By and large however we can perhaps refer to the stance exemplified here as **damning** – a strong 'take-no-prisoners' broadside of evaluative resources. As far as solidarity is concerned, this kind of stance seems designed to rally the converted, draw attention to a cause, and challenge a powerful transgressor.

Pinter's stance can be usefully contrasted with that of another British writer in the *Granta* volume, Doris Lessing. Once again we'll deal principally with the boxed in section of the text, which deals directly with the issue of America's response to 9/11.

[4.8] *Doris Lessing* – Britain

> Busily promoting my book *African Laughter* I flitted about (as authors do) on the East Coast, doing phone-ins and interviews, and had to conclude that Americans see Africa as something like Long Island, with a single government, situated vaguely south ('The Indian Ocean? What's that?'). In New York I had the heaviest, most ignorant audience of my life, very discouraging, but the day after in Washington 300 of the brightest best-informed people I can remember. To talk about 'America' as if it were a homogenous unity isn't useful, but I hazard the following generalizations.

192 *The Language of Evaluation*

> America, it seems to me, has as little resistance to an idea or a mass emotion as isolated communities have to measles and whooping cough. From outside, it is as if you are watching one violent storm after another sweep across a landscape of extremes. Their Cold War was colder than anywhere else in the West, with the intemperate execution of the Rosenbergs, and grotesqueries of the McCarthy trials. In the Seventies, Black Power, militant feminism, the Weathermen – all flourished. On one of my visits, people could talk of nothing else. Two years later they probably still flourished, but no one mentioned them. 'You know us,' said a friend. 'We have short memories'.
>
> Everything is taken to extremes. We all know this, but the fact is seldom taken into account when we try to understand what is going on. The famous Political Correctness, which began as a sensible examination of language for hidden bias, became hysterical and soon afflicted whole areas of education. Universities have been ruined by it. I was visiting a university town not far from New York when two male academics took me out into the garden, for fear of being overheard, and said they hated what they had to teach, but they had families, and would not get tenure if they didn't toe the line. A few years earlier, in Los Angeles, I found that my novel *The Good Terrorist* was being 'taught'. The teaching consisted of the students scrutinizing it for political incorrectness. This was thought to be a good approach to literature. Unfortunately, strong and inflexible ideas attract the stupid ... what am I saying! Britain shows milder symptoms of the same disease, so it is instructive to see where such hysteria may lead if not checked.
>
> The reaction to the events of 11 September – terrible as they were – seems excessive to outsiders, and we have to say this to our American friends, although they have become so touchy, and ready to break off relations with accusations of hard-heartedness. The United States is in the grip of a patriotic fever which reminds me of the Second World War. They seem to themselves as unique, alone, misunderstood, beleaguered, and they see any criticism as treachery.
>
> The judgement 'they had it coming', so angrily resented, is perhaps misunderstood. What people felt was that Americans had at last learned that they are like everyone else, vulnerable to the snakes of Envy and Revenge, to bombs exploding on a street corner (as in Belfast), or in a hotel housing a government (as in Brighton). They say to themselves that they have been expelled from their Eden. How strange they should ever have thought they had a right to one. [*Granta* 77: 52–4]

Although judgemental, Lessing's text foregrounds criticism (**social esteem**) over condemnation (**social sanction**). And almost all the **sanction** that is there involves **judgements** made by Americans, not of them.

social esteem – has ... little resistance to, intemperate, grotesqueries, have short memories, extremes, sensible, hysterical, stupid, shows milder symptoms of the same disease, such hysteria, excessive, so touchy, in the grip of a patriotic fever, unique, alone, misunderstood, beleaguered, vulnerable

social sanction – Political Correctness, bias, political incorrectness, hard-heartedness, treachery, resented, envy, right

In this respect, then, Lessing's voice is closer to the correspondent voice texts in our journalistic corpus than to the commentator voice texts. However, it does contain a number of features which, in our journalistic corpus, either only occurred in commentator voice texts or were more closely associated with commentator voice. For example,

authorial affect – *In New York I had the heaviest, most ignorant audience of my life, very **discouraging***

concurrence/proclamation – *Everything is taken to extremes. **We all know this**, but the fact is seldom taken into account when we try to understand what is going on.*

In terms of the two texts, there is some comparable amplification (Pinter/Lessing: *whole/whole, all/all, any/any, no/no one, vast/mass, endless/one after another*). But Lessing's **quantifying** deals in smaller quantities, (*one, two, few* vs Pinter's *quite a few, two million, a remarkable proportion, hundreds upon hundreds of thousands*); and her **force** is not as intense (*so touchy, so angrily, how strange* vs Pinter's *absolute contempt, infinitely more naked, quite clear, most dangerous, colossal … might*).

This softer tone is reinforced by **engagement** resources which tend to expand the discourse rather than contract it. Set against the contracting *we all know this, but the fact* we have a wide range of expansions including appearance, attribution and modality: *it seems to me, from outside it is as if, probably, said, was thought to be,* etc.

The first paragraph of Lessing's text of course establishes this heteroglossic stance (though generalising about America isn't useful, she's hazarding some generalisations anyhow); and she later goes so far as to question the trajectory of her own rhetoric, towards the end of her discussion of political correctness (*… what am I saying!*). As outlined below, voices proliferate in the final two paragraphs, which deal with the reaction to 9/11 (expansions boxed in, contractions underlined). Lessing speaks for many others here.

America, it seems to me, has as little resistance to an idea or a mass emotion as isolated communities have to measles and whooping cough. From outside, it is as if you are watching one violent storm after another sweep across a landscape of extremes. Their Cold War was colder than anywhere else in the West, with the intemperate execution of the Rosenbergs, and grotesqueries of the McCarthy trials. In the Seventies, Black Power, militant feminism, the Weathermen – all flourished. On one of my visits, people could talk of nothing else. Two years later they probably still flourished, but no one mentioned them. 'You know us,' said a friend. 'We have short memories'. Everything is taken to extremes. We all know this, but the fact is seldom taken into account when we try to understand what is going on. The famous Political Correctness, which began as a sensible examination of language for hidden bias, became hysterical and soon afflicted whole areas of education. Universities have been ruined by it. I was visiting a university town not far from New York when two male academics took me out into the garden, for fear of being overheard, and said they hated what they had to teach, but they had families, and would not get tenure if they didn't toe the line. A few years earlier, in Los Angeles, I found that my novel *The Good Terrorist* was being 'taught'. The teaching consisted of the students scrutinizing it for political incorrectness. This was thought to be a good approach to literature. Unfortunately, strong and inflexible ideas attract the stupid ... what am I saying! Britain shows milder symptoms of the same disease, so it is instructive to see where such hysteria may lead if not checked. The reaction to the events of 11 September – terrible as they were – seems excessive to outsiders, and we have to say this to our American friends, although they have become so touchy, and ready to break off relations with accusations of hard-heartedness. The United States is in the grip of a patriotic fever which reminds me of the Second World War. They seem to themselves as unique, alone, misunderstood, beleaguered, and they see any criticism as treachery.

The judgement 'they had it coming', so angrily resented, is perhaps misunderstood. What people felt was that Americans had at last learned that they are like everyone else, vulnerable to the snakes of Envy and Revenge, to bombs exploding on a street corner (as in Belfast), or in a hotel housing a government (as in Brighton). They say to themselves that they have been expelled from their Eden. How strange they should ever have thought they had a right to one. [*Granta* 77: 52–4]

This configuration of **judgement**, **graduation** and **engagement** means that where Pinter fires a broadside, Lessing deprecates. Her judgement is not that America is duplicitous and evil but rather that it is ill and naive. Deploying lexical metaphors she suggests that America has bad weather (*one violent storm after another sweep across, colder*), so it gets sick (*little resistance, measles, whooping cough, afflicted, milder symptoms, same disease, the grip of a patriotic fever*), and implies that this is what makes it react excessively. Beyond this, Americans were innocent enough to believe they lived in Eden, had a right to live there and were immune to the snakes of envy and revenge. Taken together the lexical metaphors provoke judgements of incapacity. Unflattering as these diagnoses are, they are milder **judgements** than Pinter's charges of deceit and impropriety. Lessing invites readers to try and understand Americans' pathology of excess and their naïve faith in their role as God's chosen people.

All in all we can perhaps refer to this stance as **excusing**. Lessing offers an explanation for American behaviour for those who consider it wrong. As far as solidarity is concerned, readers are positioned to back off a little from the reactions American extremism might provoke and see things from another point of view. How this aligns readers into communities of sympathy or disgust is not something she tries to control.

What then of these 'monsters' who act 'without thought, without pause for reflection, without a moment of doubt, let alone shame', and who 'see any criticism as treachery'? One exception to Pinter and Lessing's generalisations would be William Raspberry, whose article 'A few questions as we go to war' appeared in the *Guardian Weekly* early in 2003.

A few questions as we march to war

Opinion – William Raspberry

The US military, Defence Secretary Donald Rumsfeld has assured us, is quite capable of waging the virtually foreordained war with Iraq *and* taking on North Korea.

I wish someone could settle my own questions with such clarity and conviction. I've got a ton of them.

For instance: Has the decision to forgo unilateral military action against Iraq in favour of taking the matter of Iraq violations to the United Nations been cleverly subverted into some sort of Catch-22? Our government seems to be telling us that if Iraqi President Saddam Hussein denies having weapons of mass destruction, while we know he does have them, that falsehood becomes a material breach of its agreement and reason to take him out militarily. But if he admits having such weapons, he stands convicted out of his own mouth, and therefore we have no choice but to take him out.

('We know he's got those weapons of mass destruction,' satirist Mark Russell said. 'We've got the receipts!')

Is America really serious that the war we propose is for the purpose of bringing democracy to the people of Iraq? Is it hopelessly cynical to imagine that democratization is a much lower priority than controlling the Iraqi oil reserves, asserting our authority in that part of the world and (perhaps) avenging our president's father? I mean, Saddam at least *pretends* to have a democracy. Our allies such as Saudi Arabia and Kuwait don't even go through the charade.

And is it possible to call attention to our own duplicity or Saudi Arabia's lack of democracy without seeming to say that Saddam is innocent? He's not, of course. He's pretty much all the things the administration had said he is. But is he such an imminent threat to the United States as to justify unilateral military action against him? Is a war that is likely to cost thousands of innocent Iraqi lives the only way to remove whatever remains of Saddam's ability to wreak international havoc? Will our effort to take him out, even if successful, create more havoc than it prevents?

If the proposed war is less about democracy and more about opposing international terrorism, why am I mistaken in the view that it could spawn more anti-American and anti-Israeli terrorism and increase the number of terrorists who see us as the international menace?

By the way, how much of the commitment to topple Saddam is calculated to meet Israel's needs rather than our own? One must be careful not to buy into the line of those who oppose the war because they hate Israel. But if we are willing to launch a war at least partly for Israel's sake, shouldn't we have a little more clout over such matters as the Israeli settlements in the occupied territories?

A key question is how those who make our policy see the role of the United States. Are we, in their minds, the only adults in a room full of squabbling children – the only ones with the clarity of vision and the military wherewithal to undertake the unpleasant task of belling the aggressive cats of the world, as we spread democracy's joyous gospel?

Or do they see us, as I sometimes fear, as some sort of international Dirty Harry, packing lots of heat and requiring only the thinnest of pretexts (and with little patience for procedural and evidentiary niceties) to rid the world of scum?

Finally, do they think that it's too late to work at peace, that it's wimpish to wonder why so much of the world dislikes us, that it's a form of appeasement to show the world our better nature? [*Guardian Weekly* January 2–8, 2003 p. 27]

Like Pinter and Lessing, Raspberry's stance is judgemental, but more concerned with **tenacity** and **veracity** alongside **propriety**:

tenacity – conviction, serious, careful, aggressive, little patience, wimpish, appeasement

veracity – clarity, falsehood, cynical, charade, duplicity, mistaken, commitment, clarity of vision, thinnest of pretexts

propriety – innocent, not (innocent), innocent, wreak international havoc, international terrorism, terrorism, terrorists, menace, international Dirty Harry, scum, better nature

The most striking feature of his text of course is its mood, which features more than a dozen[2] interrogatives. It is as if the fear of treachery precludes declarative in favour of a stance that is explicitly dialogic, apparently inviting a range of opinions around Raspberry's propositions (MOOD realising Subject, Finite and Wh functions are underlined below, after Halliday 1994).

<u>Has the decision to forgo unilateral military action against Iraq in favour of taking the matter of Iraq violations to the United Nation been</u> cleverly subverted into some sort of Catch-22?

<u>Is America</u> really serious that the war we propose is for the purpose of bringing democracy to the people of Iraq?

<u>Is it</u> hopelessly cynical to imagine that democratization is a much lower priority than controlling the Iraqi oil reserves, asserting our authority in that part of the world and (perhaps) avenging our president's father?

And <u>is it</u> possible to call attention to our own duplicity or Saudi Arabia's lack of democracy without seeming to say that Saddam is innocent?

But <u>is he</u> such an imminent threat to the United States as to justify unilateral military action against him?

<u>Is a war that is likely to cost thousands of innocent Iraqi lives</u> the only way to remove whatever remains of Saddam's ability to wreak international havoc?

<u>Will our effort to take him out</u>, even if successful, create more havoc than it prevents?

If the proposed war is less about democracy and more about opposing international terrorism, <u>why am I</u> mistaken in the view that it could spawn more anti-American and anti-Israeli terrorism and increase the number of terrorists who see us as the international menace?

By the way, <u>how much of the commitment to topple Saddam</u> is calculated to meet Israel's needs rather than our own?

But if we are willing to launch a war at least partly for Israel's sake, <u>shouldn't we</u> have a little more clout over such matters as the Israeli settlements in the occupied territories?

<u>Are we</u>, in their minds, the only adults in a room full of squabbling children – the only ones with the clarity of vision and the military wherewithal to undertake the unpleasant task of belling the aggressive cats of the world, as we spread democracy's joyous gospel?

Or <u>do they</u> see us, as I sometimes fear, as some sort of international Dirty Harry, packing lots of heat and requiring only the thinnest of pretexts (and with little patience for procedural and evidentiary niceties) to rid the world of scum?

Finally, <u>do they</u> think that it's too late to work at peace, that it's wimpish to wonder why so much of the world dislikes us, that it's a form of appeasement to show the world our better nature?

We say 'apparently inviting a range of opinions' because so many of Raspberry's interrogatives are in fact loaded questions. His negative interrogative invites a positive response (negative interrogatives are dialogically contractive rather than expansive):

> But if we are willing to launch a war at least partly for Israel's sake, <u>shouldn't we</u> have a little more clout over such matters as the Israeli settlements in the occupied territories? [– Of course we should.]

And his graded wh interrogative presupposes that at least some of the commitment to topple Saddam serves Israel:

> By the way, <u>how much of the commitment to topple Saddam is</u> calculated to meet Israel's needs rather than our own? [– Some/a fair bit/quite a lot.]

Similarly, several of his interrogatives are involved in modalisations that favour one kind of response over another. We've rewritten these as their unmodalised variations below to highlight Raspberry's shaping of his preferred response.

> <u>Is America really serious that</u> the war we propose is for the purpose of bringing democracy to the people of Iraq?
>
> [*Is the war we propose for the purpose of bringing democracy to the people of Iraq?*]
>
> <u>Is it hopelessly cynical to imagine that</u> democratization is a much lower priority than controlling the Iraqi oil reserves, asserting our authority in that part of the world and (perhaps) avenging our president's father?
>
> [*Is democratization a much lower priority than controlling the Iraqi oil reserves, asserting our authority in that part of the world and (perhaps) avenging our president's father?*]
>
> And <u>is it possible to</u> call attention to our own duplicity or Saudi Arabia's lack of democracy without seeming to say that Saddam is innocent?
>
> [*Can we call attention to our own duplicity or Saudi Arabia's lack of democracy without seeming to say that Saddam is innocent?*]
>
> If the proposed war is less about democracy and more about opposing international terrorism, <u>why am I mistaken in the view that</u> it could spawn more anti-American and anti-Israeli terrorism and increase the number of terrorists who see us as the international menace?

[*Could the war* spawn more anti-American and anti-Israeli terrorism and increase the number of terrorists who see us as the international menace?]

In addition certain questions are followed up with advice on how to answer them. Raspberry gives reasons for his Catch-22 analysis of the UN weapons inspection, and points out that Iraq is hardly less democratic than certain of America's monarchist allies in the region:

Has the decision to forgo unilateral military action against Iraq in favour of taking the matter of Iraq violations to the United Nations been cleverly subverted into some sort of Catch-22? Our government seems to be telling us that if Iraqi President Saddam Hussein denies having weapons of mass destruction, while we know he does have them, that falsehood becomes a material breach of its agreement and reason to take him out militarily. But if he admits having such weapons, he stands convicted out of his own mouth, and therefore we have no choice but to take him out.

Is America really serious that the war we propose is for the purpose of bringing democracy to the people of Iraq? Is it hopelessly cynical to imagine that democratization is a much lower priority than controlling the Iraqi oil reserves, asserting our authority in that part of the world and (perhaps) avenging our president's father? I mean, Saddam at least *pretends* to have a democracy. Our allies such as Saudi Arabia and Kuwait don't even go through the charade.

And two questions are protected by the removal of reasons for dismissal. Raspberrry proclaims that he's not protesting Saddam's innocence, and denies he is anti-Isreal:

And is it possible to call attention to our own duplicity or Saudi Arabia's lack of democracy without seeming to say that Saddam is innocent? He's not, of course. He's pretty much all the things the administration had said he is.

By the way, how much of the commitment to topple Saddam is calculated to meet Israel's needs rather than our own? One must be careful not to buy into the line of those who oppose the war because they hate Israel.

In the context of the monoglossic certainty Pinter and Lessing attribute to America, just posing questions has to count as a challenging response. Raspberry further promotes a heteroglossic perspective by introducing a range of players into the discussion, strongly foregrounding attribution – sourcing Rumsfeld, the government (including the administration and policy makers), Saddam, Americans in general, Mark Russell and terrorists as well as himself:

> Defence Secretary Donald Rumsfeld has assured us,
> I wish
> [the decision]
> Our government seems to be telling us
> Iraqi President Saddam Hussein denies
> we know
> he admits
> We know
> satirist Mark Russell said
> to imagine
> Saddam at least pretends
> seeming to say
> the administration had said
> [the view]
> terrorists who see us as
> [a key question]
> do they see us
> I sometimes fear,
> do they think
> to wonder

But beyond this, the preferential loading on Raspberry's questions makes room for a voice of opposition – an opposition which has a few arguments against the war. Their case is mounted here as closet exposition, the overall structure of which is outlined below. The various conjunctive resources realising the logical structure of the argument are highlighted (*for instance, and, but, if ..., by the way, or, finally*). And the periodic structure of Raspberry's comment is outlined through indentation, with seven main questioning moves elaborating Raspberry's 'ton of them', and the final move in turn elaborated by three sub-queries:

> A few questions as we march to war
> The US military, Defence Secretary Donald Rumsfeld has assured us, is quite capable of waging the virtually foreordained war with Iraq *and* taking on North Korea.

I wish someone could settle my own questions with such clarity and conviction. I've got a ton of them.

[1] **For instance**: Has the decision to forgo unilateral military action against Iraq in favour of taking the matter of Iraq violations to the United Nations been cleverly subverted into some sort of Catch-22? Our government seems to be telling us that if Iraqi President Saddam Hussein denies having weapons of mass destruction, while we know he does have them, that falsehood becomes a material breach of its agreement and reason to take him out militarily. But if he admits having such weapons, he stands convicted out of his own mouth, and therefore we have no choice but to take him out.

('We know he's got those weapons of mass destruction,' satirist Mark Russell said. 'We've got the receipts!')

---

[2] Is America really serious that the war we propose is for the purpose of bringing democracy to the people of Iraq? Is it hopelessly cynical to imagine that democratization is a much lower priority than controlling the Iraqi oil reserves, asserting our authority in that part of the world and (perhaps) avenging our president's father? I mean, Saddam at least pretends to have a democracy. Our allies such as Saudi Arabia and Kuwait don't even go through the charade.

[3] **And** is it possible to call attention to our own duplicity or Saudi Arabia's lack of democracy without seeming to say that Saddam is innocent? He's not, of course. He's pretty much all the things the administration had said he is.

[4] **But** is he such an imminent threat to the United States as to justify unilateral military action against him? Is a war that is likely to cost thousands of innocent Iraqi lives the only way to remove whatever remains of Saddam's ability to wreak international havoc? Will our effort to take him out, even if successful, create more havoc than it prevents?

---

[5] **If** the proposed war is less about democracy and more about opposing international terrorism, why am I mistaken in the view that it could spawn more anti-American and anti-Israeli terrorism and increase the number of terrorists who see us as the international menace?

---

[6] **By the way**, how much of the commitment to topple Saddam is calculated to meet Israel's needs rather than our own? One must be careful not to

buy into the line of those who oppose the war because they hate Israel. But if we are willing to launch a war at least partly for Israel's sake, shouldn't we have a little more clout over such matters as the Israeli settlements in the occupied territories?

[7] A key question is how those who make our policy see the role of the United States.

[7a] Are we, in their minds, the only adults in a room full of squabbling children – the only ones with the clarity of vision and the military wherewithal to undertake the unpleasant task of belling the aggressive cats of the world, as we spread democracy's joyous gospel?

[7b] **Or** do they see us, as I sometimes fear, as some sort of international Dirty Harry, packing lots of heat and requiring only the thinnest of pretexts (and with little patience for procedural and evidentiary niceties) to rid the world of scum?

[7c] **Finally,** do they think that it's too late to work at peace, that it's wimpish to wonder why so much of the world dislikes us, that it's a form of appeasement to show the world our better nature?

Stripping away Raspberry's interrogative mood, and simplifying somewhat, we can arrive at an oppositional exposition like the following –

we shouldn't go to war

because

1. the weapons inspections are a Catch-22
2. the war's about oil, authority and revenge not democracy
3. *and* Saddam's not innocent
4. *but* he's not enough of a threat to warrant death and risk international havoc
5. (when) war could make terrorism worse
6. *by the way*, we need more control over Israel to act on their behalf
7. (critically)
   a we're not the only adults in the world
   b (nor) are we an international Dirty Harry
   c *finally* we can work at peace, determine why the world dislikes us, and show our better nature

In another world, this argument could have been put far less dialogically. But for Raspberry, putting the brakes on a 'virtually foreordained war with Iraq' required a radically heteroglossic text which made room for Americans with qualms about the war alongside their overdetermined patriots. We can perhaps refer to this replete with misgivings stance as **sceptical**, contrasting as it does with Pinter's damning tone and Lessing's excusing one.

There is of course a great deal more to say about these three texts than we have managed here, both interpersonally and multifunctionally. Our goal has simply been to move down the instantiation scale and illustrate the notion of sub-keys within one key, the commentator voice – at a level of delicacy we can usefully refer to as **stance**. We have no idea whether our notions of a damning, excusing or sceptical stance will stand the test of time. This depends of course on the extent to which the configurations of appraisal resources we have noted recur, and how they compare with related judgemental configurations we have not taken time to explore. We should also stress again at this point that instantiation is a cline, and there is no way of drawing a categorical distinction between key and stance along this cline. Having said that, in the next section we'll move further down the scale, and consider syndromes of appraisal which we come to identify with specific individuals.

4.5 Signature

At this level of delicacy we are concerned with syndromes of evaluation which characterise an individual – their appraisal signature[3] as it were. By way of illustration we'll glance at Mike Carleton, a Sydney media personality who alongside his daily radio program writes a weekly column in the 'News Review' section of the week-end broadsheet, the *Sydney Morning Herald*. Compared with Sydney's right-wing talk jocks, Carlton is relatively liberal; in Australia's contemporary 'all the way with LBJ' political scene, he might be even taken as left of centre. Carleton is irreverently outspoken about a number of issues, and regularly assumes the damning stance we introduced with Pinter's text above. Here's an example of his loud proclaiming judgemental tone, as he gets stuck into the Howard government's manipulation of insecurity and fear in place of leadership (clearly inscribed **judgements** underlined).

> Worse, this is a <u>mean</u> administration, a <u>miserly</u>, <u>mingy</u>, <u>minatory</u> bunch if ever there was one. It has a head but <u>no heart</u>, a brain but <u>no soul</u>. <u>Without generosity of spirit</u>, <u>devoid of compassion</u>, <u>absorbed in narrow self-interest</u>, the Howard Government has no concept of any over-arching duty to articulate the aspirations of the governed and to lead them, with some hope, to a happier and more complete nationhood. If the polls slump, how easy it is to

204   *The Language of Evaluation*

> play the Hansonite politics of <u>greed</u> and <u>envy</u>, to send in the bovver brigade: Herron to cosh the boongs, Tony Abbott to drop-kick the unemployed, Jocelyn Newman to savage these on social welfare.
> This is not government, it is mere management, a very different thing, and it is what will do for them in the end. A <u>cold</u> and <u>bloodless</u> lot, their veins run with piss and vinegar. [Carleton 2000: 38]

For us the key feature that makes Carleton's damning stance recognisable, at least to a Sydney readership, is its volume. It can be extremely loud. To achieve this he employs a full range of amplifying resources, including colloquial lexis (*bovver brigade, cosh the boongs, piss*), lexical metaphor (*drop-kick the unemployed, their veins run with piss and vinegar*), rhetorical triplets (*without generosity of spirit, devoid of compassion, absorbed in narrow self-interest*) and alliteration (*a mean administration, a miserly, mingy, minatory bunch*). Even more distinctive perhaps is his use of lexical proliferation to increase the mass of an evaluation (as with *mean, miserly, mingy, minatory* just noted). The longest example of this we have to hand appears to have been produced with the aid of a thesaurus (either that or Carleton's vocabulary is many times larger than ours!) as he targets politicians following the Port Arthur massacre in Tasmania in 1996 (in which dozens of people were killed by a lone gunman using automatic weapons):

> For too long – far too long – capricious, cautious, chicken-livered, cowardly, craven, duck-brained, dim-witted, faint-hearted, gutless, gormless, ignorant, indecisive, irresolute, jelly-backed, limp-wristed, namby pamby, negligent, obdurate, opportunist, perfunctory, poltroonish, pusillanimous, shallow, shameless, spineless, squeamish, timid, weak-kneed, vacuous, backsliding, bending, bickering, cheating, compromising, cringing, deal-doing, dillydallying, dithering, equivocating, failing, faking, faltering, fiddling, fidgeting, grovelling, hesitating, kowtowing, lying, obfuscating, obstructing, oscillating, paltering, pandering, posturing, quitting, quivering, resiling, see-sawing, shilly- shallying, slithering, squabbling, swivelling, tergiversating, teetering, tottering, twisting, vacillating, wavering, weaseling, wobbling, yellowing politicians have buckled to the gun lobby. [*The Sydney Morning Herald*, Saturday May 4, 1996; News Review p. 36]

In another example, Carleton sends off a corrupt senator several times by way of getting the message across that it is time to go:

> So take the hint, Senator Colston, it's time to go. Thank you and good night. Just get out. Resign. Depart. Leave. Disappear. Vanish. Rack off. Take the

money and run. You are a disgrace to the Senate and an affront to the people. [*SMH* News Review 34 Saturday April 12 Mike Carleton Delusions of grand Mal 1999]

What seems to distinguish Carleton's voice then is that he damns louder than anyone else, using a wide range of amplifying resources and featuring lexical proliferation (including colloquial and learned terms as required). It's a 'no holds barred' stance, fuelled by exasperation and designed to grab the attention of anyone listening and beat them into submission as far as sharing Carleton's opinions are concerned. A compelling signature, albeit one whose volume is bound to generate both centripetal and centrifugal reactions – depending on the **judgements** Carleton is proffering.

Loudness is not of course something Carleton owns. Stevie Ray Vaughan's fans use it to intensify their appreciation of his music in their raves on Amazon's website:

> **awesome! awesome! awesome! awesome!** it's <u>very worth</u> buying. oh did i say that it's **awesome**! thank you. stevie ray!
>
> ... and, as a bonus, a <u>**very** psychedelic, destructive</u> (literally!), <u>cathartic</u> and <u>liberatory</u> version of Jimi Hendrix's 'Third stone from the sun'.

What we are suggesting however is that Carleton's amplification strategies, combined with his irreverent judgments, do identify him to his readership – distinguishing him from other columnists in his broadsheet and the comparable print media of which we are aware. This is not to suggest that the same syndrome of evaluation cannot appear in texts elsewhere; it may. But to identify an appraiser it would need to recur across a range of texts by some individual. And to challenge Carleton's signature, it would have to cloud his identity by recurring in discourse consumed by a shared readership. At this level of delicacy then, we should clarify that signature is a concept that we need to operationalise within a specified discourse community. It names the syndrome of appraisal resources which distinguishes individuals, one from another, within that community – since it is community that aligns the relevant valeur. It's Carleton's identity as a Sydney journalist that matters here.

Moving back up the instantiation scale from signature towards stance we might generalise a loud damning stance driven by exasperation and designed to vigorously denigrate transgressors – a sub-stance which Australians might refer to colloquially as 'rubbishing'. From this perspective the question of Carleton's signature becomes a question of whether his style of rubbishing serves to identify him or not.

Ultimately, answering this kind of question depends on quantitative factor analysis, such as that exemplified in the work of Biber and his colleagues.

4.6 Evaluation and reaction

Beyond signature there is the evaluation afforded by the appraisal in a text. In Chapters 2 and 3 above and Chapter 5 below we have attempted to display in our analyses the reading we see naturalised by the text we are working on as it unfolds. Our analyses thus reflect a compliant reading, insofar as our own subjectivity enables this. Because our analyses are inevitably interested, it is probably appropriate to think of them as evaluations of appraisal. And as far as the appraisal potential of a text is concerned, such evaluations can never be the final word. There will always be people around who respond to a text in other ways; and where its appraisal is more evoked than inscribed, we might even argue that a range of readings is being facilitated, if not encouraged.

So as a final step in this chapter we need to make room for a final step on the instantiation cline which we'll refer to as reaction – which we can characterise as the reading someone makes of the evaluative meaning in a text. In terms of solidarity, this amounts to the way in which they commune with feeling and align themselves in and around the community under negotiation.

In general terms, we can recognise compliant, resistant and tactical readings (*pace* de Certeau 1984). As noted, compliaint readings accommodate the reading position naturalised by a text. As compliant readers for example we'd empathise with Pinter's condemnation of America, appreciate Lessing's explanation of excess and sympathise with Raspberry's misgivings. Resistant readings on the other hand work against the grain of this naturalisation process. It's easy to imagine 'Sheriff Shrub' and his warmongers feeling outraged by Pinter's diatribe, patronised by Lessing's deprecation, and exasperated by Raspberry's wimpishness (indeed their voice is strong enough in Raspberry's text to give us a fair indication how they might react).

Tactical readings are readings which take some aspect of the evaluation a text affords, and respond to it in an interested way that neither accepts nor rejects communion with the text as a whole. One good example of this would be our use of the Pinter, Lessing and Raspberry texts as linguistic exemplars. Our goal was to use the texts to illustrate kinds of stance, and form a community of scholars appreciating them for the concepts they exemplify. This is almost certainly not something foreseen by Pinter, Lessing and Raspberry and worked into the design of their discourse. Our reference to 'Sheriff Shrub and his warmongers' above however was deployed as a compliant reading of Pinter's text, and designed by way of illustration to provoke a tactical reading of this chapter – it's dismissal as an anti-American piece of political opportunism perhaps. We wonder as we edit our analyses here how far we have avoided provoking tactical readings of this kind. Can we in fact deal 'dispassionately' as social semioticians with volatile political discourse? Is disinterestedness just an academic con?

In retrospect our feeling is that so-called objectivity is impossible, since the mere selection of material for analysis evokes attitude and analysis cannot help but be a negotiation of interests in relation to the evaluation naturalised by a text and the social subjectivity of readers. At the same time, as modernist writers, we do strive to naturalise a reading position – in our case one which offers tools for analysis (utilitarian compliance), invites dialogue (complementarity not opposition) and minimises misunderstanding (tactical misreadings). This kind of writing is not argumentative enough for some – there's not enough coercion. But it's a stance we feel comfortable with here.

We should also keep in mind that the negotiation of feeling is a dynamic process. As a text unfolds readers align and disengage in response to a network of overlapping communalities. Recall how Pinter toned down his damning stance in his final paragraph by way of appealing to a broader readership. And Raspberry shifted gears, even within a single query as he parenthetically mitigated his charge that Bush was seeking vengeance:

> Is it hopelessly cynical to imagine that democratization is a much lower priority than controlling the Iraqi oil reserves, asserting our authority in that part of the world and (**perhaps**) avenging our president's father?

We'll look more carefully as logogenetic processes of this kind in Chapter 5.

4.7 Coda ...

Our discussion in this chapter has been directed towards an understanding of how appraisal values operate in texts, not as individual, isolated moments of meaning, but as elements integrated into broader syndromes of co-occurring meanings. This analysis of syndromes of evaluation can be conducted at greater or lesser degrees of delicacy. In identifying evaluative 'key' we attend to patterns of occurrence and co-occurrence which are conventionalised in a given discourse domain and which therefore can be observed with some regularity across a diversity of texts. In exploring key in broadsheet journalism and secondary-school history we saw how the particular configurations of evaluative meanings operating in those settings could be linked with particular rhetorical objectives. Thus the reconfiguration of the language's global meaning-making potential which constitutes reporter voice provides the grounds for the ideological claim on the part of journalism as an institution that news reporting can be 'objective', 'neutral' and 'impartial'. Recorder key has a similar functionality in secondary-school history. In identifying 'stance' and 'signature' we attend to more delicate, more localised reconfigurations of the reconfigurations which constitute evaluative 'key'. Stances are reconfigurations which we predict will be recurrent across a range of texts and a range of authors in a given discourse domain, and perhaps across different discourse domains, while signatures are the idiolectal reconfigurations of meaning-making potential by which individual authors achieve a recognisable personal style.

The appraisal framework upon which we rely for this account is dialogically oriented. It takes seriously the addressivity of so-called 'monologic' texts, attending to how authors locate themselves with respect to communities of shared feelings, tastes and values and how they present themselves as responding to, and anticipating the responses of, members of these attitudinal communities. Our account, then, of key, stance and signature is one in which evaluative style is a matter of the relationships which the author constructs with the voices and viewpoints which constitute the text's heteroglossic backdrop. In this way, the material set out in the previous chapters lays the foundations for a grammar of solidarity which integrates the lexicogrammar with the discourse semantics.

Notes

1. A rather different set of text compositional conventions operates in the tabloid media, where explicit authorial **judgement** occurs regularly in news reports.
2. The last example is actually three questions (is it too late?, is it wimpish?, is it a form of appeasement?), and projects a further question (why do they dislike

us?). And it is prefaced by a meta-question (how do those who make our policy see the role of the US?). So semantically speaking we can recognise 16 questions (13 + 2 + 1).
3. Christian Matthiessen has suggested to us that there may be a need for an additional scale alongside instantiation, ranging from the reservoir of meanings in the culture through various sub-groupings to individual repertoires; what we are calling signature here would be part of this kind of 'collectivity to individual' individuation hierarchy.

5
Enacting Appraisal: Text Analysis

5.1 Appraising discourse

In this chapter we will demonstrate some of the ways in which appraisal systems can be used to inform our interpretation of evaluation in text. In particular we are concerned here with the interaction of **attitude**, **engagement** and **graduation** in relation to the social context variable tenor. We will also comment on the interaction between appraisal and other modes of meaning, in order to make contact with more comprehensive approaches to discourse semantics (such as those outlined in Martin & Rose 2003).

In order to accomplish this, we will focus on just two texts. This of course places limits on what we can exemplify as far as the texture of appraisal in discourse is concerned; but it does allow us to undertake close readings at the level of detail we need to interpret the materialisation of evaluation as it unfolds. While both analyses will be attending to patterns in the use of appraisal resources, they will have slightly different emphases. The first analysis attends specifically to localised interactions between **attitude** and **engagement/graduation** with the purpose of developing the account begun in Chapter 3 of how, by such interactions, texts construct a model of the putative addressee and position the author with respect to that addressee. The second analysis also attends to these issues, but pays attention to more global patterns of textual organisation by which appraisal values are sequenced and made to interact so as to effect particular rhetorical outcomes. The texts we have chosen are ideologically charged, highlighting we hope the impact of evaluation on various dimensions of interpersonal politics in our troubled times.

The first of these texts is a commentary piece from the *Daily Express*, a British middle-brow tabloid newspaper which in recent times has adopted a politically and socially conservative editorial line. The article was published in October 2001 as the United States government was preparing to invade Afghanistan in the wake of the terrorist attack on the World Trade Center in New York. At the time there was substantial opposition in the United Kingdom to such an action and the author, Carol Sarler, writes to confront this position, arguing in favour of war and characterising its opponents as 'faint hearted' and 'woolly'.

The second text was published in Hong Kong on Friday September 21, 2001 – 10 days after the events of 9/11. Entitled 'Mourning', it is the editorial from *HK Magazine*, a weekly lifestyle magazine designed for expats (especially British and Australian) and Chinese returning from work or study overseas. Free copies are made available at 'fashionable' video stores, bars, coffee shops and comparable retail outlets serving this community. Its editorials represent one of the last sites in the Hong Kong print media where voices critical of the Hong Kong or Beijing governments can be heard. In this case however, it is the regional repercussions of the events of 9/11 which are in focus.

As indicated, our purpose in this chapter is to take a more global view of the operation of all three sub-systems of appraisal as they co-pattern across unfolding text. Our focus is upon certain rhetorical effects which are fundamental to the evaluative rhetoric of argumentative, mass communicative texts of this type. We are interested in understanding the interpersonal functionality of such texts as a process by which positions of potential alignment between writer and reader are constructed as the writer strategically invests the text's experiential content with the different types of attitude. Thus the actions and experiences of the social actors depicted by the text are made the grounds for the sharing of feelings, tastes and norms. We are referring here to what Maree Stenglin has called bonding (Stenglin 2002, Martin & Stenglin in press) – the investiture of attitude in activity, the resonance of attitude with events and things (abstract or concrete), around which shared reverberations we align into communing sympathies of kinship, friendship, collegiality and other of the many kinds of affinity and affiliation. By this we indicate that, in Bakhtin's terms, texts are both ideological and axiological;[1] sense bonds dynamically with sensibility, as depicted in Figure 5.1. In these terms, ideologically speaking a text unfolds as rationality – a quest for 'truth'; axiologically it unfolds rhetorically – an invitation to community.

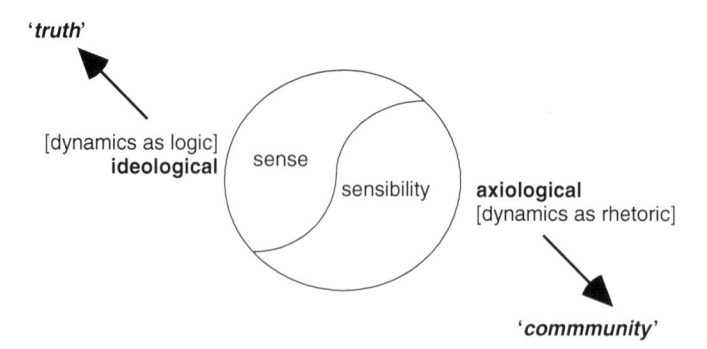

Figure 5.1   Bonding – the infusion of value in activity

5.2   War or Peace: a rhetoric of grief and hatred

As indicated, our first text is a commentary article which argues for war with Afghanistan in the wake of the destruction of the World Trade Center Towers in New York on 11 September 2001. For the purposes of analysis, we have divided the text into sections, with the divisions indicated by labels placed within square brackets at appropriate points in the text.

[Section 1. Headline]
DAMN THE PEACENIKS FOR THEIR FAINT HEARTS
By CAROL SARLER

[Section 2. Personal narrative – a lost friend]
ONCE upon a time, she sang with Duke Ellington on stage at Carnegie Hall. Last Christmas, we had her all to ourselves. Betty Farmer, mother, friend and cabaret diva, squeezed around our turkey and trim way down in the American South, and her lustrous voice led 20 of us in our most splendid round of carols: the British ones, the American ones and those few that, laughing, we shared.

At home in New York, to make meet the ends that music did not, she did some office temping. Which is how it came to be that, on September 11, she was in her third week of a job at the World Trade Center. North Tower. Floor 105.

Her only child, her daughter Kat, ashen with shock, went to collect her mother's life's belongings. Together, back in Georgia, she and I sifted and sorted them. In between the earrings over here and the nightgowns over there, Kat's grief was endlessly and relentlessly intruded upon: the local paper wanted a snap; the medical examiner wanted a DNA sample; the authorities wanted details for the death certificate ... all this, with no body to bury, not now, not ever.

[*Section 3. Observing America's response*]

And all this, too, against the bigger backdrop of a fabulous, flawed, great, gutsy nation brought to its knees by pain and bewilderment.

I would like to record that the picture was one of solemn dignity but, in fact, it was not. How could it be?

Outrage literally mangled our poor language. Defence funding, I heard, has never been 'sufficiently adequate enough'; there are folks with 'terrorist backgrounds in their past'; we had reports from 'this hellacious scene', of the railways' 'increased ridership', and of these 'terroristic activities'. And full marks to the earnest chap who announced 'help for the nose-diving airline industry'.

Commerce barely paused for breath: within a week, advertisements were urging people to buy a new car as a patriotic duty – it helps the ailing economy, so head for your nearest Chrysler dealer and God Bless America. Flags flew (and still do) from every conceivable promontory and housewives' guru Martha Stewart had her own television special to show The American People how to hang and display the Stars and Stripes correctly.

Newspaper reporters were instructed to carry tissues at all times, in case a weeping interviewee's performance be interrupted by 'embarrassment at nasal discharge'; sales figures showed that baby firemen's uniforms are to be this year's favourite Halloween costume and, last Friday, Fisher Price, to its eternal shame, launched its newest toy: to help the under-fives understand, and to offer them positive role models, they shall now have a doll dressed as a New York fireman and called ... Billy Blazes.

Soon enough, ramifications spilled out all over: the United Nations is, in case you did not know, an 'anteye-American' organisation, so come trick or treat night, you should urge your children to collect for anything that isn't Unicef. Environmentalism took a huge and early hit – well, come on, Alaskan or Arab oil? No bloody contest, is it? And then there is sheer nastiness. I heard one talk-show host introduce his programme with the fervent plea that all slain Islamic terrorists should have their bodies scrubbed raw by Jews and Christians, then have their genitals cut off and fed to pigs, so that they become pork, and see how they like that, darned Moslems, heh-heh. On the whole, however, the Gung Hos are not in charge – indeed, what strikes you most is an unaccustomed humility. I lost count of the times good and decent people asked me: why do they hate us so? And, even: did we do something to deserve this? Like soothing battered kids in the schoolyard, I told them that, no, they did nothing, ever, bad enough to deserve this. Dust yourselves down, I

214　*The Language of Evaluation*

said. Fight back, I said. Not because it's easy, not even because I am sure you will triumph. But simply because to do so will make you feel better. And that, you do deserve.

[*Section 4. The argument for war*]

IT WAS, then, with fury, that I returned home on Saturday to find my own country rumbling with the mumbles of the peaceniks; the woolliest of liberals who shake their heads and say that war is not the answer; that there can be no winners but only the loss of innocents.

Innocence, my friends, is a relative concept. The 6,000 in the World Trade Center were innocent. Afghan children are innocent. So are their displaced families and our aid, naturally, must be theirs.

But, among and around them, move the millions who are not quite guilty of murder yet are absolutely guilty of complicity; the 'innocents' about whom our peaceniks are so squeamish and I am not.

While the politically correct have stood passively by, it is these millions who have fed, nurtured and permitted fundamentalism to get us where it has today.

Those who burned Mr Rushdie's books set the scene for those who dynamited the Afghan Buddhas; those who wave their vitriolic arms through the streets of Pakistan pave the way for those who wave their guns in the name of Taliban; those who scream for jihad inspire those who yearn to sacrifice their lives upon planes impaled within skyscrapers.

And if a bunch of these rabid souls get to hook up with their 70 virgins a few years ahead of plan, I would call it mildly unfortunate, but I would shed no tears.

[*Section 5. Lost friends recalled*]

Such of those as I have left I shall keep for Kat, for Betty's memory, and for the thousands of others who will not be singing anywhere, not on the next holiday for infidels that we call Christmas.

[*Daily Express*, features pages, October 10, 2001]

5.2.1　Generic organisation and communicative objectives

The text is a typical example of a certain type of journalistic commentary – it is somewhat elusive, or at least somewhat diverse, with respect to its communicative objectives. The headline and concluding sections suggest the overarching purpose we outlined above – to criticise, and to develop an argument against, those opposed to the United State's proposed invasion of Afghanistan. The opening section immediately following the headline takes the form of a personal

Enacting Appraisal: Text Analysis 215

narrative-cum-mini-biography, as the author remembers and grieves for the friend she has lost in the 9/11 attack. There is no immediately obvious connection between this and the headline which preceded it. (We note that it is customary in the newsrooms of newspapers of this type for the headline to be added by a sub-editor after the article has been completed by the journalistic author.) The next section takes the form of a series of observations on the way Americans have reacted to the disaster. For the most part the author takes a critical view of those responses, although she ends the section praising ordinary Americans and declaring the rightness of their desire to 'fight back'. The text ends with a short wrap-up or coda in which the author returns to the theme of grief for her lost friend.

As indicated, these elements may seem diverse, even somewhat incoherent, if we are expecting a formally conducted argument with a clearly signalled hypothesis (or hypotheses) and systematically presented supporting evidence and argumentation. In fact, if we were to extract the actual line of argumentation from the text is would probably appear bare and perhaps implausible – for example, that America is right to attack Afghanistan because 'to do so will make [Americans] feel better' and that we should have no compunction about killing ordinary Afghanis because many (most?) of them are sympathetic towards Islamic extremism. Texts such as these are as much about personal recollection, observation and story telling as they are about the explicit development of an argumentative position. In order to account for, and do justice to the rhetorical functionality of such texts, it is necessary to attend to the line of evaluative positioning which runs through, and lends coherence to, these generically diverse elements.

5.2.2 Axiology – the text's value orientation

Evaluatively, the text is organised around several points of attitudinal alignment which involve the following social groupings and evaluative orientations:

> **empathy & moral outrage for** > > *Americans who are grieving over the loss of loved ones in the 9/11 attack* [sections 2 & 5]
>
> **pity/condescension** > > *Americans who have been so disturbed by the events of 9/11 that they now mangle the English language* [section 3]
>
> **condemnation** > > *Americans who have been exploiting 9/11 when developing advertising campaigns and new product lines* [section 3]

concern/sympathy >> *Americans who feel emotionally battered by 9/11* [section 3]

approval >> *Americans who want revenge for 9/11* [section 3]

contempt/anger >> *those in the UK speaking out against an attack on Afghanistan* [sections 1 (headline) & 4]

hatred >> *the millions of Muslims around the world and in Afghanistan who are supportive of acts of terror* [sections 4 & 5]

As will be demonstrated in the following discussion, the text's ultimate rhetorical potential results from the way these various value orientations are made to interconnect and interrelate as the text unfolds. By these interconnections and interactions the text constructs what Macken-Horarik has termed 'high order meaning complexes' or 'metarelations' by which the reader is positioned to adopt particular attitudes (Macken-Horarik 2003: 286).

5.2.3 The headline – damning the peaceniks

The headline unambiguously declares a position of antipathy towards those in the UK who have been speaking out against the proposed attack upon Afghanistan.

Damn the peaceniks for their faint hearts.

The colloquial *damn* conveys strong negative emotion on the part of the authorial voice, thus signalling a high degree of commitment to the pro-war position by the author. The proposition that those who are opposed to war are acting out of cowardice is construed as unproblematic and capable of being 'taken-for-granted' via the monoglossia of the headline and the presuppositional nature of the nominal *their faint hearts*. Thus the reader who is being written into the text right from the start is one who takes a negative view of those who campaign for peace. Writer and reader are construed as standing together against the antipathetic 'otherness' of the 'peaceniks'.

5.2.4 Grieving for lost friends

The body of the text proper begins with a mini narrative in which the life and death of the author's American friend Betty are recounted. We repeat it here for convenience

ONCE upon a time, she sang with Duke Ellington on stage at Carnegie Hall. Last Christmas, we had her all to ourselves. Betty Farmer, mother, friend and cabaret diva, squeezed around our turkey and trim way down in the American South, and her lustrous voice led 20 of us in our most splendid round of carols: the British ones, the American ones and those few that, laughing, we shared.

At home in New York, to make meet the ends that music did not, she did some office temping. Which is how it came to be that, on September 11, she was in her third week of a job at the World Trade Center. North Tower. Floor 105.

Her only child, her daughter Kat, ashen with shock, went to collect her mother's life's belongings. Together, back in Georgia, she and I sifted and sorted them. In between the earrings over here and the nightgowns over there, Kat's grief was endlessly and relentlessly intruded upon: the local paper wanted a snap; the medical examiner wanted a DNA sample; the authorities wanted details for the death certificate ... all this, with no body to bury, not now, not ever.

That this section is to be read by reference to an interpretative regime conventionally associated with 'story' or 'narrative' in our culture is signalled not only by the obvious *Once upon a time* but by the use of formulaic devices such as the cataphoric reference of *she* in *she sang with Duke Ellington*, the tripartite post modification in *Betty Farmer, mother, friend and cabaret diva* and the fixed phraseology of *Which is how it came to be that*. As Macken-Horarik has demonstrated, the interpretative regimes which operate for many types of narrative involve strategically sequenced combinations of attitudinal values which direct the reader to experience the narrativised world through the eyes of some central character(s), and hence to empathise with them (Macken-Horarik 2003). In the case of this mini narrative, attitudinal meanings are organised so as to align the reader into a community of shared value which grieves with and for Americans over the 9/11 attack and is morally outraged over the suffering of survivors.

The effect is achieved by firstly aligning the reader into a communality which esteems and has the warmest regard for the writer's friend 'Betty'. Tellingly this is achieved primarily via attitudinal tokens rather than inscriptions. For example,

ONCE upon a time, she sang with Duke Ellington on stage at Carnegie Hall [*factual token of +ve judgement: capacity, hence 'our' esteem for Betty*]

218   *The Language of Evaluation*

> At home in New York, <u>to make meet the ends that music did not</u>, she did some office temping [*token of Betty's +ve tenacity*]
>
> we had her all to ourselves [*indirect indication of the strongly positive feeling that 'we' had for Betty*]
>
> squeezed around our turkey and trim way down in the American South [*token of +ve affect: happiness associated with Betty*]

Where attitude is inscribed rather than invoked it is typically of values of positive **appreciation** rather than of direct positive **affect** towards, or **judgements** of, Betty. For example,

> and her **lustrous** voice
>
> led 20 of us in our most **splendid** round of carols

This is followed by an abrupt transition from the positive to the negative. The transition is marked by,

> Which is how it came to be that, on September 11, she was in her third week of a job at the World Trade Center. North Tower. Floor 105.

Under the conditioning of the reader's knowledge of what happened on this September 11, this apparently attitudinally neutral statement of fact has an obvious power to evoke a reaction of horror and dread which is, perhaps, the more strongly felt on account of only needing to be alluded to rather than directly stated.

In the short section which follows immediately after, the dominant attitudinal motif is the negative **affect** of the daughter, this time typically conveyed via inscription. For example

> ashen with <u>shock</u>; Kat's <u>grief</u>

Tellingly, this inscription is interspersed with material which has the potential to evoke a sense that 'Kat' has been wronged and hence to provoke feelings of moral outrage. For example,

> Kat's grief was endlessly and relentlessly **<u>intruded upon; the local paper wanted a snap; the medical examiner wanted a DNA sample; the authorities wanted details for the death certificate</u>**

Perhaps most tellingly, the section ends with a depiction which evokes rather than directly states high negative feelings of grief and despair.

> ... all this, with no body to bury, not now, not ever

The effect is to construe the reader as aligned into a community of feeling by which there is a compellingly 'natural' connection between there being 'no body to bury' and the experiencing of such emotions.

The section operates, therefore, to align the reader into a community of both positivity towards Americans, with 'Betty' as their exemplar, and empathetic negativity towards their loss, with 'Kat's' suffering as exemplar. The choice of narrative mode enables the writer to present this particular value orientation as arising naturally and inevitably from the 'facts' of her own personal experiences. On the face of it these experiences have no obvious relevance to the point of the article – the setting out of an argument in favour an attack upon Afghanistan. The relevance, of course, is an attitudinal one under which support for this military action is motivated by outrage that an 'only' child should have lost such an admirable and beloved parent.

Generally, then, this opening section operates to establish a bond of concern and sympathy between the British readership to which the text is directed and the people of America. With this in mind, we note the following narrative detail,

> [she] led 20 of us in our most splendid round of carols: the British ones, the American ones and those few that, laughing, we shared.

Here this communality is concretely enacted as we are shown Brits and Americans coming joyfully together to celebrate a common heritage which transcends any minor cultural differences.

5.2.5 Aligning with America – fabulous, flawed and gutsy

In the next section the writer turns to describing how America more widely and more generally responded to the World Trade Center attack. Evaluatively the section is of interest because of the way it mixes positivity with negativity and because of the way it handles that negativity. We observe this mixing of the positive and the negative in the sentence which acts as a Macro-Theme for the section,

> And all this, too, against the bigger backdrop of a fabulous, flawed, great, gutsy nation brought to its knees by pain and bewilderment.

Here is the same monoglossic taken-for-grantedness which operates in the headline. The proposition that there is an anthropomorphised entity (*brought to its knees*) called the American nation which is 'fabulous', 'flawed' and 'gutsy' is construed as not being at issue, as a position which is unproblematic an uncontentious for the audience to which the text is being directed.

The first phase of this section is concerned with the linguistic failings of Americans in the wake of the World Trade Center attack. The rhetoric here is somewhat convoluted, with both positive and negative lines of evaluation being developed. Firstly there is some suggestion of a criticism of Americans for not remaining 'solemnly dignified' (*I would like to record that the picture was one of solemn dignity but, in fact, it was not.*) The negativity, however, is immediately mitigated, even cancelled, as the writer backtracks evaluatively (*... but, in fact, it was not. How could it be?*) Here a **concurring** leading question is employed to present the unreasonableness of such a requirement as self-evident.

5.2.6 Linguistic incapacitation

The author then provides a series of factual tokens which she offers to the reader as evidence of just how upset and discombobulated the American people are.

> Outrage literally mangled our poor language. Defence funding, I heard, has never been 'sufficiently adequate enough'; there are folks with 'terrorist backgrounds in their past'; we had reports from 'this hellacious scene', of the railways' 'increased ridership', and of these 'terroristic activities'.
>
> And full marks to the earnest chap who announced 'help for the nose-diving airline industry'.

This material, then, is ostensively presented as further grounds for why 'we', the British reader, should empathise with Americans in their current emotional disarray. It enters into a meta-relationship of 'confirmation' with the preceding narrative section. (For a fuller account of attitudinal meta-relational types, see Macken-Horarik 2003: 306–7.) But there is, of course, another point of possible attitudinal alignment here for the British reader – one in which a long-standing and deep-seated view of America and Americans is invoked – namely the view which condescends to American culture, seeing it as less sophisticated, less developed or less refined than the British 'original'.[2] The attitudinal appeal, then, is to a British sense of superiority over the colonial cousin and recalls the condescending stance of Lessing discussed in the previous chapter. Thus this section is in a relationship of 'transformation' with what occurred before in that empathy (an emotional bonding between equals) is translated into pity (similar to empathy but typically involving social inequality).

We notice that, tellingly, this negativity is carefully handled so as to be significantly mitigated. The core value being invoked is one of cultural incompetence or lack of sophistication, and hence an assessment of negative **judgement: capacity**. However, in her explicit evaluative language (her inscriptions of **attitude**), the author is careful to avoid being directly critical of human agents. Rather, at the level of explicit attitude, this is construed as a matter of **appreciation** rather than **judgement**. Thus it is the *picture* which could not be *one of solemn dignity* and it is the cultural artefact *language* which is portrayed as *mangled* and warranting our sympathies (*our poor language*). Even in this mangling there is no human agent – the perpetrator of this damage is 'outrage'. It is only the final sentence of the phase,

> And full marks to the earnest chap who announced 'help for the nose-diving airline industry'

that the negativity becomes explicit, and even here the use of irony enables the overt, literal meanings to be positive (eg *full marks, earnest*) rather than negative.

In terms of attitudinal alignments and the negotiation of solidarity, this section is somewhat mixed. The negative proposition that this was not a picture of solemn dignity is multiply dialogised. For example,

> I would like to record that the picture was one of solemn dignity **but** [counter], **in fact** [counter + pronounce], it was **not** [deny]. **How could it be**? [leading question acting as concur – indicates that the answer is so obvious that it need not be declared]

Here, as we've indicated, the author is advancing a somewhat negative view of America's reaction. The dialogism acts to present this negativity as problematic and likely to be contested in the current communicative context since this is a view which the writer herself repudiates, even though she herself initially advances it. The communality into which the reader is being aligned, therefore, is very obviously one which is tolerant of a diversity of viewpoints, and more specifically of view points which would not criticise Americans in this way.

With respect to the evaluative proposition, *outrage mangled our poor language*, we notice that, while, the proposition is monoglossically

222 *The Language of Evaluation*

asserted, the author nonetheless immediately supplies several pieces of evidence by way of justification, thereby construing the proposition as in someway contentious, novel or 'at issue' for the text's putative readership. This justification takes the form of 'factual' depictions which act as tokens of **−ve judgement: incapacity** – for example, *we had reports from 'this hellacious scene', of the railways 'increased ridership'*.

Both attitudinally and dialogistically, then, this phase is mixed. Attitudinally the reader is invited to share feelings of both sympathy and condescension. Dialogistically, some propositions are held to be unproblematic for the audience (for example, that America is a fabulous, gutsy nation, and that our language has been mangled) while others are held to be somewhat more contentious and less likely to be shared, at least initially (for example, that the picture was not one of solemn dignity).

5.2.7 Crass commercialism

In the following phase, the author offers relatively straightforward negative characterisations of certain aspects of US society.

> Commerce barely paused for breath: within a week, advertisements were urging people to buy a new car as a patriotic duty – it helps the ailing economy, so head for your nearest Chrysler dealer and God Bless America. Flags flew (and still do) from every conceivable promontory and housewives guru Martha Stewart had her own television special to show The American People how to hang and display the Stars and Stripes correctly.
>
> Newspaper reporters were instructed to carry tissues at all times, in case a weeping interviewee's performance be interrupted by 'embarrassment at nasal discharge'; sales figures showed that baby firemen's uniforms are to be this years favourite Halloween costume and, last Friday, Fisher Price, to its eternal shame, launched its newest toy: to help the under-fives understand, and to offer them positive role models, they shall now have a doll dressed as a New York fireman and called ... Billy Blazes.
>
> Soon enough, ramifications spilled out all over: the United Nations is, in case you did not know, an 'anteye-American' organisation, so come trick or treat night, you should urge your children to collect for anything that isn't Unicef. Environmentalism took a huge and early hit – well, come on, Alaskan or Arab oil? No bloody contest, is it? And then there is sheer nastiness. I heard one talk-show host introduce his programme with the fervent plea that all slain Islamic terrorists should have their bodies scrubbed raw by Jews and Christians, then have their genitals cut off and fed to pigs, so that they become pork, and see how they like that, darned Moslems, heh-heh.

There is an attitudinal shift here from negative **social esteem** to negative **social sanction**, specifically **impropriety** – from the understandable, even justified, linguistic incapacitation of Americans to the much more reprehensible greed of its commercial culture and the bigotry of right-wing radio commentators. What is noteworthy is that this shift is not immediately signalled by any explicit evaluative inscription. Rather, for a paragraph and a half, all the evaluative work is done by invocation – by tokens which 'provoke', 'afford' or 'flag' an attitudinal orientation. (For the taxonomy of sub-types of attitudinal invocation, see Chapter 2, section 2.6.) Thus the reader is supplied with the attitudinal **provocation** (invocation via metaphor) of *commerce barely paused for breath* (invoking a sense of unseemly haste) and the attitudinal **flagging** (invocation via counter expectation) of *within a week, advertisements were urging people to buy a new car as a patriotic duty token*. (Here *within a week* evokes the sense that these advertisements came sooner than was to be expected.) Similarly there is the **flagging** (invocation via ironic free-indirect speech) of *so head for your nearest Chrysler dealer and God Bless America*, by which the reader's attention is drawn to the strangeness and hence wrongfulness of this particular American mentality, as well as the further **flagging** (via both intensification and counter expectation) of *Flags flew (and <u>still</u> do) from <u>every conceivable</u> promontory*, and the non-standard capitalisation of *The American People*. It is only half-way through the second paragraph that the evaluative position being naturalised is overtly stated – when the author declares, *Fisher Price, to its <u>eternal shame</u> ...* The rhetoric is one by which the author assumes that the wrongfulness of these various behaviours is so self-evident to the reader that it is only invocation, and not inscription, which is required.

When the most highly charged evaluation is formulated (the assertion of outrageous bigotry the part of the right-wing commentators) this sequence is reversed, with the inscription preceding the experiential content which exemplifies and justifies it.

And then there is <u>sheer nastiness.</u> → I heard one talk-show host introduce his programme with the fervent plea that all slain Islamic terrorists should have their bodies scrubbed raw by Jews ...

This section is monoglossic in that there is no referencing or engaging with views or voices which might not evaluate the depicted behaviours in the same way. Yet against this is the fact, just outlined, that the authorial voice typically doesn't explicitly pass judgement, relying instead on the experiential content and associated attitudinal flags and provocations. This has several important consequences for the terms under which solidarity is negotiated.

To some degree the text operates by assuming these are 'facts' which will 'speak for themselves' and accordingly that the reader will invest the presented experiential content with particular attitudinal values. We can, for example, deduce from the way in which the text unfolds evaluatively that the writer assumes of readers that they will regard as crassly and exploitatively commercial the release of a doll dressed as a New York fireman and called Billy Blazes. And yet, of course, these tokens are definitely not open-ended evaluatively. They involve **provocation** and **flagging**, not **affording**, and the evaluative meanings which the reader is expected to draw from them is eventually made quite explicit via the attitudinal inscriptions we described above. Clearly then, the reader is being aligned here into a particular attitudinal community (one strongly critical of certain elements in American society) and it is not a communality which is tolerant of alternative viewpoints – solidarity depends on the reader accepting this particular assessment. Tellingly, however, the value position is one which is not so much explicitly argued for by the writer (though she does this at a couple of points) but which for the most part is understood to arise 'naturally' or 'inevitably' from the 'factual' information with which the reader is supplied. In this there is an obvious contrast with the way in which the negative view of the British anti-war campaigners is handled. There the reader is presented simply with bare, negatively evaluative assertions unsupported and unjustified by any such 'factual' evidence.

In terms of attitudinal meta-relations, the section is in oppositional contrast with the opening section as the author shifts from positivity to negativity. The contrast is a strategic one as the author demonstrates that her pro-American orientation is not the result of undifferentiated partisanship for all things American and that she is as ready to criticise Americans as to praise them. This speaks to the vestigial British sense of superiority to America which we mentioned above and acts to establish the writer's rhetorical credentials with that British audience.

5.2.8 The battered child

This section ends with the author turning from her negativity towards selected aspects of US society to her positivity towards the population in general.

On the whole, however, the Gung Hos are not in charge – indeed, what strikes you most is an unaccustomed humility. I lost count of the times good and decent people asked me: why do they hate us so? And, even: did we do something to deserve this? Like soothing battered kids in the schoolyard, I told them that, no, they did nothing, ever, bad enough to deserve this. Dust yourselves down, I said. Fight back, I said. Not because its easy, not even because I am sure you will triumph. But simply because to do so will make you feel better. And that, you do deserve.

Once again we encounter a section which takes the form of a narrative (an account of a past sequence of actual events) rather than overt argument. Nevertheless the ultimate purpose is obviously persuasive and hortatory – to advance the view that the United States government is right to invade Afghanistan by way of a response to the World Trade Center attack. As a result of the narrative framing, this is never directly put forward as a proposition which is currently at issue but is simply presented as something the author said to some ordinary Americans she encountered. As a consequence, the text construes this as a proposition which does not need to be brought into active rhetorical play and therefore as self-evidently right and just. Once again the reader is aligned into a attitudinal communality in which, by dint of this taken-for-grantedness, there is no possibility of tolerance for alternative viewpoints.

There are several other important alignment and solidarity associated elements in play, most notably the further development of positive regard for ordinary Americans. This is achieved, both by explicit positive **judgement: propriety** (*their unaccustomed humility*) and through the sympathy invoked by the depiction of ordinary Americans as *battered kids*. Also, the author presents herself as someone to whom ordinary Americans turn to in times of need, who has the ability to soothe them, and who has the authority and social standing to offer good counsel and advice on such topics as international relations and the waging of war. An evaluative side-effect, then, is the placing of the British observer in a position of superiority over the battered and hence enfeebled ordinary American. The attitudinal community into which the British reader is aligned is one in which 'we' view ordinary Americans as clearly separate in their moral worthiness from those few sections of US society (the commercial interests and Gung Hos) which have acted inappropriately or immorally, and as deserving of our sympathy. The reader is also offered, if only in passing, a sense of British authoritativeness cum superiority over these poor troubled Americans. Once again empathy is transformed into pity.

5.2.9 Damning the peaceniks (again)

In the next section, the author returns to the theme outlined in the headline – her contempt for those opposed to military action.

> It was, then, with fury, that I returned home on Saturday to find my own country rumbling with the mumbles of the peaceniks; the woolliest of liberals who shake their heads and say that war is not the answer; that there can be no winners but only the loss of innocents.

The primary attitudinal value is one of negative **judgement: tenacity** – the 'peaceniks', who in the headline were characterised as having *faint hearts* are here depicted as *squeamish*. Once again attitudinal values operate in combination to set up an evaluative prosody which resonates across an attitudinally loaded span of text. Thus the allegation of cowardice is supported by an **affectual** value of extreme displeasure (the author is furious to discover this opposition to the United States proposed military action) and by a value of **negative judgement: incapacity** (the peace activists *mumble* and are the *woolliest of liberals*). The terms under which the reader is invited to align attitudinally with the author, then, are rather narrow – not just a matter of disagreeing with those opposed to war but of viewing them as cowards and their position as so contemptible that it warrants these extremely antipathetic emotional reactions.

Again the manner in which these evaluations are formulated is rhetorically significant. As was the case in the headline, the negative assessment of the anti-war position is construed as taken-for-granted. This is achieved by the nominalisation of the proposition that the anti-war campaigners are incoherent and otherwise incompetent in articulating their position (*the mumbles of the peaceniks*) and via the superlative formulation *woolliest of*. To suggest that these peace activists are the *most woolly of liberals* presumes that woolliness is a property which generally attaches to the liberal standpoint – the peace activists as liberals are located at the end point of a scale of woolliness along which, presumably, other liberals are situated. Again this taken-for-grantedness acts to model a putative audience for the text.

Values of **graduation: force**, specifically those of **intensification**, also have a role to play in the formulation of this point of putative writer–reader alignment. These intensifications are indicated in the following analysis. We include the headline in the analysis since it so obviously connects with this particular section of the text.

Damn [*high degree of displeasure*] the peaceniks for their faint hearts
...

It was, then, with **fury** [*high degree of displeasure*], that I returned home on Saturday to find my own country rumbling with the mumbles of the peaceniks; the **woolliest** [*superlative – heightened negative Judgement*] of liberals who shake their heads and say that war is not the answer; that there can be no winners but only the loss of innocents.

These heightened values act to signal a high degree of investment by the author in the material being presented. Specifically, she casts her negative emotional reaction to the anti-war activists as maximally intense and similarly up-scales her negative assessment of their intellectual shortcomings. This has the effect of casting this point of potential attitudinal alignment as interpersonally crucial and as a point which is likely to be central to the evaluative rhetoric by which the text naturalises its own particular reading position. The text here operates with a semantic of insistence, a kind of shouting by which attention is drawn to this point.

The evaluative syndrome, then, in play here is one of negative **judgement** and **affect** which is intensified, categorically asserted (monoglossed) and, in the case of the **judgement** values, construed as taken-for-granted. This particular combination acts to put on display the assumption of a bond between writer and reader, the assumption that readers will empathise with the writer's fury and share her contempt for those opposed to war. There is an obvious ideological effect here of presenting this negativity towards the anti-war position as natural for a given readership, namely typical readers of the *Daily Express*.

The meta-relational arrangement here is one of obvious contrast with the prior empathy for those Americans who have lost loved ones and pity for those who feel like 'battered' children. These prior attitudinal orientations provide motivation for the writer's 'righteous anger' as the opposition to war by these *mumbling, woolliest of liberals* is cast, via these latent intra-textual relations, as insensitive to, and at odds with, the suffering, loss and grief of 'our American friends'.

5.2.10 No tears for the rabid souls

The next section is devoted primarily to the argument that we should not be concerned if many ordinary Afghanis are killed as a consequence of a military attack by the West because a significant proportion of these people have taken a sympathetic view of past acts of violence and oppression by Muslim extremists. The section is repeated here for convenience.

> [the peaceniks say that war is not the answer; that there can be no winners but only the loss of innocents.]
> Innocence, my friends, is a relative concept. The 6,000 in the World Trade Center were innocent. Afghan children are innocent. So are their displaced families and our aid, naturally, must be theirs
> But, among and around them, move the millions who are not quite guilty of murder yet are absolutely guilty of complicity; the 'innocents' about whom our peaceniks are so squeamish and I am not.
> While the politically correct have stood passively by, it is these millions who have fed, nurtured and permitted fundamentalism to get us where it has today.
> Those who burned Mr Rushdie's books set the scene for those who dynamited the Afghan Buddhas; those who wave their vitriolic arms through the streets of Pakistan pave the way for those who wave their guns in the name of Taliban; those who scream for jihad inspire those who yearn to sacrifice their lives upon planes impaled within skyscrapers.
> And if a bunch of these rabid souls get to hook up with their 70 virgins a few years ahead of plan, I would call it mildly unfortunate, but I would shed no tears.
> Such of those as I have left I shall keep for Kat, for Betty's memory, and for the thousands of others who will not be singing anywhere, not on the next holiday for infidels that we call Christmas.

The argument is a simple enough one – that there is a direct line between an ideology which endorses such acts as the burning of books and the active encouragement of acts of terrorism such as the attack on the World Trade Center. Those who are seen to support in any way what is termed Islamic fundamentalism are cast as complicit in the acts of violence and murder perpetuated by terrorists. The consequences of the complicity are that we, in the West should regard it as mildly unfortunate but should shed no tears if such people 'get to hook up with their 70 virgins a few years ahead of plan'. Although the text doesn't overtly state it, there is thereby a strong implication that such fundamentalists have forfeited the right to life.

The key proposition (that fundamentalist Muslims are complicit in murder) is categorically (monoglossically) asserted but nevertheless is construed as 'at issue' or needing to be argued for by dint of the deliberateness with which the author supplies supporting evidence as justification for this claim. By this combination of monogloss and contentiousness the text projects or anticipates for itself a readership which is not strongly opposed to such a proposition (otherwise some form of dialogistically expansive engagement with heteroglossic alternatives would have been offered) but for which such a proposition would still have some novelty and hence interest. In this regard we note that readers are just as likely (if not more likely) to go to such texts, not to be persuaded to new points of view, but rather to gather material in support of views they already hold. Thus a text such as this provides material which offers support to those who are already anxious about, or antagonistic towards, what they see as Islamic fundamentalism. They are supported by this text in the way that such a prejudicial proposition is monoglossically formulated – it is formulated as a set of propositions which are essentially uncontentious in having no challenges which need to be recognised or referenced in the current communicative context.

There are, of course, instances where negativity towards the Muslim world is 'taken for granted' rather than presented as 'at issue' and by which, accordingly, there is a projection onto the intended readership of an established likemindedness with the author's position. This taken-for-grantedness can be observed in the formulation *rabid souls* (that these millions of Muslims are rabid is presumed) and in the adopting of popular cultural Western misapprehensions about the nature of the Islamic after-life (that it involves expectations of ministrations by massed virgins). Perhaps most important is the entirely unquestioned assumption that, generally, there are millions of Muslims who support terrorist acts of violence and murder and, more specifically, that a significant proportion of the population of Afghanistan is included in these millions.

Affect also has a role in this particular axis of assumed writer–reader alignment. We observe this in the strong sense of sarcasm and hence emotional alienation conveyed when the author characterises the likely deaths of many Afghanis as *get[ting] to hook up with their 70 virgins a few years ahead of plan*. This enables the reader to interpret *I would call [their deaths] mildly unfortunate, but I would shed no tears* as understatement. It suggests that the author would not simply be unmoved should these people be killed but would take some satisfaction in their deaths.

This axis of alignment, then, is one in which several lines of negativity towards the Muslim world (both **judgemental** and **affectual**) are to be taken for granted and in which another line (that millions of Muslims are complicit in acts of violence and murder), while not taken for granted, is nevertheless to be viewed as largely uncontentious and without significant challenge. Once again the reader is aligned into solidarity with an attitudinal community where the value position at stake is viewed as 'commonsensical' and where accordingly, there is no tolerance for alternative viewpoints.

5.2.11 Grieving for lost friends: the coda

It is noteworthy that the author ends the text as she began it, by reference to the same affectual motif of grief for her lost friend. This is an obvious example of meta-relational reprise and confirmation

> Such of those [tears] as I have left I shall keep for Kat, for Betty's memory, and for the thousands of others who will not be singing anywhere, not on the next holiday for infidels that we call Christmas.

In this reprise, however, the terms under which attitudinal alignment is offered the reader have been slightly adjusted. Now the author's own grief is overtly stated – via the reference to her tears – and now the grief which the reader is invited to share has been generalised to encompass not just the lost friend but all those who died in the World Trade Center attack. And perhaps most tellingly, grief for 'our lost friends' has now been directly interconnected with a rather different emotional stance – the feelings of alienation and antagonism activated via the curious use of the term infidels in *not on the next holiday for infidels that we call Christmas*. The actual rhetorical work going on here is quite complex. Infidel, of course, is a term which, according to Western popular belief, is used by Muslims to refer to all Christians and thereby to derogate them. The author purports to be defiantly taking up this term of abuse, and adopting it as her own. The effect for those who go along with the attitudinal rhetoric is to provoke a strong sense of hostility towards, those who would denigrate 'us' Westerners in this way. The **affectual** contract has thus become more complex. Solidarity now turns on the reader sharing not only the author's grief for those killed but also a feeling of hostility towards this vaguely specified Islamic constituency.

5.2.12 Bringing the analysis together

In order to provide a synoptic overview of the evaluative configuration of meta-relations in the text, we provide Table 5.1. (We have excluded the headline because the point of alignment in which it is implicated is developed later in the text.)

By this analysis, then, is revealed the complex process by which such texts construct an unfolding sequence of points of alignment and solidarity, and strategically vary the terms of these alignments. In our text it involved, for example, the strategic use of **affectually**-based alignments to equate support for the US attack on Afghanistan with the grief and sympathy which all right-minded people must be feeling for the victims of the World Trade Center attack. The text began and ended with this point of alignment, thereby giving it the maximum rhetorical force. It also involved the careful modulation of alignments associated with views of America and Americans in order to accommodate the author's rhetorically necessary positivity with the long-standing ambivalence in Britain towards aspects of American society and culture. By this modulation, the author was able to characterise America as overridingly worthy while at the same time acknowledging the unworthiness of minority elements. Since these unworthy elements have long-standingly been stereotyped targets of suspicion and criticism in British culture (for example, the crassness of US commercialism, the bigotry of its right-wing shock-jocks), the picture painted by the text was compatible with British popular cultural images of America. Tellingly, this evaluative logic also provided the compliant reader with a community of shared attitude within which British culture is understood to be still superior, at least in some respects, to its American counterpart.

The analysis also enabled us to demonstrate how such texts manipulate the resources of intersubjective positioning to construe for themselves a particular ideal audience. This text was revealed to be one which assumed a large degree of likemindedess between author and projected reader and which, in so doing, naturalised a network of value laden, rhetorically charged beliefs and assessments. It was revealed as a text which recognised no compelling need to recognise alternative voices and positions. Thus, for example, we observed the taking for granted of the unworthiness of those opposed to war and of the alien, threatening evil of millions of Muslims. The only proposition which was extensively dialogised and hence characterised as contentious was the assertion that America had responded with less 'solemn dignity' than the author had initially anticipated. Solidarity for this text, then, is overwhelmingly a matter of alignment with an axiological community for which values are to be taken for granted and in which there is very little space for alternative viewpoints. Whether such a dialogistic arrangement is to be seen as courageously forthright or, alternatively, as dogmatically narrow minded will depend, we suspect, on whether the reader shares the author's feelings, tastes and values, or abhors them.

232

Table 5.1 Overview of meta-relations

text	primary target of evaluation	attitudinal terms	dialogistic positioning
stage 1: grieving ONCE upon a time, she sang with Duke Ellington on stage at Carnegie Hall. Last Christmas, we had her all to ourselves, ...	authors friend; victims and their families	primarily **−ve affect**: evoked empathy via grief;	monoglossic narrative
Her only child, her daughter Kat, ashen with shock, went to collect her mother's life's belongings ... . all this, with no body to bury, not now, not ever.		secondary: inscribed −ve 3rd person **affect**, +ve *appreciation*, tokens of +ve **judgement**	
stage 2: America phase (i) And all this, too, against the bigger backdrop of a fabulous, flawed, great, gutsy nation brought to its knees by pain and bewilderment.	America	inscribed +ve **Judgement;**	monogloss / take-for-granted
		−ve 3rd party **affect**	monogloss:
I would like to record that the picture was one of solemn dignity but, in fact, it was not. How could it be?	the picture	inscribed −ve *appreciation*;	**heterogloss**
Outrage literally mangled our poor language. ...	our poor language		monogloss
phase (ii) Commerce barely paused for breath: within a week, advertisements were urging people to buy a new car as a patriotic duty ...	US commercialism	tokens of −ve **judgement;**	monoglossed experiential content / provoking and flagging attitude
And then there is sheer nastiness. I heard one talk-show	talk show hosts	inscribed −ve **judgement**	monogloss

Continued

Table 5.1 Continued

text	primary target of evaluation	attitudinal terms	dialogistic positioning
host introduce his programme with the fervent plea that all slain Islamic terrorists should have their bodies scrubbed raw ...			
phase (iii) what strikes you most is an unaccustomed <u>humility</u>. ... Like soothing <u>battered kids</u> in the schoolyard, I told them that, no, they did nothing, ever, bad enough to deserve this. ... Dust yourselves down, I said. Fight back, I said	ordinary Americans;	inscribed +ve **judgement**; evoked **affect** (empathy)	monogloss: narrative frame presents evaluative contents as not at issue
stage 3: damned peaceniks IT WAS, then, with <u>fury</u>, that I returned home on Saturday to find my own country rumbling with the <u>mumbles</u> of the peaceniks; the <u>woolliest</u> of liberals ...	British peace activists	inscribed −ve **affect**; inscribed −ve **judgement**	monogloss monogloss / take-for-granted
stage 4: Muslim guilt But, among and around them, move the millions who are not quite guilty of murder yet are absolutely <u>guilty of complicity</u>; the 'innocents' about whom our peaceniks are so squeamish and I am not ... And if a bunch of these <u>rabid souls</u> get to hook up with their 70 virgins	millions of Muslims (who support Islamic fundamentalism)	inscribed −ve **judgement**; −ve **judgement**;	monogloss / at-issue monogloss / take-for-granted

Continued

234 *The Language of Evaluation*

Table 5.1 Continued

text	primary target of evaluation	attitudinal terms	dialogistic positioning
a few years ahead of plan, I would call it <u>mildly unfortunate</u>, but I would <u>shed no tears</u>.		authorial −ve **affect**	monogloss
stage 1 (reprised) <u>Such of those [tears] as I have left I shall keep for Kat</u>, for Betty's memory, and for the thousands of others who will not be singing anywhere, not on the next holiday for <u>infidels</u> that we call Christmas.	victims and their families (Muslims)	−ve **affect** evoking empathy (token −ve **affect**)	monogloss

5.3 Mourning: an unfortunate case of keystone cops

We turn now to our second text, the Mourning editorial from the *HK Magazine*. It addresses another aspect of responses to the World Trade Center attack. Rather than begin with the Mourning editorial as it appeared, we'll work our way into the text – beginning with four stories:

> [a] A man was sitting peacefully at the Hotel Lisboa bar when he was spotted by undercover cops and arrested as a 'suspected Pakistani terrorist.' Under questioning, he explained to police that he was in fact a tourist, a Hindu chef from Hong Kong.
>
> [b] Two Indian nationals on a flight from Singapore to Hong Kong were chatting at Changi Airport. Before departure, they were detained by security, who had been informed by an American passenger that he had heard one of the men calling himself a 'Bosnian terrorist'. The man was eventually able to assure security that he had in fact said he was a 'bass guitarist' and been misheard by the American.
>
> [c] A dark-skinned person tried to hail a cab, but it put up an 'out of service' sign.
>
> [d] A dark-skinned person got on a bus, and people changed their seats to move away from him.

Enacting Appraisal: Text Analysis 235

As we can see, each story deals with an instance of discrimination against dark-skinned people following the events of 9/11. The first is set in Macau, the second in Singapore, and the last two, as we shall see, take place in Hong Kong. Considered from the perspective of tenor, these stories have the effect of aligning us into a community that sympathises with the victims of paranoid prejudice.

Consider now another rendering of these events, this time one which for many readers foregrounds the perpetrators of discrimination rather than its victims:[3]

[a'] The Macau police arrested and detained seven 'suspected Pakistani terrorists.' The scare was enough to close the US Consulate in Hong Kong for a day, though the men turned out to be tourists, a word which is spelled somewhat like terrorists, and we suppose to some people, just as frightening. One of the arrested people in fact was a Hindu, a chef from Hong Kong, who had been cleverly tracked down by undercover cops sitting peacefully at the Hotel Lisboa bar.

[b'] Meanwhile (and were not making this up), two Indian nationals on a flight from Singapore to Hong Kong were detained at Changi Airport after an American passenger said he heard one of the men calling himself a 'Bosnian terrorist.' (The man in fact said he was a 'bass guitarist.')

[c', d'] Similarly, there have already been reports of taxis putting up 'out of service' signs and people changing seats on buses when confronted by dark-skinned people – as if changing your seat would save you if a bomb went off, anyway.

In effect, we have shifted from stories which function as tokens of **affect** to stories invoking **judgement**, a shift that is made crystal clear if we take one more step towards the rendering of these events deployed in the Mourning editorial:

[abcd"] The Macau police found themselves in **a *Keystone Cops* episode**, arresting and detaining seven 'suspected Pakistani terrorists.' The scare was enough to close the US Consulate in Hong Kong for a day, though the men turned out to be tourists, a word which is spelled somewhat like terrorists, and we suppose to some people, just as frightening. One of the arrested people in fact was a Hindu, a chef from Hong Kong, who had been cleverly tracked down by undercover cops sitting peacefully at the Hotel Lisboa bar.

Meanwhile (and were not making this up), two Indian nationals on a flight from Singapore to Hong Kong were detained at Changi Airport after an American passenger said he heard one of the men calling himself a 'Bosnian terrorist.' (The man in fact said he was a 'bass guitarist.')

Similarly, there have already been reports of taxis putting up 'out of service' signs and people changing seats on buses when confronted by dark-skinned people – as if changing your seat would save you if a bomb went off, anyway. But such is **the logic of xenophobia**.

This time round judgement is inscribed by way of introducing the Macau episode and later commenting on the Hong Kong incidents. The Macau police are judged as bumbling fools (*Keystone Cops*); and certain taxi drivers and bus commuters in Hong Kong are branded racist (*xenophobia*). These are harsh judgments to be sure, as licensed by the commentator voice taken up by the editorial writer for HK Magazine. As noted in Chapter 4, with reporter voice explicit judgments would have to be projected; events in Macau are rendered as a comparable news story in [a″] below.

Tourist Terror

[a″] The Macau police have released seven men after arresting and detaining them as 'suspected Pakistani terrorists.' The men turned out to be tourists but the US Consulate in Hong Kong closed for a day. A Consulate spokesman reported 'Staff were frightened by the arrests.' One of the arrested people in fact was a Hindu, a chef from Hong Kong, who had been tracked down by undercover cops sitting at the Hotel Lisboa bar. His lawyer described the incident as a 'Keystone Cops episode' with 'clever cops mistakenly arresting a completely innocent man who was sitting peacefully having a quiet drink, minding his own business and not harming anyone.'

Perhaps because the **judgements** in [abcd″] are so harsh, the editorial mitigates these inscriptions by prefacing them with some tempering **appreciation**, inscribing the racist acts by fools as *unfortunate* (as inappropriate things we wish hadn't happened but did):

[abcd‴] On a smaller and closer scale, we have already begun to see **some unfortunate cases** locally of backlash against members of the Muslim community (or even just people who look like they *might* be Muslim).

The Macau police found themselves in **a *Keystone Cops* episode**, arresting and detaining seven 'suspected Pakistani terrorists.' The scare was enough to close the US Consulate in Hong Kong for a day, though the men turned out to be tourists, a word which is spelled somewhat like terrorists, and we suppose to some people, just as frightening. One of the arrested people in fact was a Hindu, a chef from Hong Kong, who had been cleverly tracked down by undercover cops sitting peacefully at the Hotel Lisboa bar.

Meanwhile (and were not making this up), two Indian nationals on a flight from Singapore to Hong Kong were detained at Changi Airport after an American passenger said he heard one of the men calling himself a 'Bosnian terrorist.' (The man in fact said he was a 'bass guitarist.')
Similarly, there have already been reports of taxis putting up 'out of service' signs and people changing seats on buses when confronted by dark-skinned people – as if changing your seat would save you if a bomb went off, anyway. But such is **the logic of xenophobia**.

By abcd''' then, we are positioned to distance ourselves from certain distasteful regional incidents, before re-positioning ourselves to mock the perpetrators; and these alignments take precedence over empathy with the victims, who we are arguably positioned to ignore. This seems a useful alignment strategy for expat and returning Chinese readers of *HK Magazine*, who would be comfortable deploring racism they do not feel responsible for, at the same time as feeling little sympathy for dark-skinned visitors and guest-workers who are not the same class of outsiders as they are.

Here, once again, what we are working with what we have termed bonding or rapport, the investing of attitude in activity in such a way as to construct communing sympathies of attitudinal likemindedness. As we have seen, **affect, judgement** and **appreciation** can all be used to form communities of feeling around shared attitudes. Rendered as [a, b, c, d] the editorial evokes empathy with the victims (**affect**). Versions [a', b', c', d'] and [abcd''] foreground **judgement** over **affect**, aligning us around shared social values concerning discrimination. By [abcd'''], **appreciation** is mobilised to construct a little social distance from these distasteful events.

As already demonstrated in the previous text analysis, this interplay between the ideational/experiential (the ideological in Bakhtin's terms) and the interpersonal (the axiological in Bakhtin's terms) needs to be textured. There are various discourse semantic systems which are used to manage this (Martin & Rose 2003). In [abcd'''], for example, conjunction is used to organise the incidents in Macau, Singapore and Hong Kong in relation to one another – as overlapping in time (*meanwhile*) and comparable (*similarly*); and these incidents spell out the cases presaged in the sentence preceding them (implicit *ie*).

On a smaller and closer scale, we have already begun to see some unfortunate cases locally of backlash against members of the Muslim community (or even just people who look like they *might* be Muslim).

[ie]

The Macau police found themselves in a *Keystone Cops* episode, arresting and detaining seven 'suspected Pakistani terrorists.' The scare was enough to close the US Consulate in Hong Kong for a day, though the men turned out to be tourists, a word which is spelled somewhat like terrorists, and we suppose to some people, just as frightening. One of the arrested people in fact was a Hindu, a chef from Hong Kong, who had been cleverly tracked down by undercover cops sitting peacefully at the Hotel Lisboa bar.

Meanwhile

(and we're not making this up), two Indian nationals on a flight from Singapore to Hong Kong were detained at Changi Airport after an American passenger said he heard one of the men calling himself a 'Bosnian terrorist.' (The man in fact said he was a 'bass guitarist.')

Similarly,

there have already been reports of taxis putting up 'out of service' signs and people changing seats on buses when confronted by dark-skinned people – as if changing your seat would save you if a bomb went off, anyway. But such is the logic of xenophobia.

This logic depends on two other discourse semantic systems which are used to manage the text. One is the use of abstract lexis (the semiotic abstractions[4] *cases* and *episode*, and the nominalisations *backlash* and *scare*) to name events – prospectively for *cases, backlash* and *episode*, retrospectively for *scare*:

On a smaller and closer scale, we have already begun to see some unfortunate **cases** locally of **backlash** against members of the Muslim community (or even just people who look like they *might* be Muslim).

The Macau police found themselves in a *Keystone Cops* **episode**, arresting and detaining seven 'suspected Pakistani terrorists.' The **scare** was enough to close the US Consulate in Hong Kong for a day, though the men turned out to be tourists, a word which is spelled somewhat like terrorists, and we suppose to some people, just as frightening. One of the arrested people in fact was a Hindu, a chef from Hong Kong, who had been cleverly tracked down by undercover cops sitting peacefully at the Hotel Lisboa bar ...

Another is the use of text reference to compare and identify passages of discourse (the comparative *smaller and closer scale* and *such*, and the identifying *the scare* and *this*) – with *smaller and closer, the* and *such* pointing back, and *this* pointing forward:

←On a small<u>er</u> and clos<u>er</u> scale, we have already begun to see some unfortunate cases locally of backlash against members of the Muslim community (or even just people who look like they *might* be Muslim).

> The Macau police found themselves in a *Keystone Cops* episode, ⌐arresting and detaining seven 'suspected Pakistani terrorists.'⌐ ←The scare was enough to close the US Consulate in Hong Kong for a day, though the men turned out to be tourists, a word which is spelled somewhat like terrorists, and we suppose to some people, just as frightening. One of the arrested people in fact was a Hindu, a chef from Hong Kong, who had been cleverly tracked down by undercover cops sitting peacefully at the Hotel Lisboa bar.
> Meanwhile (and were not making **this** → up), ⌐two Indian nationals on a flight from Singapore to Hong Kong were detained at Changi Airport after an American passenger said he heard one of the men calling himself a 'Bosnian terrorist.'⌐ (The man in fact said he was a 'bass guitarist.')
> Similarly, there have already been reports of ⌐taxis putting up 'out of service' signs and people changing seats on buses when confronted by dark-skinned people – as if changing your seat would save you if a bomb went off, anyway.⌐ But ← **such** is the logic of xenophobia.

The interaction of these conjunction, ideation and identification resources sets up the periodic structure of [abcd′″]. The passage begins with a Macro-Theme, appreciating the discrimination as unfortunate:

> On a smaller and closer scale, we have already begun to see some unfortunate cases locally of backlash against members of the Muslim community (or even just people who look like they *might* be Muslim).

The events in Macau have their own Hyper-Theme, judging the police as Keystone Cops:

> The Macau police found themselves in a *Keystone Cops* episode, arresting and detaining seven 'suspected Pakistani terrorists.'

And at least the Hong Kong incidents have a Hyper-New, judging the taxi drivers and bus passengers involved as xenophobic:

> But such is the logic of xenophobia.

This minimalist reading of the domain of *such* has been influenced by the paragraph structure of the editorial, which includes it in the paragraph about Hong Kong.

The overall effect of these interacting systems on information flow is outlined using indentation below. As far as appraisal is concerned, the critical pattern has to do with the foregrounding of inscribed **appreciation** and **judgement** as higher level Themes and New. This prominence puts them in position to prosodically colour the evaluation of the events in their domain.

On a smaller and closer scale, we have already begun to see some unfortunate cases locally of backlash against members of the Muslim community (or even just people who look like they *might* be Muslim).

The Macau police found themselves in a *Keystone Cops* episode, arresting and detaining seven 'suspected Pakistani terrorists.'

The scare was enough to close the US Consulate in Hong Kong for a day, though the men turned out to be tourists, a word which is spelled somewhat like terrorists, and we suppose to some people, just as frightening. One of the arrested people in fact was a Hindu, a chef from Hong Kong, who had been cleverly tracked down by undercover cops sitting peacefully at the Hotel Lisboa bar.

Meanwhile (and were not making this up), two Indian nationals on a flight from Singapore to Hong Kong were detained at Changi Airport after an American passenger said he heard one of the men calling himself a 'Bosnian terrorist.' (The man in fact said he was a 'bass guitarist.')

Similarly, there have already been reports of taxis putting up 'out of service' signs and people changing seats on buses when confronted by dark-skinned people – as if changing your seat would save you if a bomb went off, anyway.

But such is the logic of xenophobia.

As the comparative text reference *smaller and closer scale* noted above indicates, there is more to this editorial than the stories of regional discrimination we've been exploring. The global events being referred to are included below, along with the editorials title and its final comment. This rendering establishes the wording as it appeared on page 5 of *HK Magazine* on Friday September 21, 2001.

Mourning

> The terrible events of the past week have left us with feelings – in order of occurrence – of horror, worry, anger, and now, just a general gloom. The people of America are grieving both over the tragedy itself and over the loss – perhaps permanently – of a trouble-free way of life.
>
> While that grief is deeply understood, the problem with tragedies like this one is that they become a heyday for the overly-sincere, maudlin, righteous-indignation crowd. We've been appalled, perplexed and repulsed by some of the things we've heard said in the media this week. The jingoistic, flag-waving, 'my way or the highway' rhetoric is enough to make thinking people retch. That said, the polls aren't going our way. 89 percent of Americans surveyed are thrilled and delighted by all the tub-thumping. We suppose that every episode of 'Letterman' from now until doomsday is going to open with another weepy rendition of 'God Bless America.'
>
> Those who have the good fortune to live in the international world – that is, the world outside the U.S. – know that we are not all of one

> religion, one language or one political system. We live in a big world where people have diverse, and often, diametrically opposed views. And while it is commendable to want to stamp out terrorism, it might also be a good idea to pause and reflect on some of the grievances that people in the rest of the world have towards the U.S. Of course, there's precious little chance of that happening in America any time soon.

←On a smaller and closer scale, we have already begun to see some unfortunate cases locally of backlash against members of the Muslim community (or even just people who look like they might be Muslim).

The Macau police found themselves in a Keystone Cops episode, arresting and detaining seven 'suspected Pakistani terrorists.' The scare was enough to close the U.S. Consulate in Hong Kong for a day, though the men turned out to be tourists, a word which is spelled somewhat like terrorists, and we suppose to some people, just as frightening. One of the arrested people in fact was a Hindu, a chef from Hong Kong, who had been cleverly tracked down by undercover cops sitting peacefully at the Hotel Lisboa bar.

Meanwhile (and we're not making this up), two Indian nationals on a flight from Singapore to Hong Kong were detained at Changi Airport after an American passenger said he heard one of the men calling himself a 'Bosnian terrorist.' (The man in fact said he was a 'bass guitarist.')

Similarly, there have already been reports of taxis putting up 'out of service' signs and people changing seats on buses when confronted by dark-skinned people – as if changing your seat would save you if a bomb went off, anyway. But such is the logic of xenophobia.

> If, as all the pundits are saying, there is no hope of normalcy returning soon, let's at least hope that sanity does.

One difference we can note about the first half of the editorial as opposed to the second is that the first has much more inscribed **attitude**. Rather than establishing **attitude** in higher level Themes and New which dominate the stories in their domain, the editorial begins by spreading inscribed **attitude** throughout the text. The evaluation saturates the text rather than dominating it. **Affectual** inscriptions are foregrounded first, as highlighted below. For this analysis, weve taken *appalled, repulsed, retch* and *xenophobia* as inscribing affect as well as judgement.

Mourning – inscribed affect

> The terrible events of the past week have left us with feelings – in order of occurrence – of horror, worry, anger, and now, just a general gloom. The people of

242   *The Language of Evaluation*

America are ⸢grieving⸣ both over the tragedy itself and over the loss – perhaps permanently – of a trouble-free way of life.

While that ⸢grief⸣ is deeply understood, the problem with tragedies like this one is that they become a heyday for the overly-sincere, maudlin, righteous-indignation crowd. We've been ⸢appalled⸣, perplexed and ⸢repulsed⸣ by some of the things we've heard said in the media this week. The jingoistic, flag-waving, 'my way or the highway' rhetoric is enough to make thinking people ⸢retch⸣. That said, the polls aren't going our way. 89 percent of Americans surveyed are ⸢thrilled⸣ and ⸢delighted⸣ by all the tub-thumping. We suppose that every episode of 'Letterman' from now until doomsday is going to open with another ⸢weepy⸣ rendition of 'God Bless America.'

Those who have the good fortune to live in the international world – that is, the world outside the U.S. – know that we are not all of one religion, one language or one political system. We live in a big world where people have diverse, and often, diametrically opposed views. And while it is commendable to ⸢want⸣ to stamp out terrorism, it might also be a good idea to pause and reflect on some of the grievances that people in the rest of the world have towards the U.S. Of course, there's precious little chance of that happening in America any time soon.

On a smaller and closer scale, we have already begun to see some unfortunate cases locally of backlash against members of the Muslim community (or even just people who look like they *might* be Muslim).

The Macau police found themselves in a *Keystone Cops* episode, arresting and detaining seven 'suspected Pakistani terrorists.' The ⸢scare⸣ was enough to close the U.S. Consulate in Hong Kong for a day, though the men turned out to be tourists, a word which is spelled somewhat like terrorists, and we suppose to some people, just as ⸢frightening⸣. One of the arrested people in fact was a Hindu, a chef from Hong Kong, who had been cleverly tracked down by undercover cops sitting peacefully at the Hotel Lisboa bar.

Meanwhile (and we're not making this up), two Indian nationals on a flight from Singapore to Hong Kong were detained at Changi Airport after an American passenger said he heard one of the men calling himself a 'Bosnian terrorist.' (The man in fact said he was a 'bass guitarist.')

Similarly, there have already been reports of taxis putting up 'out of service' signs and people changing seats on buses when confronted by dark-skinned people – as if changing your seat would save you if a bomb went off, anyway. But such is the logic of **xeno**⸢phobia⸣.

If, as all the pundits are saying, there is no ⸢hope⸣ of normalcy returning soon, let's at least ⸢hope⸣ that sanity does.

As we can see, the editorial begins by empathising with Americans which, in our experience, remains a next-to-obligatory rhetorical move for anyone dealing with these events – especially if they want to say anything critical about America. It is as if one's right to speak on the events of 9/11 depends on first establishing one's humanity, thereby aligning with people (and against the barbarous hordes outside). The editor follows this move by inscribing his disgust with the mainstream American response to the attack, communing at this point we must presume with readers alienated by the tub-thumping rhetoric.

This reaction resonates strongly through the **judgement** inscribed in the second paragraph and continuing with less intensity throughout the text. Most of the **judgement** is negative, beginning with criticism of America. One of the most interesting of these **judgements** is the sarcastic *cleverly* used to mock Macaus undercover cops, which we have to read as the opposite of what it literally means precisely because it is dominated by the Keystone Cops prosody of negative **capacity**. For this analysis we've taken *terrorist* as inscribing negative **judgement** (contrasting with alternative positive terms like *freedom fighter* or *martyr*).

Mourning – inscribed judgement

> The terrible events of the past week have left us with feelings – in order of occurrence – of horror, worry, anger, and now, just a general gloom. The people of America are grieving both over the tragedy itself and over the loss – perhaps permanently – of a trouble-free way of life.
>
> While that grief is deeply understood, the problem with tragedies like this one is that they become a heyday for the overly-sincere, maudlin, righteous-indignation crowd. We've been appalled, perplexed and repulsed by some of the things we've heard said in the media this week. The jingoistic, flag-waving, 'my way or the highway' rhetoric is enough to make thinking people retch. That said, the polls aren't going our way. 89 percent of Americans surveyed are thrilled and delighted by all the tub-thumping. We suppose that every episode of 'Letterman' from now until doomsday is going to open with another weepy rendition of 'God Bless America.'
>
> Those who have the good fortune to live in the international world – that is, the world outside the U.S. – know that we are not all of one religion, one language or one political system. We live in a big world where people have diverse, and often, diametrically opposed views. And while it is commendable to want to stamp out terrorism, it might also be a good idea to pause and reflect on some of the grievances that people in the rest of the world have towards the U.S. Of course, there's precious little chance of that happening in America any time soon.
>
> On a smaller and closer scale, we have already begun to see some unfortunate cases locally of backlash against members of the Muslim community (or even just people who look like they *might* be Muslim).
>
> The Macau police found themselves in a *Keystone Cops* episode, arresting and detaining seven 'suspected Pakistani terrorists.' The scare was enough to close the U.S. Consulate in Hong Kong for a day, though the men turned out

to be tourists, a word which is spelled somewhat like [terrorists,] and we suppose to some people, just as frightening. One of the arrested people in fact was a Hindu, a chef from Hong Kong, who had been [cleverly] tracked down by undercover cops sitting [peacefully] at the Hotel Lisboa bar.

Meanwhile (and we're not making this up), two Indian nationals on a flight from Singapore to Hong Kong were detained at Changi Airport after an American passenger said he heard one of the men calling himself a 'Bosnian [terrorist].' (The man in fact said he was a 'bass guitarist.')

Similarly, there have already been reports of taxis putting up 'out of service' signs and people changing seats on buses when confronted by dark-skinned people – as if changing your seat would save you if a bomb went off, anyway. But such is the logic of [xeno]phobia.

If, as all the pundits are saying, there is no hope of [normalcy] returning soon, let's at least hope that [sanity] does.

Appreciation in the editorial is a less prominent motif. Its deployment to distance readers from regional discrimination has been discussed above (*unfortunate cases*).

Mourning – inscribed appreciation

The [terrible] events of the past week have left us with feelings – in order of occurrence – of horror, worry, anger, and now, just a general gloom. The people of America are grieving both over the [tragedy] itself and over the loss – perhaps permanently – of a [trouble-free] way of life.

While that grief is deeply understood, the problem with [tragedies] like this one is that they become a heyday for the overly-sincere, maudlin, righteous-indignation crowd. We've been appalled, perplexed and repulsed by some of the things we've heard said in the media this week. The jingoistic, flag-waving, 'my way or the highway' rhetoric is enough to make thinking people retch. That said, the polls aren't going our way. 89 percent of Americans surveyed are thrilled and delighted by all the tub-thumping. We suppose that every episode of 'Letterman' from now until doomsday is going to open with another weepy rendition of 'God Bless America.'

Those who have the good fortune to live in the international world – that is, the world outside the U.S. – know that we are not all of one religion, one language or one political system. We live in a big world where people have [diverse,] and often, [diametrically opposed] views. And while it is commendable to want to stamp out terrorism, it might also be a [good] idea to pause and reflect on some of the grievances that people in the rest of the world have towards the U.S. Of course, there's precious little chance of that happening in America any time soon.

On a smaller and closer scale, we have already begun to see some [unfortunate] cases locally of backlash against members of the Muslim community (or even just people who look like they *might* be Muslim).

...

Saturation of the first half of the text (the global scene) with **attitude** is further reinforced by **graduation** resources which intensify the prosodies of evaluation. Taken together these amplifications add mass to the **affect** and **judgement** saturating paragraphs 1, 2 and 3. At this point the text is very loud as far as positioning readers to sympathise with and then criticise Americans. It compels, with strong views. For the local scene on the other hand, the volume is turned down. Inscribed **attitude** dominates the discourse from its positioning in higher level Themes and New; but it doesn't achieve the same kind of critical mass. Prosodically speaking the editorial seems to be suggesting that whereas people's behaviour in America has been absolutely appalling, the regional response has simply been humorously remiss.

Mourning – graduation: force (and focus)

[Key to analyses] force: inherently intense lexis – BOLD, SMALL CAPS; intensifiers – **bold, underlined**; intensifying triplets – boxed; focus – *italics, underlined*]

> The TERRIBLE events of the past week have left us with feelings – in order of occurrence – of HORROR, worry, anger, and now, just a *general* GLOOM. The people of America are grieving both over the tragedy itself and over the loss – perhaps permanently – of a trouble-free way of life.
>
> While that grief is **deeply** understood, the problem with tragedies like this one is that they become a heyday for the overly-sincere, maudlin, RIGHTEOUS-INDIGNATION crowd. We've been APPALLED, perplexed and repulsed by some of the things we've heard said in the media this week. The JINGOISTIC, flag-waving, 'my way or the highway' rhetoric is **enough** to make thinking people retch. That said, the polls aren't going our way. 89 percent of Americans surveyed are THRILLED and DELIGHTED by all the TUB-THUMPING. We suppose that every episode of 'Letterman' from now until doomsday is going to open with another weepy rendition of 'God Bless America.'
>
> Those who have the good fortune to live in the international world – that is, the world outside the U.S. – know that we are not all of one religion, one language or one political system. We live in a big world where people have diverse, and often, **diametrically** opposed views. And while it is commendable to want to STAMP OUT terrorism, it might also be a good idea to pause and reflect on some of the grievances that people in the rest of the world have towards the U.S. Of course, there's **precious** little chance of that happening in America any time soon.
>
> On a smaller and closer scale, we have already begun to see some unfortunate cases locally of backlash against members of the Muslim community (or even just people who look like they *might* be Muslim).

The Macau police found themselves in a *Keystone Cops* episode, arresting and detaining seven 'suspected Pakistani terrorists.' The scare was **enough** to close the U.S. Consulate in Hong Kong for a day, though the men turned out to be tourists, a word which is spelled <u>somewhat</u> like terrorists, and we suppose to some people, just as frightening. One of the arrested people in fact was a Hindu, a chef from Hong Kong, who had been cleverly tracked down by undercover cops sitting peacefully at the Hotel Lisboa bar.

Meanwhile (and were not making this up), two Indian nationals on a flight from Singapore to Hong Kong were detained at Changi Airport after an American passenger said he heard one of the men calling himself a 'Bosnian terrorist.' (The man in fact said he was a 'bass guitarist.')

Similarly, there have already been reports of taxis putting up 'out of service' signs and people changing seats on buses when confronted by dark-skinned people – as if changing your seat would save you if a bomb went off, anyway. But such is the logic of XENOPHOBIA.

If, as all the pundits are saying, there is no hope of normalcy returning soon, let's at least hope that sanity does.

For this analysis we've taken the following attitudinal inscriptions as employing terms which involve infused up-scaling and hence are inherently intensified:

Terrible, horror, gloom, righteous-indignation, appalled, jingoistic, thrilled, delighted, tub-thumping, stamp out, xenophobia …

Submodification is also used to intensify:

<u>deeply</u> understood
<u>overly</u>-sincere
<u>enough</u> (to make …)
<u>diametrically</u> opposed
<u>precious</u> little
<u>enough</u> (to close …)

And a number of rhetorical triplets are also deployed:

horror, worry, anger
overly-sincere, maudlin, righteous-indignation
appalled, perplexed and repulsed

jingoistic, flag-waving, 'my way or the highway'
one religion, one language or one political system

To these we might add the three examples of local backlash (the discrimination in Macau, Singapore and Hong Kong); but our sense is that three paragraphs serve more to itemize regional incidents than to amplify their **appreciation** as unfortunate cases. Tripling in other words is more of a grammatical resource for intensification (parataxis) than a discourse one (listing).

Up-scaled **force: quantification** adds further weight to this loud-to-soft motif. The global scene features extremes of amount, size and distance in time:

both, some, 89 percent, all, every, all, one, one, one, some
little
permanently, from now until doomsday, any time soon

The local scene on the other hand features ungraduated digital numbering (7, 1, 2) and comparative size and spatial distance:

seven, one, two,
smaller
closer

Graduation via **quantification**, however, returns in the final paragraph, readjusting the volume upwards for the editorials culminative plea.

all, no,
soon

Mourning – quantification (amount, spatio-temporal distance underlined)

The terrible events of the past week have left us with feelings – in order of occurrence – of horror, worry, anger, and now, just a general gloom. The people of America are grieving both over the tragedy itself and over the loss – perhaps permanently – of a trouble-free way of life.

While that grief is deeply understood, the problem with tragedies like this one is that they become a heyday for the overly-sincere, maudlin, righteous-indignation crowd. We've been appalled, perplexed and repulsed by some of the

248 *The Language of Evaluation*

things we've heard said in the media this week. The jingoistic, flag-waving, 'my way or the highway' rhetoric is enough to make thinking people retch. That said, the polls aren't going our way. <u>89 percent</u> of Americans surveyed are thrilled and delighted by <u>all</u> the tub-thumping. We suppose that <u>every</u> episode of 'Letterman' <u>from now until doomsday</u> is going to open with another weepy rendition of 'God Bless America.'

Those who have the good fortune to live in the international world – that is, the world outside the U.S. – know that we are not <u>all</u> of <u>one</u> religion, <u>one</u> language or <u>one</u> political system. We live in a big world where people have diverse, and often, diametrically opposed views. And while it is commendable to want to stamp out terrorism, it might also be a good idea to pause and reflect on <u>some</u> of the grievances that people in the rest of the world have towards the U.S. Of course, there's precious <u>little</u> chance of that happening in America <u>any time soon</u>.

On a <u>smaller</u> and <u>closer</u> scale, we have already begun to see some unfortunate cases locally of backlash against members of the Muslim community (or even just people who look like they *might* be Muslim).

The Macau police found themselves in a *Keystone Cops* episode, arresting and detaining <u>seven</u> 'suspected Pakistani terrorists.' The scare was enough to close the U.S. Consulate in Hong Kong for a day, though the men turned out to be tourists, a word which is spelled somewhat like terrorists, and we suppose to some people, just as frightening. <u>One</u> of the arrested people in fact was a Hindu, a chef from Hong Kong, who had been cleverly tracked down by undercover cops sitting peacefully at the Hotel Lisboa bar.

Meanwhile (and were not making this up), <u>two</u> Indian nationals on a flight from Singapore to Hong Kong were detained at Changi Airport after an American passenger said he heard one of the men calling himself a 'Bosnian terrorist.' (The man in fact said he was a 'bass guitarist.')

Similarly, there have already been reports of taxis putting up 'out of service' signs and people changing seats on buses when confronted by dark-skinned people – as if changing your seat would save you if a bomb went off, anyway. But such is the logic of xenophobia.

If, as <u>all</u> the pundits are saying, there is <u>no</u> hope of normalcy returning <u>soon</u>, let's at least hope that sanity does.

Whereas **attitude** and **graduation** shift gears in consort as the editorial moves from global to regional concerns, **engagement** systems operate continuously throughout the text. As we would expect from an editorial, the text is very dialogic, with a range of resources used to expand and contract the voices at play. We'll look at expanding options first.

As far as values of **engagement: entertain** involving modal meanings are concerned, there is a full spectrum of objective and subjective selections, alongside modalised causality (*if*):

explicit subjective	*we suppose*
implicit subjective	*might, would*
implicit objective	*perhaps, often*
explicit objective	*little chance, no hope*
modalised cause	*if*

Modalisation of probability (what might happen) is mainly used in relation to future events, where alternative predictions about possible futures are **entertained** – for example:

the loss – perhaps permanently – of a trouble-free way of life

there's precious little chance of that happening in America any time soon

there is no hope of normalcy returning soon

Modulation of obligation (what should happen) is less common, and can arguably be read in each instance as **attitudinal** (and has been coded as such above):

be a good idea to (appreciation)

is commendable to want to (judgement)

let's at least hope (affect)

The selections which **entertain** alternative positions are highlighted below (to which we might have added the closely related realisations of appearance, *look like* and *turned out*).

Mourning – expand: entertain (modality)
> The terrible events of the past week have left us with feelings – in order of occurrence – of horror, worry, anger, and now, just a general gloom. The people of America are grieving both over the tragedy itself and over the loss – perhaps permanently – of a trouble-free way of life.
> While that grief is deeply understood, the problem with tragedies like this one is that they become a heyday for the overly-sincere, maudlin, righteous-indignation crowd. We've been appalled, perplexed and repulsed by some of

250 *The Language of Evaluation*

the things we've heard said in the media this week. The jingoistic, flag-waving, 'my way or the highway' rhetoric is enough to make thinking people retch. That said, the polls aren't going our way. 89 percent of Americans surveyed are thrilled and delighted by all the tub-thumping. We suppose that every episode of 'Letterman' from now until doomsday is going to open with another weepy rendition of 'God Bless America.'

Those who have the good fortune to live in the international world – that is, the world outside the U.S. – know that we are not all of one religion, one language or one political system. We live in a big world where people have diverse, and often, diametrically opposed views. And while it is commendable to want to stamp out terrorism, it might also be a good idea to pause and reflect on some of the grievances that people in the rest of the world have towards the U.S. Of course, there's precious little chance of that happening in America any time soon.

On a smaller and closer scale, we have already begun to see some unfortunate cases locally of backlash against members of the Muslim community (or even just people who look like they might be Muslim).

The Macau police found themselves in a *Keystone Cops* episode, arresting and detaining seven 'suspected Pakistani terrorists.' The scare was enough to close the U.S. Consulate in Hong Kong for a day, though the men turned out to be tourists, a word which is spelled somewhat like terrorists, and we suppose to some people, just as frightening. One of the arrested people in fact was a Hindu, a chef from Hong Kong, who had been cleverly tracked down by undercover cops sitting peacefully at the Hotel Lisboa bar.

Meanwhile (and we're not making this up), two Indian nationals on a flight from Singapore to Hong Kong were detained at Changi Airport after an American passenger said he heard one of the men calling himself a 'Bosnian terrorist.' (The man in fact said he was a 'bass guitarist.')

Similarly, there have already been reports of taxis putting up 'out of service' signs and people changing seats on buses when confronted by dark-skinned people – as if changing your seat would save you if a bomb went off, anyway. But such is the logic of xenophobia.

If, as all the pundits are saying, there is no hope of normalcy returning soon, let's at least hope that sanity does.

Alongside expanding the discourse by entertaining alternative positions, the editorial also makes use of projection to attribute text to sources. Discourse is attributed in various ways:

[graphology]
The Macau police found themselves in a *Keystone Cops* episode, arresting and detaining seven '**suspected Pakistani terrorists**.'

Enacting Appraisal: Text Analysis 251

[circumstance of angle]
    though the men turned out to be tourists, a word which is spelled somewhat like terrorists, and we suppose **to some people**, just as frightening.

[semiotic nouns]
    Similarly, there have already been **reports** of taxis putting up 'out of service' signs

[projecting mental process]
    an American passenger **said he heard** one of the men

[projecting verbal process]
    an **American passenger said** he heard ...

[agentive relational process]
    one of the men calling himself a 'Bosnian terrorist.'

Several sources are explicitly **acknowledged**, including the editor, people frightened by tourists, pundits, the American passenger and his accused, the media and the polls:

    the things ⃞we'⃞ve heard said in the media this week.
    ⃞let's⃞ at least hope that sanity does.
    and we suppose ⃞to some people⃞, just as frightening.
    If, as ⃞all the pundits⃞ are saying, there is no hope ...
    ⃞an American passenger⃞ said ⃞he⃞ heard one of the men
    ⃞one of the men⃞ calling himself a 'Bosnian terrorist.'
    (⃞The man⃞ in fact said he was a 'bass guitarist.')
    the things we've heard said in ⃞the media⃞ this week.
    That said, ⃞the polls⃞ aren't going our way.

For some sources the attribution is implicit, but recoverable (the editor, Americans, the Macau police and the media):

    that said (by the editor)
    it might also be a good idea (for Americans) to pause and reflect on some of the grievances

The Macau police found themselves in a *Keystone Cops* episode, arresting and detaining seven (people they described as) 'suspected Pakistani terrorists.'

The jingoistic, flag-waving, 'my way or the highway' rhetoric (said in the media)

The great majority of these projections acknowledge alternative sources, thereby expanding the range of voices in the text. Some however contract, by committing us to a particular point of view – as something we *know*, something *all the pundits* are saying or something that is *in fact* the case:

Those who have the good fortune to live in the international world – that is, the world outside the U.S. – know that we are not all of one religion, one language or one political system.

If, as all the pundits are saying, there is no hope of normalcy returning soon

The man in fact said he was a 'bass guitarist.'

To these **proclamations** we can add examples which **pronounce** in non-projecting environments:

One of the arrested people in fact was a Hindu, a chef from Hong Kong,

The scare was enough to close the U.S. Consulate in Hong Kong for a day, though the men turned out to be tourists

(and we're not making this up)

And in addition the **concurring** realization *of course*:

Of course, theres precious little chance of that happening in America any time soon.

To these contracting resources we need to add polarity resources which **deny** alternative positions:

the polls are**n't** going our way

we are **not** all of one religion, one language or one political system we're **not** making this up

there is **no** hope of normalcy returning soon

And finally the text uses conjunctions (*while, though, in fact, as if, anyway, but, at least*) and continuatives (*just, already, even*) to adjust reader expectations, countering predictions they might be making about the way in which the discourse will unfold. These **countering** contracting resources are highlighted below (taking *that said* as realizing counter-expectation).

Mourning – conceding and countering (conjunction & continuity)

The terrible events of the past week have left us with feelings – in order of occurrence – of horror, worry, anger, and now, just a general gloom. The people of America are grieving both over the tragedy itself and over the loss – perhaps permanently – of a trouble-free way of life.

While that grief is deeply understood, the problem with tragedies like this one is that they become a heyday for the overly-sincere, maudlin, righteous-indignation crowd. We've been appalled, perplexed and repulsed by some of the things we've heard said in the media this week. The jingoistic, flag-waving, 'my way or the highway' rhetoric is enough to make thinking people retch. That said, the polls aren't going our way. 89 percent of Americans surveyed are thrilled and delighted by all the tub-thumping. We suppose that every episode of 'Letterman' from now until doomsday is going to open with another weepy rendition of 'God Bless America.'

Those who have the good fortune to live in the international world – that is, the world outside the U.S. – know that we are not all of one religion, one language or one political system. We live in a big world where people have diverse, and often, diametrically opposed views. And while it is commendable to want to stamp out terrorism, it might also be a good idea to pause and reflect on some of the grievances that people in the rest of the world have towards the U.S. Of course, there's precious little chance of that happening in America any time soon.

On a smaller and closer scale, we have already begun to see some unfortunate cases locally of backlash against members of the Muslim community (or even just people who look like they *might* be Muslim).

The Macau police found themselves in a *Keystone Cops* episode, arresting and detaining seven 'suspected Pakistani terrorists.' The scare was enough to close the U.S. Consulate in Hong Kong for a day, though the men turned out to be tourists, a word which is spelled somewhat like terrorists, and we suppose to some people, just as frightening. One of the arrested people in fact was a Hindu, a chef from Hong Kong, who had been cleverly tracked down by undercover cops sitting peacefully at the Hotel Lisboa bar.

254 *The Language of Evaluation*

> Meanwhile (and we're not making this up), two Indian nationals on a flight from Singapore to Hong Kong were detained at Changi Airport after an American passenger said he heard one of the men calling himself a 'Bosnian terrorist.' (The man ⟨in fact⟩ said he was a 'bass guitarist.')
> Similarly, there have ⟨already⟩ been reports of taxis putting up 'out of service' signs and people changing seats on buses when confronted by dark-skinned people – ⟨as if⟩ changing your seat would save you if a bomb went off, ⟨anyway⟩. ⟨But⟩ such is the logic of xenophobia.
> If, as all the pundits are saying, there is no hope of normalcy returning soon, let's ⟨at least⟩ hope that sanity does.

This extensive array of **engagement** resources is typical of discourse which is negotiating alignment and rapport with a complex readership. As noted above, the readers of *HK Magazine* consist largely of British and Australian expats working in Hong Kong on short and longer term contracts, and of returning Chinese, including ABCs (American born Chinese) and some of the Chinese who have studied and worked in western institutions overseas. Dislocated in these ways, they can appreciate the irreverent tone of the magazines editorials – a useful stimulus for dinner party, bar and coffee shop conversation. But dislocation also makes their identity a complex issue: are they from Hong Kong or somewhere else, eastern or western, Chinese or gweilo ('white ghosts' as the local Cantonese call Europeans), permanent residents or residents, employees or guest-workers, educators or business people, workers or visitors, home owners or renters, etc? What holds this community together is its taste for leisure activities, as reflected in the lifestyles offered for consumption in *HK Magazine*. That said, hybrid subjectivites of this order generate a range of voices for the editor to deal with, more so perhaps for international than regional politics. And being irreverent means flying in the face of others, who need to be drawn into the fray.

So instead of baldly stating that Americans have permanently lost their trouble-free way of life or that every episode of Letterman will end with God Bless America, the editor modalises, entertaining other possibilities:

> The people of America are grieving both over the tragedy itself and over the loss – ⟨perhaps⟩ permanently – of a trouble-free way of life.
> ⟨We suppose⟩ that every episode of 'Letterman' from now until doomsday is going to open with another weepy rendition of 'God Bless America.'

Enacting Appraisal: Text Analysis 255

Instead of stating directly that the Pakistani tourists were suspected of terrorism or taxis were putting up out of service signs, he attributes these claims to others:

> The Macau police found themselves in a *Keystone Cops* episode, arresting and detaining seven ⌈'suspected Pakistani terrorists.'⌉
> there have already been ⌈reports⌉ of taxis putting up 'out of service' signs and people changing seats on buses when confronted by dark-skinned people

These expansions are complemented by contractions which pronounce on the identity of suspects (discarding the opinions of Macau's Keystone Cops):

> the men ⌈turned out⌉ to be tourists
> One of the arrested people ⌈in fact⌉ was a Hindu

And what otherwise might be taken as contentious positions are confirmed and endorsed (challenging potential dissenters to disagree):

> ⌈Of course⌉, there's precious little chance of that happening in America any time soon.
> If, as ⌈all the pundits⌉ are saying, there is no hope of normalcy returning soon,

In order to interpret the overall effect of this dialectic, let's return to the global organisation of the editorial and consider its rhetoric. One of the first things to deal with here is who's who, including the less than determinate issue of who 'we' identifies as the text unfolds. As noted above the first paragraph of the editorial aligns us with the people of America, whereas the second and third paragraphs oppose us to them. The ideational construction of us and them is outlined for this part of the text below.

- align us with Americans as human; **affect** (empathising)
  [us & the people of America]

  > The terrible events of the past week have left *us* with feelings – in order of occurrence – of horror, worry, anger, and now, just a general gloom. <u>The people of America</u> are grieving both over the tragedy itself and over the loss – perhaps permanently – of a trouble-free way of life.

- oppose us thinking people to jingoistic Americans; judgement (castigating)
[we; thinking people; our way; we; those who have the good fortune to live in the international world – that is, the world outside the U.S.; we; we; people; people in the rest of the world]

versus

[the overly-sincere, maudlin, righteous-indignation crowd; 89 percent of Americans; the U.S.; America]. The construction of us and them is highlighted for this part of the editorial below.

While that grief is deeply understood, the problem with tragedies like this one is that they become a heyday <u>for the overly-sincere, maudlin, righteous-indignation crowd</u>. *We've* been appalled, perplexed and repulsed by some of the things *we've* heard said in the media this week. <u>The jingoistic, flag-waving, 'my way or the highway' rhetoric</u> is enough to make *thinking people* retch. That said, the polls aren't going *our* way. <u>89 percent of Americans surveyed</u> are thrilled and delighted by all the tub-thumping. *We* suppose that every episode of 'Letterman' from now until doomsday is going to open with another weepy rendition of 'God Bless America.'

Those who have the good fortune to live in the international world – that is, the world outside the U.S. – know that *we* are not all of one religion, one language or one political system. *We* live in a big world where *people have diverse, and often, diametrically opposed views*. And while it is commendable to want to stamp out terrorism, it might also be a good idea to pause and reflect *on some of the grievances that people in the rest of the world* have <u>towards the U.S.</u> Of course, there's precious little chance of that happening in <u>America</u> any time soon.

The main opposition here seems to be between thinking people who live in the rest of the world and self-righteous jingoistic Americans. It's pretty clear which community readers are being positioned to belong to here. Turning to the local scene, a further distinction has to be made between victims of discrimination and the perpetrators (overzealous security forces and racist residents).

- oppose us to backlash perpetrators; judgement (mocking)
[we & members of the Muslim community; people who look like they *might* be Muslim; seven 'suspected Pakistani terrorists.'; the men;

tourists; the arrested people; a Hindu; a chef from Hong Kong; two Indian nationals; one of the men-himself; a Bosnian terrorist; the man-he; a bass guitarist; dark-skinned people]. The construction of us and them is highlighted for this part of the editorial below.

versus

[the Macau police; some people; undercover cops; an American passenger-he; taxis (drivers); people (on buses)]. The construction of us and them is highlighted for this part of the editorial below.

> On a smaller and closer scale, *we* have already begun to see some unfortunate cases locally of backlash against *members of the Muslim community* (or even just *people who look like they might be Muslim*).
> The Macau police found themselves in a Keystone Cops episode, arresting and detaining *seven 'suspected Pakistani terrorists.'* The scare was enough to close the U.S. Consulate in Hong Kong for a day, though *the men* turned out to be *tourists*, a word which is spelled somewhat like terrorists, and *we* suppose to some people, just as frightening. *One of the arrested people* in fact was *a Hindu, a chef from Hong Kong*, who had been cleverly tracked down by undercover cops sitting peacefully at the Hotel Lisboa bar.
> Meanwhile (and *we're* not making this up), *two Indian nationals* on a flight from Singapore to Hong Kong were detained at Changi Airport after an American passenger said *he* heard *one of the men* calling *himself a 'Bosnian terrorist.'* (*The man* in fact said *he* was *a 'bass guitarist.'*)
> Similarly, there have already been reports of taxis putting up 'out of service' signs and people changing seats on buses when confronted by *dark-skinned people* – as if changing your seat would save you if a bomb went off, anyway. But such is the logic of xenophobia.

This section of the text repositions thinking internationals as antiracists, certainly a compatible communality for the expat and returning Chinese community. As a final step the editorial endorses the pundits, and enters a plea for rationality – presumably on behalf of the thinking people readers were positioned to align with above.

[all the pundits & us]

> If, as *all the pundits* are saying, there is no hope of normalcy returning soon, *let's* at least hope that sanity does. [*HK Magazine* Friday Sept. 21, 2001: 5]

Alongside this ideational re/construction of us and them, the text plays out an important dialectic of concession. To begin, this has to do with the American response to 9/11. Readers are positioned to understand Americans' grief, but be appalled by their jingoism – although the polls aren't going our way. Similarly readers are commended to stamp out terrorism, but to reflect on grievances as well – although there's little chance of Americans taking a critical look at themselves. Thinking people in other words know the right way to feel, but that's not going to affect unthinking Americans.

> While that grief is deeply understood, // the problem with tragedies like this one is that they become a heyday for the overly-sincere, maudlin, righteous-indignation crowd. *We've* been appalled, perplexed and repulsed by some of the things *we've* heard said in the media this week. The jingoistic, flag-waving, 'my way or the highway' rhetoric is enough to make *thinking people* retch. / That said, the polls aren't going *our* way. 89 percent of Americans surveyed are thrilled and delighted by all the tub-thumping. *We* suppose that every episode of 'Letterman' from now until doomsday is going to open with another weepy rendition of 'God Bless America.'
>
> *Those who have the good fortune to live in the international world – that is, the world outside the U.S.* – know that *we* are not all of one religion, one language or one political system. *We* live in a big world where *people have diverse, and often, diametrically opposed views.* And while it is commendable to want to stamp out terrorism, // it might also be a good idea to pause and reflect *on some of the grievances that people in the rest of the world* have towards the U.S. / Of course, there's precious little chance of that happening in America any time soon.

Turning to the local scene, this concessive dialectic plays out as fact countering suspicion. There's backlash against Muslims, including people who just look like Muslims; against 'Pakistani' terrorists who turn out to be tourists; against Bosnian terrorists, who are in fact Indian; against dark-skinned people, when changing seats won't actually save you from a bomb.

> On a smaller and closer scale, *we* have already begun to see some unfortunate cases locally of backlash against members of the Muslim community // (or even just people who look like they *might* be Muslim).
>
> The Macau police found themselves in a Keystone Cops episode, arresting and detaining seven 'suspected Pakistani terrorists.' The scare was enough to close the U.S. Consulate in Hong Kong for a day, // though the men turned out to be tourists, a word which is spelled somewhat like terrorists, and *we* suppose to some people, just as frightening. One of the arrested people in fact

was a Hindu, a chef from Hong Kong, who had been cleverly tracked down by undercover cops sitting peacefully at the Hotel Lisboa bar.

Meanwhile (and *we're* not making this up), two Indian nationals on a flight from Singapore to Hong Kong were detained at Changi Airport after an American passenger said he heard one of the men calling himself a 'Bosnian terrorist.' // (The man in fact said he was a 'bass guitarist.')

Similarly, there have already been reports of taxis putting up 'out of service' signs and people changing seats on buses when confronted by dark-skinned people – // as if changing your seat would save you if a bomb went off, any- way. But such is the logic of xenophobia.

This kind of rhetoric has the effect of putting readers in the know – letting them in on things they might not otherwise have picked up from the mainstream print and electronic media.[5] Reinforcing this is the use of asides though which the writer steps out of his editorial role for a moment to confide in readers, expat to expat as it were:

(or even just people who look like they *might* be Muslim)

(and we're not making this up)

(The man in fact said he was a 'bass guitarist.')

As a final concessive move, the editor endorses the idea that hope for a return to normalcy is forlorn, settling instead upon a plea for sanity:

If, as all the pundits are saying, there is no hope of normalcy returning soon, *let's* at least hope that sanity does.

At this point in the discourse we can return to the title of the editorial, *Mourning*, and ask what it is exactly that readers are being positioned to mourn? What began as communion with Americans over their loss of life and way of life now looks more like mourning for the loss of normalcy and sanity which has the potential to affect *HK Magazine* readers' way of life. The main reaction in Hong Kong to 9/11, after all, was concern over the effect it would have on business – and by extension on the huge salaries, low taxes, heavily subsidized accommodation and schooling and cheap cleaning, cooking and nanny services enjoyed by expat professionals, returning Chinese and their families. Were the events of 9/11 an economic hiccough? Or was the gravy train at risk? In the face of uncertainty of this order readers could be counted on to hope for a return to business as usual. Thus the *Mourning* discourse comes to rest, consolidating its heartland, however contentious the opinions it has proffered along the way.

This concern with equilibrium sits nicely with the play of **attitude** and **graduation** discussed above: first loudly chastise Americans (who are at a safe distance), then softly mock the local discrimination (without stirring up too much fuss) – as a backdrop to what really matters, namely a return to an order in which thinking people can get on with their jobs.

5.4 Envoi

In this concluding chapter we have concentrated on the interplay of the appraisal resources we built up in Chapters 2 and 3 above, working with texts deploying the commentator key introduced in Chapter 4. In particular we were concerned to show the contingency of **attitude**, **engagement** and **graduation** choices as texts unfold, and the way in which these contingencies negotiate complex communities of readership. As such our analysis has been a qualitative exercise, oriented to the solidarity dimension of the register variable tenor.

The complement to qualitative analysis of this order is a quantitative approach, which would focus on fewer variables across a corpus of texts. Although we have not undertaken large scale studies we hope that our appraisal framework will encourage a reconsideration of evaluative meaning, factored out as **attitude**, **engagement** and **graduation** (see, for example, Taboada & Grieve, 2004). Studies of this kind will play a crucial role in the development of the instantiation cline proposed in Chapter 4, as work by Miller (see, for example, Miller 2002a, 2002b) has already indicated.

Finding the right balance between qualitative and quantitative analysis is an important challenge as we try to deepen our understanding of evaluation in discourse. Computer-assisted automation is improving all the time (see for example, Shanahan *et al.* to appear) and even semi-automated work-benches make the job of coding data and analysing results easier than it has ever been before. By the same token, we still feel a generation away from the computer-assisted discourse analysis we need to explore how appraisal choices synergise with one another, dynamically accumulating and nuancing evaluation in relation to tenor from one moment in discourse to the next. It remains important for qualitative analysts to establish the challenges of interpretation which quantitative work can learn to manage over time.

In particular we are concerned that appraisal analysis provokes a rehabilitation of the study of rhetoric within linguistic theory, which for most of the twentieth century has privileged a concern with ideational semantics and the logic of sentences. This truth functional philosophical orientation wouldn't be such a problem if it affected only linguistics. But we expect that a preoccupation with ideational meaning encourages a critical discourse analysis which focuses on deceit, as if drawing attention to the lies of the powerful and the truths hidden by spin is the kind of exercise we need to make the world a better place. To our mind this needs to be balanced by intersubjective analysis that focuses rhetorically on evaluation, interprets how people are disposed by feelings and looks for ways to negotiate more productive alignments – sensitive to our ever more pressing need to share this world and its depleting resources with one another. Analysis that moves beyond conspiracy and critique towards a more constructive, more hopeful vision of possible futures.

Notes

1. This is of course Halliday's complementarity of ideational and interpersonal meaning; Bakhtin's terms have the advantage of denaturalising the ideational as political (ideology), and foregrounding evaluation over interaction (axiology).
2. We should, perhaps, point out that Jim is Canadian (though living in Australia) and Peter is Australian (though living in the UK at the time), and hence we are somewhat reluctant to pronounce too definitively on such British attitudes. That the British maintain at least a vestigial condescension with regards to US culture and that this was reflected in this text was suggested to Peter by Susan Hunston (born and living in the UK). Lessing's diagnosis of America's reaction to 9/11 (Chapter 4) seems to us to confirm this suggestion.
3. This point was drawn to Jim's attention by Angel Lim, who was struck by the way in which the second rendering backgrounded a concern with the victims of the hysterical prejudice generated by 9/11.
4. A further example of metadiscourse in this passage is the word *word*, which enables the editor to comment on his own discourse, by way of mocking hysterical fear of the other.
5. Jim was living as an expat in Hong Kong at the time and carefully following events in the daily English broadsheet, *The South China Morning Post*, and watching evening news on TV; from these he certainly learned about the arrests in Macau and attendant closure of the American Consulate in Hong Kong, but not about the actual identity of the suspects.

References

Achugar, M. 2004. 'The events and actors of September 11, 2001, as seen from Uruguay: analysis of daily newspaper editorials'. *Discourse & Society* 15.2/3 (Special Issue on 'Discourse around 9/11'). 291–320.

Aijmer, K. 1997. 'I think – an English modal particle', in T. Swan & O. Westvik (eds), *Modality in Germanic Languages. Historical and Comparative Perspectives.* Berlin/New York: Mouton de Gruyter. 1–47.

Bakhtin, M. M. 1981. *The Dialogic Imagination* (translated by C. Emerson & M. Holquist) Austin: University of Texas Press.

Baldry, A. (ed.) 1999. *Multimodality and Multimediality in the Distance Learning Age.* Campo Basso: Lampo.

Biber, D. 1995. *Dimensions of Register Variation: A Cross-linguistic Comparison.* Cambridge: Cambridge University Press.

Biber, D. S. Conrad & R. Reppen, 1998. *Corpus Linguistics: Investigating Language Structure and Use.* Cambridge: Cambridge University Press.

Biber, D. & E. Finegan, 1988. 'Adverbial stance types in English'. *Discourse Processes* 11.1. 1–34.

Biber, D. & E. Finegan, 1989. 'Styles of stance in English: lexical and grammatical marking of evidentiality and affect'. *Text* 9.1. (Special Issue on the pragmatics of affect) 93–124.

Bringing Them Home: National Inquiry into the Separation of Aboriginal and Torres Strait Islander Children from their Families. 1997. Sydney, Human Rights and Equal Opportunity Commission.

Brown, R. & A. Gilman, 1960. 'The pronouns of power and solidarity' in T. Sebeok (ed.), *Style in Language.* Cambridge, Mass.: MIT Press. 253–76.

Brown, P. & S. Levinson, 1987. *Politeness: Some Universals in Language Usage.* Cambridge: Cambridge University Press.

Butler, C. S. 2003. *Structure and Function: a Guide to Three Major Structural–functional Theories. Part 1: Approaches to the Simplex Clause. Part II: From Clause to Discourse and Beyond.* Amsterdam: Benjamins (Studies in Language Companion Series).

Bybee, J. & S. Fleischman, 1995. *Modality in Grammar and Discourse.* Amsterdam: Benjamins.

Caffarel, A. J. R. Martin & C. M. I. M. Matthiessen (eds), 2004. *Language Typology: A Functional Perspective.* London & New York: Continuum.

Caldas-Coulthard, C. R. 1994. 'On reporting reporting: the representation of speech in factual and factional narratives', in M. Coulthard (ed.), *Advances in Written Text Analysis.* London & New York: Routledge. 295–309.

Carleton, M. 1996. 'Let us all be sheep'. *The Sydney Morning Herald* Saturday May 4 (News Review), 36.

Carleton, M. 1999. 'Delusions of grand Mal'. *The Sydney Morning Herald* Saturday April 12 (News Review), 34.

Carleton, M. 2000. 'Thin edge of wedge politics'. *The Sydney Morning Herald* April 8, 38.

Chafe, W. L. 1982. 'Integration and involvement in speaking, writing and oral literature', in D. Tannen (ed.), *Spoken and Written Language: Exploring Orality and Literacy*. Norwood. N.J.: Albex. 35–54.
Chafe, W. 1986. 'Evidentiality in English conversation and academic writing', in W. Chafe and J. Nichols (eds) *Evidentiality: the Linguistic Coding of Epistemology*. Norwood, N.J.: Ablex (Advances in Discourse Processes XX), 261–72.
Chafe, W. & J. Nichols (eds), 1986. *Evidentiality: The Linguistic Coding of Epistemology*. Norwood, N.J.: Ablex. (Advances in Discourse Processes XX)
Channel, J. 1994. *Vague Language*. Oxford: Oxford University Press. (Describing English Language.)
Channel, J. 2000. 'Corpus-based analysis of evaluative lexis' in Hunston & Thompson 2000. 38–55.
Christie, F. (ed.), 1999. *Pedagogy and the Shaping of Consciousness: Linguistic and Social Processes*. London: Cassell (Open Linguistics Series).
Christie, F. & J. R. Martin (eds), 1997. *Genres and Institutions: Social Processes in the Workplace and School*. London: Cassell (Open Linguistics Series).
Clark, C., P. Drew & T. Pinch, 2003. 'Managing prospect affiliation and rapport in real-life sale encounters'. *Discourse Studies* 5.1. 5–32.
Coates, J. 1983. *The Semantics of Modal Auxiliaries*. London & Canberra: Croom Helm.
Coffin, C. 1997. 'Constructing and giving value to the past: an investigation into second school history', in Christie, F. & J. R. Martin (eds), *Genre and Institutions – Social Processes in the Workplace and School*. London: Cassell. 196–230.
Coffin, C. 2003. 'Reconstruals of the past – settlement or invasion? The role of JUDGEMENT analysis', in J. R. Martin & R. Wodak (eds), *Re/reading the Past: Critical and Functional Perspectives on Discourses of History*. Amsterdam: John Benjamins. 219–46.
Colquhoun, D. 1995. THAT GARETH – WE'LL SHOW THE FRENCH! *The Sydney Morning Herald*. June 19 (Stay in Touch).
Column 8. 2002. *The Sydney Morning Herald*. Friday August 30.
Conrad, S. & D. Biber, 2000. 'Adverbial marking of stance in speech and writing'. H&T. 56–73.
Coppock P. (ed.), 2001. *The Semiotics of Writing: Transdisciplinary Perspectives on the Technology of Writing*. Brepols (Semiotic & Cognitive Studies X).
Coulthard, M. 1994. 'On analysing and evaluating text', in M. Coulthard (ed.), *Advances in Written Text Analysis*, London: Routledge. 1–11.
Davidse, K. 1991. *Categories of Experiential Grammar*. PhD Dissertation. Department of Lingusitics, University of Leeuwen.
de Beaugrande, R. 1997. 'Society, education, linguistics and language: inclusion and exclusion in theory and practice', *Linguistics and Education* c 9.2, 99–158.
de Certeau, M. 1984. *The Practice of Everyday Life*. Berkeley: University of California press.
Doughty, P., J. Pearce, J. John & M. Geoffrey, 1971. *Language in Use*. London: Arnold (Schools Council Programme in Linguistics and English Teaching).
Doyle, A. C. 1981a. 'The valley of fear.' Part 1 'The tragedy of birlstone.' Chapter 1 'The warning.' *The Penguin Complete Sherlock Holmes*. Harmondsworth: Penguin.
Eco, U. 1984. *The Role of the Reader. Explorations in the Semiotics of Texts*. Bloomington: Indiana University Press.

Eggins, S. 1994/2004. *An Introduction to Systemic Functional Linguistics*. London: Pinter.
Eggins, S. & D. Slade, 1997. *Analysing Casual Conversation*. London: Cassell.
Ellis, B. 1998. 'Opinion: what's race got to do with it?', *The Sydney Morning Herald* June 6. 17.
Fairclough, N. 1992. *Discourse and Social Change*. Cambridge: Polity Press.
Flowerdew, L. 2003. 'A combined corpus and systemic-functional analysis of the problem–solution pattern in a student and professional corpus of technical writing', *TESOL. Quarterly* 37.3, 489–511.
Fuller, G. 1995. *Engaging Cultures: Negotiating Discourse in Popular Science*. University of Sydney Ph.D. Thesis.
Fuller, G. 1998. 'Cultivating science: negotiating discourse in the popular texts of Stephen Jay Gould' in J. R. Martin and R. Veel, *Reading Science: Critical and Functional Perspectives on Discourses of Science*. London: Routledge, 35–62.
Fuller, G. 2000. 'The textual politics of good intentions', in Lee, A & C. Poynton (eds). 2000. *Culture & Text: Discourse and Methodology in Social Research and Cultural Studies*. Sydney: Allen & Unwin, 81–98.
Fuller, G. & A. Lee, 1997. 'Textual collusions', *Discourse: Studies in the Cultural Politics of Education* 18.2, 409–23.
Goatly, A. 2000. *Critical Reading and Writing – An Introductory Coursebook*. London & New York: Routledge.
Goodman, S. 1996. 'Visual English'. in S. Goodman & D. Graddol (eds), *Redesigning English: New Texts, New Identities*. London: Routledge. 38–105.
Gratton, M. (ed.), 2000. *Reconciliation: Essays on Australian Reconciliation*. Melbourne: Black Inc.
Gregory, M. 1995. *Before and Towards Communication Linguistics: Essays by Michael Gregory and Associates* (Jin Soon Cha ed.) Seoul: Sookmyng Women's University.
Gregory, M. 2000. 'Phasal analysis within communication linguistics: two contrastive discourses', in P. Fries, M. Cummings, D. Lockwood & W. Sprueill (eds), *Relations and Functions in Language and Discourse*. London: Continuum.
Halliday, M. A. K. 1967. *Intonation and Grammar in British English*. The Hague: Mouton.
Halliday, M. A. K. 1970a. 'Language structure and language function' in J. Lyons (ed.), *New Horizons in Linguistics*. Harmondsworth: Penguin. 140–65.
Halliday, M. A. K. 1970b. *A Course in Spoken English: Intonation*. London: Oxford University Press.
Halliday, M. A. K. 1975. *Learning How to Mean: Explorations in the Development of Language*. London: Edward Arnold (Explorations in Language Study).
Halliday, M. A. K. 1976a. *Halliday: System and Function in Language* (G. Kress ed.). London: Oxford University Press.
Halliday, M. A. K. 1976b. 'Anti-languages'. *American Anthropologist* 78.3. 570–84. (reprinted in Halliday 1978. 164–82).
Halliday, M. A. K. 1978. *Language as a Social Semiotic: The Social Interpretation of Language and Meaning*. London: Edward Arnold.
Halliday, M. A. K. 1979. 'Modes of meaning and modes of expression: types of grammatical structure, and their determination by different semantic functions'. in D. J. Allerton, E. Carney & D. Holdcroft (eds), *Function and Context in Linguistic Analysis: Essays Offers to William Haas*. Cambridge: Cambridge University Press, 57–79. (Republished in Halliday 2002: 196–218).

Halliday, M. A. K. 1981a. 'Text semantics and clause grammar: some patterns of realisation'. in J. E. Copeland & P. W. Davis (eds), *The Seventh LACUS. Forum*. Columbia, S.C.: Hornbeam Press. 31–59.
Halliday, M. A. K. 1981b. 'Types of structure' in M. A. K. Halliday & J. R. Martin (eds), *Readings in Systemic Linguistics*. London: Batsford. 29–41.
Halliday, M. A. K. 1981c. 'Structure'. In M. A. K. Halliday & J. R. Martin (eds), *Readings in Systemic Linguistics*. London: Batsford. 122–31.
Halliday, M. A. K. 1982. 'How is a text like a clause?' *Text Processing: Text Analysis and Generation, Text Typology and Attribution* (Proceedings of Nobel Symposium 51). S. Allen (ed.), Stockholm: Almqvist & Wiksell International. 209–47.
Halliday, M. A. K. 1984. 'Language as code and language as behaviour: a systemic–functional interpretation of the nature and ontogenesis of dialogue'. in R. Fawcett, M. A. K. Halliday, S. M. Lamb & A. Makkai (eds), *The Semiotics of Language and Culture: Vol 1: Language as Social Semiotic*. London: Pinter. 3–35.
Halliday, M. A. K. 1985a. *Spoken and Written Language*. Geelong, Victoria: Deakin University Press (republished by Oxford University Press 1989).
Halliday, M. A. K. 1985b, 'Context of situation', in M. A. K. Halliday & R. Hasan, *Language, Context and Text*. Geelong, Vic.: Deakin University Press. 3–14. (republished by Oxford University Press 1988/9).
Halliday, M. A. K. 1992. 'A systemic interpretation of peking syllable finals', in P. Tench (ed.), *Studies in Systemic Phonology*. London: Pinter. 98–121.
Halliday, M. A. K. 2004/1994. *An Introduction to Functional Grammar*. London: Edward Arnold. (2004 third edition revised by C. M. I. M. Matthiessen).
Halliday, M. A. K. 2002. *Linguistic studies of Text and Discourse* (edited by J. Webster). (The collected works of M. A. K. Halliday Series, volume 2), London & New York: Continuum.
Halliday, M. A. K. & J. R. Martin, 1993. *Writing Science: Literacy and Discursive Power* (with M. A. K. Halliday) London: Falmer (Critical perspectives on literacy and education) & Pittsburg: University of Pittsburg Press. (Pittsburg Series in Composition, Literacy, and Culture).
Halliday, M. A. K. & C. M. I. M. Matthiessen, 1999. *Construing Experience Through Meaning: a Language-based Approach to Cognition*. London: Continuum.
Harré, R. (ed.), 1987. *The Social Construction of Emotions*. Oxford: Blackwell.
Hasan, R. & G. Williams (eds), 1996. *Literacy in Society*. London: Longman (Language and Social Life).
Hood, S. 2004. *Appraising Research: Taking a Stance in Academic Writing*. University of technology Sydney PhD. Thesis.
Hood, S. 2004. 'Managing attitude in undergraduate academic writing: a focus on the introductions to research reports', in L. Ravelli and R. Ellis (eds), *Analysing Academic Writing: Contextualised Frameworks*. London: Continuum.
Horvath, B. & S. Eggins, 1995. 'Opinion texts in conversation'. In P. Fries & M. Gregory (eds), *Discourse in Society: Systemic Functional Perspectives*. Norwood, N.J.: Ablex (Advances in Discourse Processes L: Meaning and Choices in Language – studies for Michael Halliday). 29–46.
Hunston, S. 1993. 'Evaluation and ideology in scientific writing.' In M. Ghadessy (ed.), *Register Analysis: Theory and Practice*. London: Pinter (Open Linguistics Series). 57–73.

Hunston, S. 1994. 'Evaluation and organisation in a sample of written academic discourse'. In M. Coulthard (ed.), *Advances in Written Text Analysis*. London: Routledge. 191–218.

Hunston, S. 2000. 'Evaluation and the planes of discourse: status and value in persuasive texts'. In Hunston, S. & G. Thompson (eds), 2000. *Evaluation in Text: Authorial Stance and the Construction of Discourse*. Oxford: Oxford University Press, 176–207.

Hunston, S. & G. Thompson (eds), 2000. *Evaluation in Text. Authorial Stance and the Construction of Discourse*. Oxford: Oxford University Press.

Hunston, S. & G. Thompson, 2000a. 'Evaluation: an introduction', in Hunston, S. & G. Thompson (eds), 2000. *Evaluation in Text: Authorial Stance and the Construction of Discourse*. Oxford: Oxford University Press, 1–27.

Hunston, S. in press, 'Phraseology and system: a contribution to the debate', in Thompson, G. & Hunston, S. (eds), *System and Corpus: Exploring connections*, London: Equinox.

Hyland, K. 1998. *Hedging in Scientific Research Articles*. Amsterdam: Benjamins. (Pragmatics & Beyond New Series 54).

Hyland, K. 1996. 'Writing without conviction: hedging in science research articles', *Applied Linguistics* 17 (4), 433–54.

Hyland, K. 2000. *Disciplinary Discourses: Social Interactions in Academic Writing*. London: Longman.

Iedema, R. 1995. *Literacy of Administration (Write it Right Literacy in Industry Research Project – Stage 3)*. Sydney: Metropolitan East Disadvantaged Schools Program.

Iedema, R. 1997. 'The history of the accident news story'. *Australian Review of Applied Linguistics* 20.2. 95–119.

Iedema, R., S. Feez & P. R. R. White, 1994. *Media Literacy (Write it Right Literacy in Industry Research Project – Stage 2)*. Sydney: Metropolitan East Disadvantaged Schools Program.

Irvine, J. 1982. 'Language and affect: some cross-cultural issues'. In H. Byrnes (ed.), *Contemporary Perceptions of Language: Interdisciplinary Dimensions*. Washington, D.C.: Georgetown University Press. 31–47.

Irvine, J. 1990. 'Registering affect: heteroglossia in the linguistic expression of emotion'. In C. A. Lutz & L. Abu-Lughod, *Language and the Politics of Emotion*. Cambridge: Cambridge University Press (Studies in Emotion and Social Interaction). 126–61.

Jakobson, R. 1957. *Shifters, Verbal Categories and the Russian Verb*. Russian Language Project. Harvard: Dept of Slavic Languages and Literature.

Jordens, C. 2002. *Reading Spoken Stories for Values: a Discursive Study of Cancer Survivors and Their Professional Carers*. University of Sydney PhD. Thesis.

Jewitt, C. & R. Oyama, 2001. 'Visual meaning: a social semiotic approach'. In van Leeuwen, T. & C. Jewitt, (eds), 2001. *The Handbook of Visual Analysis*. London: Sage, 134–56.

Keating, P. 1992. Redfern Park Speech. Paul Keating Website. (Edited version in Gratton 2000: 60–4).

Kempson, R. M. 1975. *Presupposition and the Delimitation of Semantics*, Cambridge: Cambridge University Press.

Kiparsky, P. & C. Kiparsky, 1970. 'Fact', in M. Bierwisch & K. Heidolph (eds), *Progress in Linguistics*, The Hague: Mouton, 143–73.

Körner, H. 2000. *Negotiating Authority: the Logogenesis of Dialogue in Common law Judgments*. University of Sydney PhD. Thesis.

Körner, H. & C. Treloar, 2003. 'Needle and syringe programmes in the local media: "needle anger" versus "effective education in the community" '. *The International Journal of Drug Policy* 15. 46–55.

Kress, G. & T. van Leeuwen, 1996. *Reading Images: the Grammar of Visual Design*. London: Routledge.

Kress, G. & T. van Leeuwen, 2001. *Multimodal Discourse – The Modes and Media of Contemporary Communication*. London: Arnold.

Kress, G. & T. van Leeuwen, 2002. 'Colour as a semiotic mode: notes for a grammar of colour.' *Visual Communication* 1.3. 343–68.

Kuno, S. 1993. *Functional Syntax: Anaphora, Discourse and Empathy*. Chicago: University of Chicago Press.

Labov, W. 1972. 'The transformation of experience in narrative syntax'. *Language in the Inner City*. Philadelphia: Pennsylvania University Press. 354–96.

Labov, W. 1982. 'Speech actions and reactions in personal narrative'. In D. Tannen (ed.), *Analysing Discourse: Text and Talk* (Georgetown University Round Table on Language and Linguistics 1981). Washington, D.C.: Georgetown University Press.

Labov, W. 1984. 'Intensity'. In D. Schiffrin (ed.), *Meaning, Form, and Use in Context: Linguistic Applications* (Georgetown University Roundtable on Language and Linguistics) Washington, D.C.: Georgetown University Press. 43–70.

Labov, W. 1997. 'Some further steps in narrative analysis'. *Journal of Narrative and Life History* 7.1–4. 1997. 395–415.

Labov, W. & J. Waletzky, 1967. 'Narrative analysis'. In J. Helm (ed.), *Essays on the Verbal and Visual Arts* (Proceedings of the 1966 Spring Meeting of the American Ethnological Society). Seattle: University of Washington Press. 12–44.

Lakoff, G. 1972. 'Hedges: a study in meaning criteria and the logic of fuzzy concepts', *Proceedings of the Chicago Linguistics Society* 8: 183–228.

Lakoff, G. & Z. Kovecses, 1987. 'The cognitive model of anger inherent in American English'. In D. Holland & N. Quinn (eds), *Cultural Models in Language and Thought*. Cambridge: Cambridge University Press. 195–221.

Lee, A. & C. Poynton (eds), 2000. *Culture & Text: Discourse and Methodology in Social Research and Cultural Studies*. Sydney: Allen & Unwin.

Leech, G. 1983. *The Principles of Pragmatics*. London & New York: Longman.

Lemke, J. L. 1992. 'Interpersonal meaning in discourse: value orientations'. In M. Davies & L. Ravelli (eds), *Advances in Systemic Linguistics: Recent Theory and Practice*. London: Pinter (Open Linguistics Series). 82–194.

Lemke, J. L. 1995. *Textual Politics: Discourse and Social Dynamics*. London: Taylor & Francis (Critical Perspectives on Literacy and Education).

Lemke, J. L. 1998. 'Resources for attitudinal meaning: evaluative orientations in text semantics'. *Functions of Language* 5.1. 33–56.

Lessing, D. 2002. Doris Lessing: Britain. *Granta* 77. 52–4.

Lock, G. 1996. *Functional English Grammar: an Introduction for Second Language Teachers*. Cambridge: Cambridge University press (Cambridge Language Education).

Lutz, C. A. 1982. 'The domain of emotion words in Ifaluk'. *American Ethnologist* 9. 113–28.

Lutz, C. A. 1986. 'Emotion, thought and estrangement: emotion as a cultural category'. *Cultural Anthropology* 1. 405–36.

Lutz, C. A. 1987. 'Goals, events and understanding in Ifaluk emotion theory'. In D. Holland & N. Quinn (eds), *Person, Self and Experience: Exploring Pacific Ethnopsychologies*. Berkeley: University of California Press. 35–79.

Lutz, C. A. 1988. *Unnatural Emotions: Everyday Sentiments on a Micronesian Atoll and their Challenge to Western Theory*. Chicago: University of Chicago Press.

Lutz, C. A. & L. Abu-Lughod, 1990. *Language and the Politics of Emotion*. Cambridge: Cambridge University Press (Studies in Emotion and Social Interaction).

Lutz, C. A. & G. White, 1986. 'The anthropology of emotions'. *Annual Review of Anthropology* 15. 405–36.

Lyons, J. 1977. *Semantics*. Cambridge: Cambridge University Press.

Macken-Horarik, M. & J. R. Martin (eds), 2003. *Negotiating Heteroglossia: Social Perspectives on Evaluation*. (Special Issue of *Text* 23.2.)

Manne, R. 1998. 'The stolen generations'. *Quadrant* No. 343. Volume XLII. Number 1–2. 53–63.

Manne, R. 2001. *In Denial: the Stolen Generations and the Right*. Melbourne: Black Inc. (First published in *Quarterly Essay*.)

Markkanen, R. & H. Schröder, 1997. *Hedging and Discourse: Approaches to the Analysis of a Pragmatic Phenomenon in Academic Texts*. The Hague: Walter De Gruyter.

Martin, J. R. 1992a. 'Macro-proposals: meaning by degree'. In W. C. Mann & S. Thompson (eds), *Discourse Description: Diverse Analyses of a Fund Raising Text*. Amsterdam: Benjamins. 359–95.

Martin, J. R. 1992b. *English Text: System and Structure*. Amsterdam: Benjamins.

Martin, J. R. 1995a. 'Text and clause: fractal resonance'. *Text* 15.1. 5–42.

Martin, J. R. 1995b. 'Interpersonal meaning, persuasion and public discourse: packing semiotic punch'. *Australian Journal of Linguistics* 15.1. 33–67.

Martin, J. R. 1996. 'Types of structure: deconstructing notions of constituency in clause and text'. In E. H. Hovy & D. R. Scott (eds), *Computational and Conversational Discourse: Burning Issues – an Interdisciplinary Account*. Heidelberg: Springer. 39–66.

Martin, J. R. 1997a. 'Linguistics and the consumer: theory in practice'. *Linguistics and Education* 9.4. 409–46.

Martin, J. R. 1997b. 'Analysing genre: functional parameters'. in Christie & Martin. 3–39.

Martin, J. R.1997c. 'Register and genre: modelling social context in functional linguistics – narrative genres'. In E. R. Pedro (ed.), *Discourse Analysis: Proceedings of First International Conference on Discourse Analysis*. Lisbon: Colibri/Portuguese Linguistics Association. 305–44.

Martin, J. R. 1999a. 'Modelling context: a crooked path of progress in contextual linguistics (Sydney SFL)'. In M. Ghadessy (ed.), *Text and Context in Functional Linguistics*. Amsterdam: Benjamins (CILT. Series IV). 1999. 25–61.

Martin, J. R. 1999b. 'Grace: the logogenesis of freedom'. *Discourse Studies* 1.1. 31–58.

Martin, J. R. 2000a. 'Beyond exchange: appraisal systems in English'. In Hunston, S. & G. Thompson (eds), 2000. *Evaluation in Text. Authorial Stance and the Construction of Discourse*. Oxford: Oxford University Press, 142–75.

Martin, J. R. 2000b. 'Factoring out exchange: types of structure'. In M. Coulthard (ed.), *Working with Dialogue*. Tubingen: Niemeyer.

Martin, J. R. 2000c. 'Design and practice: enacting functional linguistics in Australia'. *Annual Review of Applied Linguistics* 20 (20th Anniversary Volume 'Applied Linguistics as an Emerging Discipline'). 116–26.

Martin, J. R. 2001a. 'Fair trade: negotiating meaning in multimodal texts' in P. Coppock (ed.), *The Semiotics of Writing: Transdisciplinary Perspectives on the Technology of Writing*. Brepols (Semiotic & Cognitive Studies X). 311–38.

Martin, J. R. 2001b. 'Writing history: construing time and value in discourses of the past'. In C. Colombi & M. Schleppergrell (eds), *Developing Advanced Literacy in First and Second Languages*. Mahwah, N.J.: Erlbaum.

Martin, J. R. 2001c. 'Giving the game away: explicitness, diversity and genre-based literacy in Australia'. In R. Wodak *et al.* (eds), *Functional Il/literacy*. Vienna: Verlag der Osterreichischen Akadamie der Wissenschaften. 155–74.

Martin, J. R. 2002a. 'Blessed are the peacemakers: reconciliation and evaluation'. In C. Candlin (ed.), *Research and Practice in Professional Discourse*. Hong Kong: City University of Hong Kong Press. 187–227.

Martin, J. R. 2002b. 'Writing history: construing time and value in discourses of the past'. In C. Colombi & M. Schleppergrell (eds), *Developing Advanced Literacy in First and Second Languages*. Mahwah, N.J.: Erlbaum. 2002. 87–118.

Martin, J. R. 2004. 'Sense and sensibility: texturing evaluation'. In J. Foley (ed.), *Language, Education and Discourse*. London: Continuum. 270–304.

Martin, J. R. & G. Plum, 1997. 'Construing experience: some story genres'. *Journal of Narrative and Life History* 7.1–4. (Special Issue: Oral Versions of Personal Experience: three decades of narrative analysis; M. Bamberg Guest Editor). 299–308.

Martin, J. R. & D. Rose, 2003 [Second, revised edition, 2007]. *Working with Discourse: Meaning Beyond the Clause*. London: Continuum.

Martin, J. R. & M. Stenglin, in press (now 2006). 'Materialising reconciliation: negotiating difference in a post-colonial exhibition'. In T. Royce & W. Bowcher (eds), *New Directions in the Analysis of Multimodal Discourse*. Mahwah, New Jersey: Lawrence Erlbaum Associates. 215–238.

Martin, J. R. & R. Veel, 1998. *Reading Science: Critical and Functional Perspectives on Discourses of Science*. London: Routledge.

Martin, J. R. & R. Wodak (eds), 2003. *Re/reading the Past: Critical and Functional Perspectives on Discourses of History*. Amsterdam: Benjamins.

Martinec, R. 1998. 'Cohesion in action'. *Semiotica* 120. 1/2. 161–80.

Martinec, R. 2000a. 'Rhythm in multimodal texts'. *Leonardo* 33 (4), 289–97.

Martinec, R. 2000b. 'Types of process in action'. *Semiotica* 130–3/4, 243–68.

Martinec, R. 2000c. 'Construction of identity in M. Jackson's "Jam" '. *Social Semiotics* 10.3. 313–29.

Martinec, R. 2001. Interpersonal resources in action. *Semiotica*, 135–1/4. 117–45.

Matthiessen, C. M. I. M. 1995. *Lexicogrammatical Cartography: English Systems*. Tokyo: International Language Sciences Publishers.

McGregor, W. 1997. *Semiotic Grammar*. Oxford: Clarendon.

Meyer, P. G. 1997. 'Hedging Strategies in Written Academic Discourse: Strengthening the Argument by Weakening the Claim', in Markkanen, R. & H. Schröder (eds), *Hedging and Discouse – Approaches to the Analysis of a Pragmatic Phenomenon in Academic Texts*, Berlin & New York: Walter de Gruyter. 21–42.

Michaels, E. 1987. Afterword *Yuendumu Doors*. Canberra: Australian Institute of Aboriginal Studies.

Miller, D. M. 1999. 'Meaning up for grabs: value-orientation patterns in British parliamentary debate on Europe', in J. Verschueren (ed.), *Language and Ideology: Selected Papers from the 6th International Pragmatics Conference*, vol. I, Antwerp, International Pragmatics Association, 1999: 386–404.

Miller, D. M. 2002a. 'Ways of meaning "yea" and "nay" in parliamentary debate as register: a cost-benefit analysis', in M. Bignami, G. Iamartino, C. Pagetti (eds), *The Economy Principle in English: Linguistic, Literary, and Cultural Perspectives*. Milano: Edizioni Unicopli. 220–33.

Miller, D. M. 2002b, 'Multiple judicial opinions as specialized sites of engagement: conflicting paradigms of valuation and legitimation in Bush v. Gore 2000'. In M. Gotti, D. Heller and M. Dossena (eds), *Conflict and Negotiation in Specialized Texts*, Bern: Peter Lang, Linguistic Insights Series. 119–41.

Miller, D. M. 2004. ' "Truth, Justice and the American Way": The APPRAISAL SYSTEM of JUDGEMENT in the House debate on the impeachment of the President, 1998', in P. Bayley (ed.), *Cross-cultural Perspectives on Parliamentary Discourse*. Amsterdam & Philadelphia: John Benjamins. 271–300.

Miller, D. M. forthcoming, ' "... to meet our common challenge": ENGAGEMENT strategies of alignment and alienation in current US international discourse', in M. Gotti & C. Candlin (eds), *Intercultural Discourse in Domain-specific English*, Textus XVIII (2004) n.1: 39–62.

Miller, D. M. forthcoming, 'From concordance to text: appraising "giving" in Alma Mater donation requests'. In G. Thompson & S. Hunston (eds), *System and Corpus: Exploring Connections*. London: Equinox.

Mourning 2000. *HK Magazine*. Hong Kong: Asia City Publishing Ltd. 5.

Myers, G. 1989. 'The pragmatics of politeness in scientific articles.' *Applied Linguistics* 10. 1–35.

Niemeier, S. & R. Dirven (eds), 1997. *The Language of Emotions: Conceptualisation, Expression, and Theoretical Foundation*. Amsterdam: Benjamins.

O'Brian, P. 1997a. *The Letter of Marque*. London: HarperCollins.

O'Brian, P. 1997b. *The Reverse of the Medal*. London: HarperCollins.

Ochs, E. (ed.), 1989. *Text* 9.1 (Special Issue on the pragmatics of affect).

Ochs, E. & B. Schiefflen, 1989. 'Language has a heart'. *Text* 9.1 (Special Issue on the pragmatics of affect) 7–25.

Ondaatje, M. 2000. *Anil's Ghost*. Toronto: Vintage.

O'Toole, M. 1994. *The Language of Displayed Art*. London: Leicester University Press (a division of Pinter).

Pagano, A. 1994. 'Negatives in written text', in M. Coulthard (ed.), *Advances in Written Text Analysis*. London: Routledge. 250–65.

Painter, C. 1984. *Into the Mother Tongue: a Case Study of Early Language Development*. London: Pinter.

Painter, C. 1998. *Learning Through Language in Early Childhood*. London: Cassell.

Painter, C. 2003. 'Developing attitude: an ontogentic perspetive on APPRAISAL'. *Text* 23.2. 183–210.

Palmer, F. R. 1986. *Mood and Modality*. Cambridge, UK: Cambridge University Press.

Pinter, H. 2002. Harold Pinter: Britain. *Granta* 77. 66–9.

Pike, K. L. 1982. *Linguistic Concepts: an Introduction to Tagmemics*, Lincoln Nebraska & London: University of Nebraska Press.

Plum, G. 1988. *Text and Contextual Conditioning in Spoken English: a Genre-based Approach*. Unpublished doctoral dissertation, Department of Linguistics, University of Sydney. (Also published Nottingham: Department of English Studies, University of Nottingham (Monographs in Systemic Linguistics).)

Poynton, C. 1984. *Names as Vocatives: Forms and Functions*. Nottingham Linguistic Circular 13 (Special Issue on Systemic Linguistics). 1–34.

Poynton, C. 1985. *Language and Gender: Making the Difference*. Geelong, Vic.: Deakin University Press (republished London: Oxford University Press. 1989).
Poynton, C. 1990a. *Address and the Semiotics of Social Relations: a Systemic–functional Account of Address Forms and Practices in Australian English*. PhD. Thesis. Department of Linguistics, University of Sydney.
Poynton, C. 1990b. 'The privileging of representation and the marginalising of the interpersonal: a metaphor (and more) for contemporary gender relations'. in T. Threadgold & A. Cranny-Francis (eds), *Feminine/Masculine and Representation*. Sydney: Allen & Unwin. 231–55.
Poynton, C. 1993. 'Grammar, language and the social: poststructuralism and systemic functional linguistics'. *Social Semiotics* 3.1. 1–22.
Poynton, C. 1996. 'Amplification as a grammatical prosody: attitudinal modification in the nominal group'. In M. Berry, C. Butler & R. Fawcett (eds), *Meaning and Form: Systemic Functional Interpretations*. Norwood, N.J.: Ablex (Meaning and Choice in Language: studies for Michael Halliday). 211–27.
Precht, K. 2003. 'Stances moods in spoken English: evidentiality and affect in British and American conversation'. *Text* 23.2. 239–57.
Proulx. A. 1993. *The Shipping News*. London: Fourth Estate.
Quirk, R., S. Greenbaum G. Leech & J. Svartvik 1985. *A Comprehensive Grammar of the English Language*. London: Longman.
Raspberry, W. 2003. 'A few questions as we go to war'. *Guardian Weekly*. Jan. 2–8.27.
Roach, A. 1990. Took the Children Away. *Charcoal Lane*. Sydney: Mushroom Records (produced by P. Kelly & S. Connolly).
Roget's Thesaurus of English Words and Phrases. 1972. London: Longman (revised by R. A. Dutch).
Rose, D. B. 1996. *Nourishing Terrains: Australian Aboriginal Views of Landscape and Wilderness*. Canberra: Australian Heritage Commission.
Rothery, J. & M. Stenglin, 1997. 'Entertaining and instructing: exploring experience through story'. In Christie, F. & J. R. Martin (eds). 1997. *Genres and Institutions: Social Processes in the Workplace and School*. London: Cassell (Open Linguistics Series), 231–63.
Rothery, J. & M. Stenglin, 2000. 'Interpreting literature: the role of appraisal'. In Unsworth L. (ed.) 2000. *Researching Language in Schools and Communities: Fictional Linguistic Perspectives*. London: Cassell, 222–44.
Sadock, J. M. 1974. *Toward a Linguistic Theory of Speech Acts*, New York & London: Academic Press.
Sayers, D. L. 1991. *On the Case with Lord Peter Wimsey: Three Complete Novels: Strong Poison, Have his Carcase, Unnatural Death*. New York: Wings Books.
Shanahan, J. G., Yan Qu & J. Wiebe. To appear 2005. *Computing Attitude and Affect in Text*. The Netherlands Springer, Dordrecht.
Simon-Vandenbergen, A. -M. 1998. 'I think and its Dutch equivalents in parliamentary debates', in S. Joansson & S. Oksefjell (eds), *Corpora and Cross-Linguistic Research. Theory, Method and Case Studies*, Amsterdam/Atlanta: Rodopi. 297–331.
Simon-Vandenbergen, A. -M 2000. 'The function of I think in political discourse', *International Journal of Applied Linguistics* 10 (1): 41–63.
Sinclair, J. M. 1986. 'Fictional worlds', in M. Coulthard (ed.), *Talking About Text: Studies Presented to David Brazil on His Retirement*. Birmingham: Discourse

Analysis Monographs No. 13 University of Birmingham: English Language Research. 43–60.

Sinclair, J. M. 1994. 'Trust the text', in M. Coulthard (ed.), *Advance in Written Text Analysis*, London: Routledge. 12–25.

Sitka, C. 1998. 'Letter from Melbourne'. *Guardian Weekly* June 7. 25.

Stenglin, M. 2002. 'Comfort and security: a challenge for exhibition design.' in L. Kelly & J. Barratt (eds), *Uncover: Vol 1 of the Proceedings of the UNCOVER: Graduate Research in the Museum Sector Conference, Australian Museum, Sydney, May 24*. Sydney: Australian Museum/University of Sydney. 23–30.

Stenglin, M. 2004. *Packaging Curiosities: Towards a Grammar of Three-dimensional Space*. University of Sydney PhD.

Stenglin, M. & R. Iedema, 2001. 'How to analyse visual images: a guide for TESOL. teachers'. In A. Burns & C. Coffin (eds), *Analysing English in a Global Context: a Reader*. London: Routledge (Teaching English Language Worldwide). 194–208.

Stillar, G. F. 1998. *Analyzing Everyday Texts: Discourse, Rhetoric and Social Perspectives*. London: Sage.

Stubbs, M. 1996. 'Towards a modal grammar of English: a matter of prolonged fieldwork', in M. Stubbs, *Text and Corpus Analysis*, Oxford: Blackwell.

Taboada, M. and J. Grieve, 2004. 'Analyzing appraisal automatically', in *Exploring Attitude and Affect in Text: Theories and Applications Papers from 2004 AAAI Spring Symposium* Stanford. AAAI Technical Reports (http://www.aaai.org/Press/Reports/Symposia/Spring/ss-04-07.html).

Tadros, A. 1993. 'The pragmatics of text averal and attribution in academic texts', in M. Hoey (ed.), *Data, Description, Discourse: Papers on English Language in Honour of John Sinclair*, London: HarperCollins. 98–114.

The Dad Department 1994. *Mother & Baby* June/July. Sydney: A Bounty Publication.

Thibault, P. J. 1989. 'Semantic variation, social heteroglossia, intertextuality: thematic and axiological meaning in spoken discourse'. *Critical Studies (A Journal of Critical Theory, Literature and Culture)* Vol. 1.2. 181–209.

Thibault, P. 1992. 'Grammar, ethics and understanding: functionalist reason and clause as exchange'. *Social Semiotics* 2.1. 135–75.

Thompson, G. 2001. 'Interaction in academic writing: learning to argue with the reader', *Applied Linguistics* 22 (1): 58–78.

Tottie, G. 1982. 'Where do negative sentences come from', *Studia Linguistica* 36 (1): 88–105.

Tottie, G. 1987. 'Rejections, denials and explanatory statements – a reply to fretheim', *Studia Linguistica* 41 (2): 154–63.

Tucker, G. 1999. *The Lexicogrammar of Adjectives: a Systemic Functional Approach to Lexis*. London: Cassell.

Unsworth, L. (ed.), 2000. *Researching Language in Schools and Communities: Functional Linguistic Perspectives*. London: Cassell.

van Leeuwen, T. 1982. *Professional Speech: Accentual and Junctural Style in Radio Announcing*. MA. Hons Thesis. School of English and Linguistics, Macquarie University.

van Leeuwen, T. 1999. *Speech, Music, Sound*. London: Palgrave Macmillan.

Veltman, R. 1998. Lars Porsena and my bonk manager: a systemic-functional study in the semogenesis of the language of swearing. Sanchez-Macarro, A. & R. Carter (eds) *Linguistic Choice Across Genres: Variation in Spoken and Written*

English (Current Issues in Linguistic Theory). Amsterdam: John Benjamins, 301–16.
Ventola, E. 1998. 'Interpersonal choices in academic work'. In A. Sanchez-Macarro & R. Carter (eds), *Linguistic Choices Across Genres*. Amsterdam: Benjamins (CILT. 158). 117–36.
Voloshinov, V. N. 1995. *Marxism and the Philosophy of Language, Bakhtinian Thought – an Introductory Reader*. S. Dentith, L. Matejka & I. R. Titunik (trans.), London: Routledge.
White, P. R. R. 1997. 'Death, disruption and the moral order: the narrative impulse in mass "hard news" reporting'. In Christie, F. & J. R. Martin (eds). 1997. *Genres and Institutions: Social Processes in the Workplace and School*. London: Cassell (Open Linguistic Series), 101–33.
White, P. R. R. 1998. *Telling Media Tales: The News Story as Rhetoric*. PhD. Thesis, Sydney: University of Sydney.
White, P. R. R. 2000. 'Dialogue and inter-subjectivity: reinterpreting the semantics of modality and hedging'. In M. Coulthard, J. Cotterill & F. Rock (eds), *Working With Dialogue*. Tubingen: Neimeyer. 67–80.
White, P. R. R. 2002a. 'Appraisal – the language of evaluation and stance'. In J. Verschueren, J. Östman, J. Blommaert & C. Bulcaen (eds), *The Handbook of Pragmatics*. Amsterdam: John Benjamins. 1–27.
White, P. R. R. 2002b. 'News as history – Your daily gossip'. In J. R. Martin & R. Wodak (eds), *Re-reading the Past: critical and Functional Perspectives on Time and Value*. Amsterdam: John Benjamins. 61–89.
White, P. R. R. 2003. 'Beyond modality and hedging: a dialogic view of the language of intersubjective stance'. *Text – Special Edition on Appraisal*. 259–84.
White, P. R. R. 2004. 'Subjectivity, evaluation and point of view in media discourse' in C. Coffin, A. Hewings & K. O'Halloran (eds), *Applying English Grammar*. London: Hodder Arnold.
White, P. R. R. 2004b. Appraisal web site: www.grammatics.com/appraisal
White, P. R. R. to appear, 'Modality as dialogue – a Bakhtinian reanalysis of "epistemic" stance'. *Word – Journal of the International Linguistics Association*.
Wierzbicka, A. 1986. 'Human emotions: universal or culture-specific?', *American Anthropologist* 88.3. 584–94.
Wierzbicka, A. 1990a. 'The semantics of emotions: *fear* and its relatives in English'. *Australian Journal of Linguistics* 10.2 (Special Issue on the Semantics of Emotions). 359–75.
Wierzbicka, A. (ed.), 1990b. *Australian Journal of Linguistics* 10.2 (Special Issue on the Semantics of Emotions).

Index

acknowledge (attribution), 112
see also engagement
addressivity, 208
adjudicator key (history), 184–5
affect, 2, 8, 31, 35, 39, 43, 45–56
  dis/inclination, 48
  dis/satisfaction, 49
  in/security, 49
  tokens of affect (invoking versus inscribing), 61–8
  un/happiness, 49
Aijmer, K., 108
alignment, 92, 95, 97, 114, 118, 129, 152
amplification, 20, 29, 193, 245, 271
  see also intensification, force, graduation
appreciation, 56–68
  border with judgement, 58–61
  composition (balance or complexity), 56
  reaction (impact or quality), 56
  tokens of appreciation (invoking versus inscribing), 61–8
  valuation, 56
attitude, 35–8, 42–69
  see also affect, judgement, appreciation,
attribution, 98, 111–17
  see also engagement
axiology (axiological), 109, 121, 211, 215, 231, 237, 272
axis, 12–13

Bakhtin, M., 37, 93, 99
balance, *see* appreciation
bare assertion, 94, 98, 99, 100
  see also monogloss
Biber, D., 38–40
booster, 94, 133, 138
  see also intensification, intensifier

Caldas-Coulthard, C., 103, 113

capacity, 52–5
  see also judgement
Chafe, N., 39, 104, 159
Coates, J., 104, 105
Coffin, C., 33, 164, 184, 185
commentator voice, 164–84
  see also evaluative key
complexity, *see* appreciation
compliant reading, 6, 231
composition (balance or complexity), *see* appreciation
concession (concede), 36, 94, 97, 124, 125, 134, 257
  see also engagement
concur (proclaim), 98, 121, 122–6
  see also engagement
connotation, 27, 66
  see also attitudinal flags
context, 26–7
contract (dialogic), 102, 104, 117, 135
  concur (proclaim), 98, 121, 122–6
  counter (disclaim), 97, 120–4, 182
  deny (disclaim), 97, 118–20
  endorse (proclaim), 98, 121, 126–7
  pronounce (proclaim), 98, 121, 127–33
  see also engagement
core vocabulary, 65
corpus linguistics, 40, 46, 58, 165, 173
correspondent voice, 164–84
  see also evaluative key
counter (disclaim), 97, 120–4, 182
  see also engagement
counter-expectancy, 67, 118, 156, 183, 253

Davidse, K., 48
delexicalisation, 143, 152
denotation, 27, 66
deny (disclaim), 97, 118–20
  see also engagement
desiderative, 46, 48, 57
  see also affect

Index

dialogic, 5, 36, 40, 92, 98, 102–33, 155
  see also dialogism, heterogloss, Bakhtin
dialogism, *see* engagement
disclaim, 118–21
  see also engagement
discourse semantics, 9
disposition, *see* affect
distance (attribution), 113
  see also engagement
distribution (extent), 141, 151, 154
  see also graduation
domination, 20–4

Eggins, S., 7, 28, 33, 57, 90
emotion, *see* affect
endorse (proclaim), 98, 121, 126–7
  see also engagement
engagement, 35–8, 40, 92–137
  acknowledge (attribution), 112
  affirm (concur), 125, 134
  attribution, 98, 111–17
  concession (concede), 36, 94, 97, 124, 125, 134, 257 (*see also* counter)
  concur (proclaim), 98, 121, 122–6
  counter (disclaim), 97, 120–4, 182
  deny (disclaim), 97, 118–20
  dialogism, 40, 92, 126, 221
  dialogic contraction, 102, 104, 117, 135
  dialogic expansion, 102, 104, 111, 117, 135
  disclaim, 118–21
  distance (attribution), 113
  endorse (proclaim), 98, 121, 126–7
  entertain, 98, 104–10, 117, 122, 133, 182
  proclaim, 98, 117, 121–33
  pronounce (proclaim), 98, 121, 127–33
  entertain, 98, 104–10, 117, 122, 133, 182
  see also engagement
epistemic modality, 2, 38, 39, 104–7
evaluative key, *see* key
evidential, 2, 39, 40, 94, 104, 159
  see also engagement

expand (dialogic), 102, 104, 111, 117, 135
  acknowledge (attribution), 112
  attribution, 98, 111–17
  distance (attribution), 113
  entertain, 98, 104–10, 117, 122, 133, 182
  see also engagement
expository question, 98, 105, 110, 122, 159
  see also rhetorical question
extent (quantification), 148, 150
  see also graduation

fact, 39, 108
Fairclough, N., 118
Feez, S., 8, 165
field, 27–8
Finnegan, E., 38
flag judgement, *see* tokens of judgement
focus, 37, 40, 137–40, 245
  see also graduation
force, 37, 40, 67, 137, 140–53, 226, 245
  see also graduation
Fuller, G., 94

genesis, 25
genre, 24, 26, 32–3
gradability, 33, 37, 44, 58, 68, 135
graduation, xi, 35, 37, 39, 40, 67, 92, 94, 97, 135–59
  distribution (extent), 141, 151, 154
  extent (quantification), 148, 150
  focus, 37, 40, 137–40, 245
  force, 37, 40, 67, 137, 140–53, 226, 245
  infused intensification, 143–5
  infused quantification, 151
  intensification, 2, 20, 23, 37, 40, 65, 94, 140, 141–8
  isolated intensification, 141–3
  isolated quantification, 151
  mass (quantification), 150–2
  number (quantification), 141, 148–51
  proximity (extent), 137, 141, 151, 154

276 *Index*

graduation – *continued*
   quantification, 140, 148–52
   sharpen (focus), 37, 138
   soften (focus), 37, 138
   grammatical metaphor, 10–12

Halliday, M.A.K., 7, 11–15, 18–28, 106, 133, 249
happiness, *see* affect
hedge, 39, 40, 94, 108, 159, 266
   see also engagement, entertain
heterogloss, 26, 37, 38, 93, 97–117, 124, 128, 155, 193, 199, 208
   see also engagement, Bakhtin
history, 184–6
Hunston, S., 38, 39, 159, 261
Hyland, K., 28, 39, 108, 133

ideal reader, *see* putative reader
ideational meaning, 7
ideology (ideological), 93, 96, 101, 109, 184, 208, 211, 212, 227, 237, 261
Iedema, R., 8, 29, 33, 54, 165, 169
imagined reader, *see* putative reader
impact, *see* appreciation
inclination, *see* affect
infused intensification, 143–5
   see also graduation
infused quantification, 151
   see also graduation
inscribe judgement, 61–8
   see also judgement
interjection, 69
interpersonal meaning, 7–8
instantiation, 23–5, 162–4, 186, 203, 205, 206
intensification, 2, 20, 23, 37, 40, 65, 94, 140, 141–8
   see also graduation
intensifier, 39, 94, 127, 138, 145, 245
interpersonal metaphor, 22, 54
interpreter key (history), 184, 185
interrogative, 21, 22, 198
intertextuality, 114, 133, 272
   see also heterogloss, attribution
invite judgement, *see* tokens of judgement

invoke judgement (tokens, indirect realisation), 61–8
   see also judgement
involvement, 33–5
isolated intensification, 141–3
   see also graduation
isolated quantification, 151
   see also graduation

journalistic discourse, 164–83
judgement, 35, 38, 40, 42–5, 52–6, 58–68
   afford judgement (tokens), 66–7
   border with appreciation, 58–61
   capacity, 52–5
   flag judgement (tokens), 66–7
   inscribing versus invoking judgement, 61–8
   invite judgement (tokens), 61–4, 67
   invoke judgement (tokens), 61–8
   judgement and modality, 54
   normality, 52–4
   provoke judgement (tokens), 65–7
   propriety, 52–5
   social esteem, 52–3
   social sanction, 52–3
   tenacity, 52–5
   text analysis methods, 69
   tokens of judgement (invocation, indirect realisation), 61–8
   veracity, 52–4

key, evaluative, 26, 28, 161

Labov, W., 39, 159
Lakoff, G., 39, 138
Leech, G., 118
Lemke, J., 4, 54, 59
Lessing, D., 191
lexicogrammar, 9
logogenesis, 26
Lyons, J., 99, 105

Macken-Horarik, M., 37, 186, 216, 217
Martin, J.R., 1, 7, 8, 13, 26, 28, 29, 32, 37, 41, 54, 56, 69, 94, 161, 162, 171, 181, 210, 237, 262

mass (quantification), 150–2
   see also graduation
Matthiessen, C.M.I.M., 24, 26, 209
media discourse, *see* journalistic discourse
metafunction, 7–8
metaphor (lexical), 64, 66, 67, 76, 79, 86, 194, 204
   see also provoked judgement
Miller, D., 260
modality, 2, 11, 13–17, 19, 21, 36, 38, 54–6, 94, 104–6, 193, 253
   lexicalisation and judgement, 54–6
   permission and obligation (deontic), 110
mode, 28–9
monogloss, 37, 38, 99–111, 155–8, 199, 220, 228, 232–4
   see also engagement, Bakhtin
monologic, 5, 8, 28, 92, 208
   see also monogloss
Myers, G., 108

negatives, *see* deny
negotiation, 9, 33–4
news reporting, *see* journalistic discourse
non-core vocabulary, 65–7
normality, 52–4
   see also judgement
number (quantification), 141, 148–51
   see also graduation

objectivity, *see* reporter voice
Ochs, E., 38, 39, 40
ontogenesis, 26

Pagano, A., 118, 119, 121
Painter, C., 26, 45, 69
Palmer, F. R., 104, 105
paradigmatic relations, 13
phylogenesis, 26
Pinter, H., 186
polarity, 21, 35, 36, 94
power, 30
Poynton, C., xi, 20, 29–33
probability, 11, 13–15, 17, 54, 104, 109
   see also engagement

proclaim, 98, 117, 121–33
   see also engagement
projection, 36, 105, 126, 133
   see also reported speech, attribution
proliferation, 30, 31, 204
pronounce (proclaim), 98, 121, 127–33
   see also engagement
propriety, 52–5
   see also judgement
prosody, 19–24, 26, 33, 64, 88, 226, 243
provoke judgement, *see* tokens of judgement
proximity (extent), 137, 141, 151, 154
   see also graduation
putative audience, 97, 226
   see also putative reader
putative reader, 95, 118, 119, 125, 140, 222
   see also putative audience

quality, *see* appreciation
quantification, 140, 148–52
   see also graduation

rapport, 2, 112, 157, 237, 254
reaction (impact or quality), *see* appreciation
realisation, 8–19
recorder key (history), 184, 208
register, 24, 27–32, 162–4
reported speech, 103, 111, 113, 126, 133
   see also projection, attribution
reporter voice, 164–85
   see also evaluative key
resistant reading, 206
rhetorical question, 110
   see also expository question
Rothery, J., 186,

satisfaction, *see* affect
saturation, 19, 23, 24
security, *see* affect
sharpen (focus), 37, 138
   see also graduation
signature, 25, 203–6
Simon-Vandenbergen, A-M., 108

Sinclair, J., 135, 143, 159
Slade, D., 28, 33
social esteem, 52–3
    see also judgement
social sanction, 52–3
    see also judgement
soften (focus), 37, 138
    see also graduation
solidarity, 29–35, 92–7, 121, 125, 130, 139, 140, 152, 158, 191, 206, 221, 224, 230
Spock (not Doctor), 41, 50
stance, 2, 39, 40, 97, 161, 163, 186
Stenglin, M., 29, 186, 211
strata, 9
Stubbs, M., 92, 95
surge of behaviour, *see* affect
swearing, 68–9
syntagmatic relations, 13
system network, 14–15
system, 12–17
Systemic Functional Linguistics (SFL), 1, 6, 7, 8, 11, 12, 17, 23, 26, 27, 28, 33, 40, 126, 146, 161, 177

tactical reading, 206
tenacity, 52–5
    see also judgement

tenor, 27–34, 210, 235, 260
textual meaning, 7
Thompson, G., 38, 39, 159
tokens of attitude (affect, appreciation and judgement), 61–8
tokens of judgement (invoked judgement, indirect realisation), 61–8
    see also judgement
topology, 16–17
types of structure, 18–19

usuality, 54, 140, 150
    see also modality

valuation, *see* appreciation
veracity, 52–4
    see also judgement
voice, journalistic, 164–84
    see also evaluative key, reporter voice, correspondent voice, commentator voice
Voloshinov, V., 92, 93

White, P.R.R., 8, 33, 40, 135, 159, 165, 169, 266, 268
Wierzbicka, A., 39, 40

Yoda, 20